977.5004 A nation within a
NATIO   nation.

$34.95   12/12   2

A Nation
within
a Nation

Voices of the
Oneidas in Wisconsin

A Nation within a Nation

Voices of the Oneidas in Wisconsin

Edited by

L. Gordon McLester III
Oneida Indian Historical Society
Oneida, Wisconsin

and

Laurence M. Hauptman
SUNY Distinguished Professor of History
SUNY New Paltz

WISCONSIN HISTORICAL SOCIETY PRESS

Published by the Wisconsin Historical Society Press
Publishers since 1855
© 2010 by the State Historical Society of Wisconsin

Publication of this book was made possible in part by the
Oneida Nation of Indians of Wisconsin

wisconsinhistory.org

Photographs identified with WHi or WHS are from the Society's collections; address requests to reproduce these photos to the Visual Materials Archivist at the Wisconsin Historical Society, 816 State Street, Madison, WI 53706.

Karim Tiro's "Claims Arising: The Oneida Nation of Indians of Wisconsin and the Indian Claims Commission, 1951–1982" previously appeared in the *American Indian Law Review 32* (2008).

Printed in Canada

Cover and interior design and typesetting by Jane Tenenbaum

14   13   12   11   10   1   2   3   4   5

Library of Congress Cataloging-in-Publication Data

A nation within a nation : voices of the Oneidas in Wisconsin / edited by L. Gordon McLester III and Laurence M. Hauptman.

p. cm.

Includes bibliographical references and index.

ISBN 978-0-87020-454-8 (hardcover : alk. paper) 1. Oneida Indians — Wisconsin — History — 20th century. 2. Oneida Indians — Politics and government. 3. Indians of North America — Wisconsin — History — 20th century. I. McLester, L. Gordon. II. Hauptman, Laurence M.

E99.O45N38 2010

977.500497'5543 — dc22

2010010592

♾ The paper used in this publication meets the minimum requirements of the American National Standard for Information Sciences — Permanence of Paper for Printed Library Materials, ANSI Z39.48-1992.

To the Oneida elders,
for all the treasures they have left for us

Contents

Part 2 Wisconsin Oneidas Polish the Chain of Alliance, 1917–1975

Part 3 Wisconsin Oneida Responses to Federal Policies, 1900–1975

Part 4 Portraits of Wisconsin Oneida Leadership

Preface

Throughout the Indigenous nations located within the United States, the term "sovereignty" is invariably used when describing the inherent authority of their nations. Usually, the term is invoked in the course of protecting some right — as in, "The application of the state's taxes to our land will undermine our sovereignty!" — or as a justification for an assertion of power — as in, "Building this casino is an exercise of our sovereignty!" It is referenced in whole and absolute terms and on occasion is tailored to suit a particular purpose, e.g., to assert the nation's "cultural sovereignty" or its "economic sovereignty." — Robert Odawi Porter, "Conceptions of Indigenous Sovereignty"

THIS BOOK IS THE FOURTH AND CONCLUDING VOLUME in a series on the history of the Oneida Nation. In 1988, Syracuse University Press published *The Oneida Indian Experience: Two Perspectives,* which provided a historical overview of Oneida communities in the United States and Canada. In 1999, the University of Wisconsin Press published *The Oneida Indian Journey: From New York to Wisconsin, 1784–1860,* which described the pressures on those Indians during the time they made treaties with the federal government (1784 to 1838), the reasons for their migration out of the Empire State, and their adjustment to their new home in the Badger State. In 2006, the University of Oklahoma Press published *The Oneida Indians in the Age of Allotment, 1860–1920,* which focused on the Wisconsin community's loss of more than sixty-five thousand acres as a result of congressional and state legislative actions in the wake of the Dawes Act of 1887. As was true in the preceding volumes in this series, the editors of *A Nation Within a Nation: Voices of the Oneidas in Wisconsin* do not simply view these Native Americans as victims acted upon by white outsiders; they present the Oneidas as actors in their own history.

Although not new by any means, the term "sovereignty" has been used more frequently in Indian country over the past four decades. Anyone spending time in a Native American community soon realizes that the word has a distinct, solemn meaning when used by Indians, and has little to do with its use in a Euro-American context. In western thought, sover-

eignty connotes a political-legal reality and refers to the supreme and ultimate authority that exists within any political unit or association or territory. A sovereign power is deemed free from all other authorities and
possesses no rivals within its jurisdiction.

Native Americans have never accepted this definition, believing instead
that they can retain elements of sovereignty even if they are not free from
all other authorities. As scholars David Wilkins and K. Tsianina Lomawaima note, not even an international superpower such as the United
States possesses truly "unlimited sovereignty." The American federalist
system reserves certain rights and powers to the states and people rather
than to the federal government, for example, and treaties made with
foreign nations or with Indian nations also limit Washington's powers. "In
the real world, sovereignty operates within constraints." Certainly the
colonial process known as frontier expansion has imposed severe restraints
on Native Americans. The United States Supreme Court has added to
these constraints, deeming Indian nations "domestic dependent nations"
since 1831, and, in 1903, declaring that the Congress had plenary power
allowing it to abrogate federal-Indian treaties without tribal consent. Nevertheless, Native Americans emphasize that they were sovereign nations at
the time of European contact and that they remain sovereign nations now.

But too often, federal, state, and local authorities have attempted to
subvert Oneida autonomy. According to Wilkins and Lomawaima, the
"relationship between American Indian tribes and the U.S. federal government is an ongoing contest over sovereignty. At stake are fundamental
questions of identity, jurisdiction, power, and control."

Wilkins and Lomawaima define a sovereign nation as one that "exer-
cises self government and the right to treat with other nations, applies its
jurisdiction over the internal affairs of its citizens and subparts (such as
states), claims political jurisdiction over the land within its borders, and
may define certain rights that inhere in its citizens (or others)." Consequently, the two authors conclude:

> American Indian tribes are sovereign nations. Their sovereignty is inher-
> ent, pre- or extraconstitutional, and is explicitly recognized in the Con-
> stitution. What do these terms mean? Inherent sovereignty inheres in

self-governing human groups — various scholars no doubt define different criteria of political organization as requisite for sovereign status. Tribes existed before the United States of America, so theirs is a more mature sovereignty, predating the Constitution; in that sense, tribal sovereignty exists "outside" the Constitution. The drafters of the Constitution, in express wording in the commerce clause, recognized Indian nations as something distinct from the United States...this clause and the treaty and property clauses add a constitutional basis to understandings of tribal sovereignty. Are tribes today unlimited sovereigns? Certainly not. The political realities of relations with the federal government, relations with state and local governments, competing jurisdictions, complicated local histories, circumscribed land bases, and overlapping citizenships all constrain their sovereignty.[1]

The focus of this book is on how one Native American nation perceives and maintains its sovereignty, operating, in effect, as a sovereign nation within a nation. To the more than sixteen thousand members of the Oneida Nation of Indians of Wisconsin, the definition of "sovereignty" is not limited to the political-legal arena but includes other elements: (1) retaining a landbase, however reduced, and defending it at all costs; (2) maintaining a kinship structure that separates Wisconsin Oneidas from both non-Indian and other Indian communities; (3) stressing their historic government-to-government relationship with the United States, the reciprocal bonds symbolized to the Oneidas by wampum, the metaphor of an iron-link chain dating back to first contact with the Europeans, and/or the Treaty of Canandaigua of 1794 (associated with this relationship is the sacrifice of their Indian ancestors as loyal allies fulfilling an obligation in war, from the American Revolution to Iraq); and (4) emphasizing community leadership that is supposed to concern itself with more than immediate goals and to look to future generations — as the Oneidas would say, "seven generations to come."

The Wisconsin Oneidas posit that, based on their presence as Native peoples on the North American continent prior to the European invasion, they have inherent sovereignty. Moreover, despite outsiders' policies aimed at eradicating the tribe's existence, on their lands guaranteed by federal treaty in 1838, the Wisconsin Oneidas have always remained a visible and definable Indian community. They are, in other words, a sovereign nation.

As in the previous volumes in this series, the current book has several unique features. First, the project is a joint effort of more than thirty years between the academic community and a Native American nation. Second, one of the editors and many of the authors are Wisconsin Oneidas. Alongside the contributions of non-Indian scholars — two historians, two anthropologists, and a specialist in women's studies and literature — Wisconsin Oneida community voices are well represented. They include four tribal chairmen, two tribal attorneys, two tribal secretaries, two tribal treasurers, three tribal historians, one library director, one education department administrator, one tribal linguist instructor, two college administrators, and two major federal administrators of national American Indian policies. In addition, a prominent Menominee, Ada Deer, the former assistant secretary of the interior for Indian affairs and noted educator at the University of Wisconsin–Madison, provides a portrait of federal termination policies that stands in marked contrast with the Wisconsin Oneida experience. Third, despite the growing literature on twentieth-century American Indian policies, in the editors' opinions, few if any historians have placed federal and state policies within the full context of tribal life. By combining archival research on policy decisions with tribal perspectives, oral and written, the editors have attempted to provide a fuller, more rounded Native American history, one that is not totally dependent on one side of the divide.

The historical records amassed by the Wisconsin Oneidas are second to none in Indian country. Working under contract from the Wisconsin Oneida tribal government, L. Gordon McLester III, an Oneida public historian and one of the editors of this collection, has administered conferences since 1987, focusing on every aspect of his nation's history. He has also conducted more than five hundred interviews with tribal elders, now on videotape, about events, festivities, people, places, and traditions. This massive project builds on the earlier Oneida Language and Folklore Project (1938–1942), funded by the Works Progress Administration (WPA) and administered by anthropologists Morris Swadesh, Floyd Lounsbury, and Harry Basehart, a remarkable and extensive oral history collection covering every aspect of Oneida life from the time of their arrival in Wisconsin — then Michigan Territory — from New York in the 1820s. Both the WPA stories and the videotaped interviews are housed in the Oneida Cultural Heritage Department, which publishes a newsletter dealing with a variety of subjects, including the (Dawes) General Allotment Act, famous Oneida leaders, treaties, and Iroquoian cultural and religious traditions. *A Nation Within a Nation: Voices of the Oneidas in Wisconsin* has benefited from these collections, which provide a unique inside perspective on community life.

Unlike the three previous books, this volume concentrates exclusively on the Wisconsin Oneidas, not on the other related communities at Southwold, Ontario, Canada, and at Oneida, New York. Even though Oneidas have always had what Jack Campisi has termed a "common estate," reflected in their joint history before the 1820s as well as their common kinship, land claims, language, religious expression, and singing societies, the Wisconsin community has had its own unique experience. Besides being the largest in population, the Wisconsin community, unlike the other Oneida territories, is split into two counties — Oneida and Outagamie — and five separate school districts — Pulaski, West DePere, Seymour, Freedom, and the Oneida Nation school system.

. . .

A Nation Within a Nation: Voices of the Oneidas in Wisconsin focuses on the years 1900 to 1975. The editors did not arbitrarily choose the beginning and end dates. The year 1900 marks the start of several events that led to a devastating loss of land for the Wisconsin Oneidas. Over the next seventy-five years, they weathered these cataclysms and began the process of creating the modern-day Wisconsin Oneida Nation.

In 1900–1901, the Wisconsin state legislature first considered creating the town of Hobart in Brown County and the town of Oneida in Outagamie County out of lands reserved to the Oneidas under the amended Treaty of Buffalo Creek of February 3, 1838. In 1903, these two new towns were established by state law. This state statutory action, questionable under federal Indian law, was a disaster to the Oneidas in the long run. By 1934, the year of the Indian Reorganization Act, the Wisconsin Oneida reservation had been reduced by more than sixty-five thousand acres.

By 1975, however, the Wisconsin Oneidas were well under way at rebuilding their modern nation. National Indian policies had changed and, as we will see, Wisconsin Oneidas were in Washington, D.C., and involved in the design of this new "age of self-determination." Tribal member Robert L. Bennett, whose oral history account is included in Part 4, was the first American Indian since Reconstruction to be appointed commissioner of Indian affairs, serving in that capacity during the administration of President Lyndon Johnson. In the mid-1970s, Ernest Stevens Sr., also represented in this volume, served on the American Indian Policy Review Commission established by the United States Congress. The Wisconsin Oneidas' leadership role in national Indian policy making has continued since the 1970s as well: Richard Hill and Ernest Stevens Jr. have both headed the National Indian Gaming Association, and Carl Artman served as assistant secretary of the interior for Indian affairs in 2007–2008.

Long before the civil rights revolution or red power activism of the 1960s and '70s, Wisconsin Oneidas were developing strategies of survival — maintaining a vibrant community life, attempting to preserve their language by working with anthropologists and organizing singing societies, adapting to Milwaukee city life but never losing touch with kin at the Oneida reservation, learning new artistic traditions such as lacework that engendered pride and provided some money in hard times, and pursuing centuries-old land claims in federal courts. Hence, the Wisconsin Oneidas were and are still highly adaptable people. They changed their political governing system in the 1820s, 1870s, early twentieth century, during the Indian New Deal of the 1930s, and again in 1969, all to maintain sovereignty within their territory and meet the challenges they faced in each era. From a hereditary council of chiefs in the 1820s brought from New York state to a nine-member elected tribal council in 1969, they adjusted to new circumstances while maintaining their status as a sovereign nation. It is little wonder that the Wisconsin Oneidas were among the first Indian nations to take advantage of the decision in the Cabazon case of 1987 that led to the Indian Regulatory Gaming Act of 1988. Nor is it a surprise that the Wisconsin Oneidas have aggressively pursued their land claims in New York state and defended their sovereignty against local and Wisconsin state efforts to extend jurisdiction.

These accomplishments of Wisconsin Oneidas, individually and collectively, have significance beyond recent history. They reveal a recurring theme brought out in this book: namely, the Oneidas' ability to adapt to change while remaining an Iroquoian people. This adaptability was clearly evident in the period 1900 to 1975. Although there has been a recent setback in the courts related to the New York land claim, the Wisconsin Oneidas have retained their culture and remained a sovereign nation, and they have begun to overcome the limitations on their self-rule imposed by outsiders in Washington, D.C.; Albany, New York; and Madison, Wisconsin. Today, the Wisconsin Oneidas are committed to providing for their people's future by bringing educational, economic, and social betterment to tribal members. They encourage tribal members to seek greater economic opportunities through higher education that is available only off the reservation. In this strategy, however, the Wisconsin Oneidas, and most Native Americans, face the dilemma of maintaining a unique culture in the face of outside values that often are distinct from Oneida traditions. In this respect and in others, the Wisconsin Oneidas follow the Iroquoian creed: they have a responsibility to ensure their survival as a people by concerning themselves with the "seven generations to come."

L. Gordon McLester III
Laurence M. Hauptman

Note

1. David E. Wilkins and K. Tsianina Lomawaima, *Uneven Ground: American Indian Sovereignty and Federal Law* (Norman: University of Oklahoma Press, 2001), 117.

Acknowledgments

THE EDITORS WOULD LIKE TO THANK the Oneida Nation of Indians of Wisconsin's Business Committee for supporting and promoting the historical conference that led to the publication of this volume. Our friend David Jaman provided the editors with good cheer, excellent wit, and technical expertise. The editors would also like to acknowledge the staff of the Lyndon B. Johnson Presidential Library for allowing us to reprint the Robert L. Bennett oral history that is in Part 4 of this book. Dr. Robert W. Venables kindly allowed us to use an excerpt from his lengthy interview with Oscar Archiquette conducted in 1970.

Although more than 95 percent of the material presented here is new, there are exceptions. Laurence M. Hauptman's article "The Wisconsin Oneidas and Termination, 1943–1956" is partially reprinted in Part 3. Two earlier versions appeared in the *Journal of Ethnic Studies* 14 (Fall 1986): 31–52; and in his *The Iroquois Struggle for Survival: World War II to Red Power* (Syracuse, NY: Syracuse University Press, 1986), chapter 5. The article in this current book is an edited revision of the previous two analyses. In addition, Karim M. Tiro's "Claims Arising: The Oneida Nation of Wisconsin and the Indian Claims Commission" appeared in *American Indian Law Review* 32 (2008).

Most important, the two editors would like to thank their wives, Ruth and Betty, who have put up with their husbands' obsession with Oneida history for too long!

Abbreviations

AIPRC	American Indian Policy Review Commission
ARCIA	Annual Reports of the Commissioner of Indian Affairs
BIA	Bureau of Indian Affairs
CCF	Central Classified Files
Cong.	Congress
GLAR	Great Lakes Agency Records
GPO	U.S. Government Printing Office
ICC	Indian Claims Commission
IRA	Indian Reorganization Act
JL	Johnson Library, Austin, Texas
KAR	Keshena Agency Records
LC	Library of Congress
MSS	Manuscript Collection
NA	National Archives, Washington, D.C.
NCAI	National Congress of American Indians
OIA	Office of Indian Affairs
OLFP	Oneida Language and Folklore Project
ONIW	Oneida Nation of Indians of Wisconsin
ONIWBC	Oneida Nation of Indian of Wisconsin Business Committee
ONIWCHD	Oneida Nation of Indians of Wisconsin Cultural Heritage Department
ONIWEC	Oneida Nation of Indians of Wisconsin Executive Committee
ONIWGTC	Oneida Nation of Indians of Wisconsin General Tribal Council
P.L.	Public Law
RG	Record Group

RGLCA	Records of the Great Lakes Consolidated Agency
sess.	session
SHSW	State Historical Society of Wisconsin (Wisconsin Historical Society), Madison
Stat.	United States Statutes at Large
TL	Truman Library, Independence, Missouri
WHS	Wisconsin Historical Society (previously SHSW)
WPA	Works Progress Administration

Wisconsin Oneida Time Line

1887–1933 Allotment era Wisconsin Oneidas' land loss totals sixty-five thousand acres in this period, beginning with the (Dawes) General Allotment Act.

1893 United States Indian Industrial School (Oneida Boarding School/Government School) at Oneida, Wisconsin, opens.

1898 The Sybil Carter Lace Association is established among the Wisconsin Oneidas and funded by New York philanthropists until 1926; lacemaking activities and the enterprise continue to the early 1950s.

1903 Wisconsin state legislature formally creates the town of Hobart in Brown County and the town of Oneida in Outagamie County, dividing the Oneida reservation into two townships.

1903 Chief Cornelius Hill is ordained as an Episcopal priest.

1906 Bishop Grafton Parish Hall is built.

1906 Burke Act converts trust patents to fee simple title; large-scale Oneida land loss begins.

1907 Chief Cornelius Hill dies.

1909–1911 Federal efforts to buy out Oneida treaty obligations through one lump-sum payment are unsuccessful; U.S. Congressional report on the matter March 3, 1911.

1911 Society of American Indians is founded.

1917–1918 World War I; hundreds of Wisconsin Oneidas serve.

1917 Federal competency commission meets at Oneida; James McLaughlin and two other commissioners recommend immediate conversion of most of the remaining trust patents to fee simple titles.

1918 President Woodrow Wilson, by executive order, carries out the federal competency commission's recommendation on most of the remaining trust patents.

1918 The Oneida Boarding School (Government School) closes.

1920–1922   Holy Apostles Episcopal Church is struck by lightning, and everything but the stone walls and foundation is destroyed; the church is rebuilt and consecrated in 1922 by Bishop Weller.

1922   Centennial celebration includes One Hundred Years of Oneidas in Wisconsin festivities.

1922   New York state assembly report (Everett Report) states unequivocally that the Six Nations have legitimate claims to millions of acres in New York state.

1924   U.S. Congress passes the Indian Citizenship Act.

1924   Despite Oneida protests, the BIA approves the sale of the Oneida Boarding School for twenty-four thousand dollars to the Murphy Land and Investment Company, which acquired the property for the Catholic Archdiocese of Green Bay.

1925   Wisconsin Oneida chiefs are condoled.

1927   In Deere v. St. Lawrence Power, a federal court dismisses the Six Nations land claim.

1934   New Wisconsin Oneida government is formed under state charter; Oscar Archiquette is elected tribal chairman.

1934   The Indian Reorganization Act (IRA) constitution and bylaws modify tribal governmental structure; Morris Wheelock is elected first tribal chairman under the federal incorporation of the IRA.

1937–1940   Wisconsin Oneidas begin to repurchase former tribal lands under the provisions of the federal incorporation of the IRA.

1938–1942   Drs. Morris Swadesh, Floyd Lounsbury, and Harry Basehart direct the WPA Oneida Language and Folklore Project.

1941–1945   World War II; hundreds of Wisconsin Oneidas serve.

1944   National Congress of American Indians is established.

1944   John Collier presents "federal withdrawal" recommendations to Congress.

1945   Oneida Methodist church is severely damaged by fire; rebuilding efforts begin.

1947   The BIA's Zimmerman Plan to "emancipate" American Indian nations is announced; the Oneida Nation of Indians of Wisconsin is listed in the second group, "Great Lakes Indians," to be terminated.

1950–1953   Korean War; hundreds of Oneidas serve.

1950–1975   American involvement in Vietnam becomes war by 1964–1965; hundreds of Oneidas serve.

1950–1956   Federal government renews efforts to buy out treaty obligations by lump-sum payment of annuities to the Oneidas.

1953   (U.S. Congress) House Concurrent Resolution 108 declares that federal policy will be directed to abolishing federal supervision over Indian nations and that the Indians would be subjected to the same laws, privileges, and responsibilities as other United States citizens.

1953   Public Law 280 transfers criminal and civil jurisdiction over Indians to the state of Wisconsin.

1953   Oneida Methodist church parsonage is consecrated.

1954   U.S. Congress passes the Menominee Termination Act.

1956   At a Des Moines, Iowa, meeting, BIA officials meet with Wisconsin Oneidas to push termination.

1961   American Indian Chicago Conference is a national forum for American Indian concerns.

1962   Eva Danforth and other Native Americans present petition of American Indian Chicago Conference to President Kennedy at the White House.

1963–1965   Wisconsin Oneida Housing Authority is formed under the federal Housing and Urban Development (HUD) program. U.S. Congress passes Economic Opportunity Act. Under Lyndon Johnson's "War on Poverty," the Office of Economic Opportunity provides for youth programs, community action programs, rural assistance, small loans, job training, and VISTA (Volunteers in Service to America) as well as the creation of Neighborhood Youth Corps, Job Corps, and Head Start programs; Head Start begins at Parish Hall in 1965.

1966   Site 1 HUD housing is built.

1966   President Johnson names Robert L. Bennett, Wisconsin Oneida, commissioner of Indian affairs.

1967   Wisconsin Oneidas purchase industrial park (former tribal lands) in Green Bay; today, the land is a major part of Oneida economic development that includes Mason Street Casino and Sam's Club/Wal-Mart.

1969   "Indians of All Nations" take over Alcatraz Island.

1970   President Nixon's historic speech formally ends termination.

1970   Iroquois longhouse is established at Oneida, Wisconsin.

1971   American Indian Movement seizes vacant Milwaukee coast guard station.

1972   "Trail of Broken Treaties" caravan takes over BIA.

1973   Wounded Knee is taken over and occupied.

1973   U.S. Congress passes the Menominee Restoration Act.

1973–1984 Wisconsin Oneidas negotiate for and purchase the Sacred Heart building back from the Roman Catholic Diocese of Green Bay; they rename it the Norbert Hill Center and establish their tribal governmental offices, along with their high school, there.

1974   U.S. Supreme Court decides Oneida Indian land-claims case and overturns 134 years of federal law by giving the Oneida Nation access to federal courts.

1975   The Oneida Nation of Indians of Wisconsin tribal government establishes the Oneida Tribal Development Corporation (OTDC), which helped construct, in 1976–1977, the post office, the nursing home, the tribal museum, and the ongoing housing program.

1975   Ernest Stevens Sr. is named to the American Indian Policy Review Commission.

1975   U.S. Congress passes the Indian Self-Determination and Education Assistance Act.

Oneida Nation Geographic Land Information Systems Department

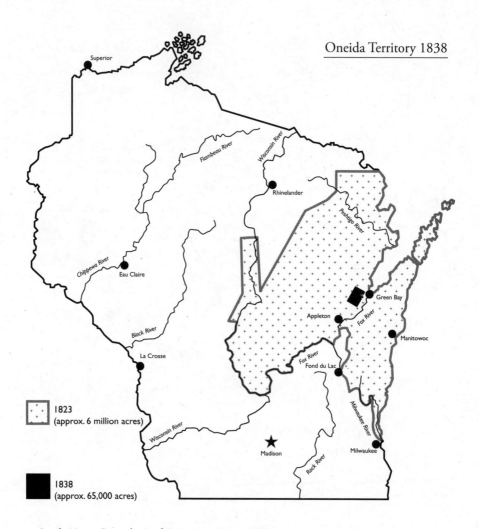

Oneida Territory 1838

Superior

Flambeau River

Wisconsin River

Rhinelander

Pestigo River

Chippewa River

Eau Claire

Green Bay

Appleton   Fox River

Black River

Manitowoc

La Crosse

Fox River

Fond du Lac

Milwaukee River

☆ Madison

Milwaukee

Rock River

Wisconsin River

⊞ 1823
(approx. 6 million acres)

◼ 1838
(approx. 65,000 acres)

Oneida Nation Geographic Land Information Systems Department

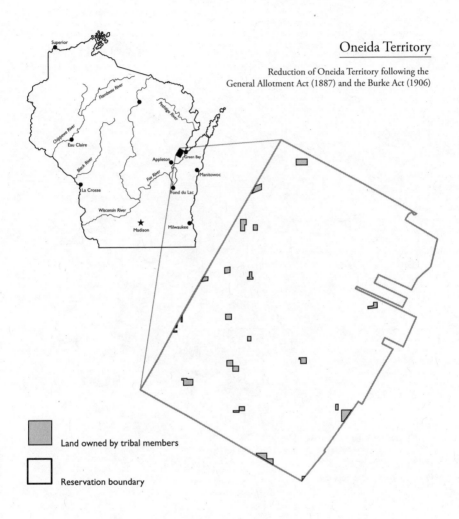

Oneida Territory

Reduction of Oneida Territory following the
General Allotment Act (1887) and the Burke Act (1906)

Land owned by tribal members

Reservation boundary

Oneida Nation Geographic Land Information Systems Department

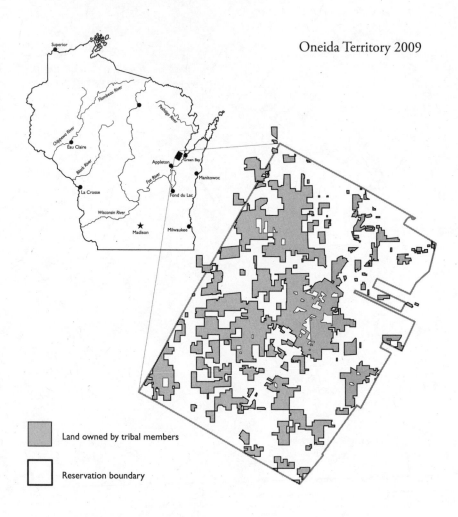

Oneida Territory 2009

Land owned by tribal members

Reservation boundary

Oneida Nation Geographic Land Information Systems Department

Introduction

A Bumpy Road: Overview of
Wisconsin Oneida History, 1900–1975

by Laurence M. Hauptman

THE WISCONSIN ONEIDAS ARE A REMARKABLE Native American community. Despite their separation from their ancient Iroquois homeland in central New York — the Oneidas are one of the original Six Nations of the Iroquois Confederacy that also include the Mohawks, Onondagas, Cayugas, Senecas, and Tuscaroras — they have persevered, retaining their family connections and sense of community; maintaining their tribal government, one that has been modified in form over the years; and asserting their long-standing treaty relationship with and obligations to the United States. In the face of overbearing outside influences that included federal policies of removal, assimilation, and threats to end their tribal existence, they have always maintained their status as a sovereign nation.

Well before their first federal treaty with the United States in 1784, the Oneidas had extensive diplomatic experiences with European and other Indian nations. Today, the Oneida Nation of Indians of Wisconsin have a government-to-government relationship with Washington, one that can be traced back to its alliance with the patriot cause in the American Revolution. In times of the American nation's struggles, Oneidas have come to the aid of their ally, paying a high price for their valiant efforts on battlefields, from Oriskany in 1777 to Iraq and Afghanistan.[1] Yet, as this collection shows, too often federal, state, and local officials have attempted to undermine the Oneidas' status as a sovereign nation composed of the original occupants of North America who are tied by kinship and a common culture. They maintained their Iroquoian way of life at home on the reservation and in their sizable Indian community in Milwaukee, but Wisconsin Oneida tribal existence was constantly threatened. They were particularly beset beginning in the last decades of the nineteenth century, when local, state, and federal governments tried to forcibly amalgamate them into the American polity.

The Oneidas first migrated to Wisconsin in the 1820s and 1830s and built their community on a sixty-five-thousand-acre landbase in and around today's city of Green Bay. Their lands were protected under federal treaty law, most specifically Article 2 of the amended Buffalo Creek Treaty of February 3, 1838; however, things were to change dramatically after 1887.[2] The Dawes or General Allotment Act of 1887 was designed to initiate the breakup of reservation lands after a twenty-five-year trust period. Lands were to be parceled out to individual tribal members, an effort that was tied to forcibly acculturating the Indians, encouraging capitalist values, and, at times, allowing outsiders, such as railroad and lumber companies, to get at Indian resources. In return the Indians were to be awarded United States citizenship.

In the same year as the (Dawes) General Allotment Act, the Office of Indian Affairs concluded that most Oneidas were eligible to receive allotments. Two years later, the Interior Department sent a special agent to administer the allotment policy at Oneida, though some acreage — approximately 40 acres that were used as an Episcopalian mission and approximately 120 acres reserved for a now abandoned railroad easement — was not allotted.[3] By 1892, most allottees were issued patents to a parcel of reservation land, which was supposed to be held in trust for twenty-five years, after which the allottees would be able to sell the land.

Even before the end of the twenty-five-year trust period, local and state politicians were maneuvering to gain an advantage for when the reservation was to be parceled out to individual Oneida allottees. They advocated that the Oneidas become United States citizens, accept individual fee patent title rather than tribal title to reservation lands (essentially cutting short the twenty-five-year trust period), and pay their "fair share" of taxes to support roads, schools, and planned townships to be carved partly out of Oneida tribal lands.[4] At the urging of J. C. Hart, superintendent of the Oneida Government School who also served as federal Indian agent, as well as local political and business leaders, in the spring of 1903 the Wisconsin state legislature created two townships — Oneida in Outagamie County and Hobart in Brown County — out of Wisconsin Oneida lands.[5] While some Oneidas initially participated in the workings of these new governmental entities and even were elected to major town offices, many others objected, arguing that the state legislative action violated federal treaty rights. Eventually, the Oneidas who had originally been elected to these town offices lost out when a rush of non-Indian settlement to the new townships tipped the political balance away from the Indians. The Oneidas did not have a majority to hold power in the two towns, and the result was disaster for the tribe.[6]

On May 8, 1906, Congress passed the Burke Act, which authorized the secretary of the interior to issue a fee patent to any Indian deemed "competent and capable of managing his or her affairs" before the end of the twenty-five-year trust period required by the Dawes General Allotment Act of 1887.[7] As fee simple patentees, individuals, not the tribe as a whole, received title to the land; however, this new arrangement made these individually held lands taxable, and too often the impoverished Oneidas were unable to pay, making their lands subject to foreclosure. Numerous poor Indians were now faced with foreclosure or were forced to sell their lands to pay off their debts; some others saw little future in the dwindling landbase of the reservation, sold their lands, and left for the cities of the Midwest. Solomon Wheelock, an Oneida, later described exactly what happened to his impoverished people under the workings of the Burke Act and other federal legislation that followed it:

> At the time we were made citizens of our country we were called together at one big meeting and we were asked to line up in a row, and all that was in favor of becoming citizens should step up ahead and form a new line. The majority stepped out and just a few stayed in their places. And all of us that stepped out got our deeds for our properties. Lots of people sold their land in just a short time, and as we were not used to paying taxes on anything we had, we just neglected it and left our taxes unpaid, and the money men got a chance to buy up our taxes, and quite a number of them lost their lands in just a few years. You see we were just not used to paying on anything that we thought was ours, and after three or four years our taxes were so high that we were not able to redeem it. And businessmen in town offered to give us anything we need in machinery even if we didn't have any money as long as we had deeds for our lands.[8]

In 1907, Congress also authorized the sale of restricted lands of "noncompetent" Indians under rules set by the secretary of the interior.[9] Moneys from the sales of these lands were supposed to benefit the "noncompetent" Indian; however, as historian Francis Paul Prucha brings out, it "became an effective instrument in the dissipation of Indian landholdings."[10] Often so-called competency was arbitrarily defined based on how many years an Oneida had spent at the government school on the reservation or if he or she had attended Carlisle, Hampton, Haskell, or Flandreau Indian schools. As a result, specifically named individual Oneidas were deemed ready to receive fee simple patents without trust restrictions. By 1908, the Office of Indian Affairs had converted more than half of the Oneida allotments to fee simple patents.[11] A third modification of the Dawes General Allotment Act was passed on June 25, 1910. Now any Indian allottee twenty-one years of age or older who had a trust patent could obtain a fee simple patent and could will or sell his or her land.[12]

Once trust patents were converted to fee simple patents, the Oneida lands became subject to taxation, and numerous allotments were lost to the two towns for nonpayment. Oneidas, using their new fee simple patents as collateral, were encouraged to take out cash loans or to mortgage their property, ideas promoted by local real estate brokers and land jobbers in collusion with the federal Indian agent, local politicians in the Green Bay area, and even a few Oneida tribal members themselves. When they could not repay the loan or mortgage, their lands were foreclosed.[13] Excited by the possibility of acquiring Indian lands once fee simple conversion took place, the Wisconsin state legislature passed two laws in 1907 calling for an appraisal of Indian lands and timber on Wisconsin reservations and a report to the state commissioner of public lands. This transparent act clearly indicated that state officials expected that Madison officials would soon assume greater jurisdiction over the Indians and their lands.[14]

Federal policies were consistently inconsistent. As early as October 16, 1909, officials of the Office of Indian Affairs (also known as the Bureau of Indian Affairs) were indicating to the Wisconsin Oneidas that they had no intention of challenging state laws creating the townships of Oneida and Hobart.[15] Despite this federal opinion, the United States government continued to be deeply involved with the Wisconsin Oneidas. It maintained a government-to-government treaty relationship with the Wisconsin Oneida nation and frequently received reports from Indian agents stationed in the community and region, or from those federal personnel who were inspecting conditions at Oneida. Nearly every commissioner of Indian affairs' Annual Report between 1887 and 1933 devoted some attention to the Wisconsin Oneidas. Moreover, the Office of Indian Affairs continued to maintain and administer the federal Indian boarding school at Oneida until it was closed in 1918. On the other hand, between 1909 and 1911, Washington was attempting to relinquish its trust responsibilities to the Wisconsin Oneidas by trying to convince tribal leaders to accept a lump-sum payout of their annuities under the Treaty of Canandaigua (1794). The Oneidas soundly rejected this early form of termination in 1911, further indicating their determination to maintain their separate sovereign existence as a federally recognized Indian nation.[16]

The year 1917 was a major turning point for the Wisconsin Oneidas; the federal government appeared to be making its final push for the total allotment of the reservation. In that year, a federal Indian competency commission under the chairmanship of James McLaughlin had arrived in Oneida, Wisconsin. McLaughlin's efforts were a clear attempt by the Interior Department to speed up the integration process, a plan strongly supported by both Wisconsin state politicians and Washington officials. The federal competency commissions nationwide were disbanded in 1921 because of Indian resistance, but by then the Wisconsin Oneida reservation had already been reduced by more than fifty thousand acres.[17]

By 1930, 77 percent of the Wisconsin Oneida Indians were receiving public assistance. In the early 1930s, in order to alleviate starvation, the federal government sent 1,500 Navajo sheep to Oneida. Unfortunately, the sheep were too scrawny to yield much meat after butchering.[18] Other relief efforts included sending Red Cross flour and surplus army clothing, but despite these efforts, conditions worsened.[19] By the mid-1930s, the superintendent of the Keshena Indian Agency appealed to Washington on the Oneidas' behalf, claiming he knew "of no condition within this area that is in such dire need of assistance."[20] By the time Franklin D. Roosevelt took office in 1933, the Wisconsin Oneidas possessed less than ninety acres of tribal lands and approximately seven hundred acres of land held by individual allottees.[21]

The Wisconsin Oneidas were a severely divided community during this age of allotment. Five hundred Oneidas had attended the Carlisle Indian Industrial School at Carlisle, Pennsylvania; while others had been sent off to Flandreau, Hampton, Haskell, Pipestone, and Tomah boarding schools. Many, but not all, had been inculcated with the assumption that reservation life was wrong for the Indians, that tribal land bases would soon come to an end, and that full integration of the Indians into the American polity was possible and even inevitable. One such Wisconsin Oneida was the prominent musician and attorney Dennison Wheelock. Other Wisconsin Oneidas, such as Laura Minnie Cornelius Kellogg, reacted to these troubled times by attempting to renew ties to the Iroquois Confederacy in New York and advocating the pursuit of land claims. Still others in the Oneida Indian Party, including Paul and Henry Doxtator and later "Willie Fat" Skenandore, challenged the legality of the creation of the towns of Hobart and Oneida, the imposition of taxation, and the resulting foreclosures during the allotment period. Consequently, measures required for tribal relief, reform, and economic development were postponed during this bitter and highly charged time.[22]

Out of the chaos came a new group of Wisconsin Oneida leaders who saw the political and economic advantages of tribal incorporation under the Indian Reorganization Act (IRA), which had been passed by Congress in 1934 and was sometimes called the "Indian New Deal." This new leadership included Morris Wheelock, a Carlisle-educated and prominent urban Oneida from Milwaukee. The IRA resulted in the establishment of a new tribal governing body, the Oneida Tribal Business Committee, under a constitution and bylaws.[23]

The "Indian New Deal" era at Oneida was marked by several positive developments. The Oneidas established a new elected system of tribal government and repurchased and reclaimed a small portion of former tribal lands. IRA programs also built so-called New Deal homes to replace dilapidated log cabins and drilled wells for each new home to end the need to haul water from springs. The Civilian Conservation Corps and the Works Progress Administration (WPA) sponsored relief employment. The WPA administered the Oneida Language and Folklore Project, one of the earliest and most extensive language and oral history programs among the Indians of the United States. Yet, for all its important changes, the Indian New Deal was not true self-determination, nor did it accomplish a complete economic turnaround.[24] Anthropologist Robert Ritzenthaler noted that the Oneida unemployment rate in 1939 was at 86 percent, 7 percent higher than it had been in 1930.[25]

By the end of the 1930s, the limitations of the Indian New Deal were evident. The IRA did not go far enough in helping the Indians' efforts to reclaim submarginal lands or provide money for repurchase of additional lands; moreover, smothering federal supervision retarded the efforts of the Oneida Business Committee to make decisions on its own. It was time to clean house, but the Bureau of Indian Affairs (BIA) was standing in the way. Significantly responsible for the situation in the first place, BIA had both sponsored the IRA and was now put in charge of carrying out its own reforms. Although Congress and the White House were largely responsible for the limitations of the IRA, the act itself was another in-house reorganization for BIA, following a century of mismanagement and mistaken policies that had severely depleted Indian resources and impoverished the Indian population. Much of the IRA's focus had involved changes in ad hoc rules and regulations that had accumulated over the preceding century. Four decades after its passage, the American Indian Policy Review Commission reported that only 595,157 acres had been purchased for tribal use under the IRA, while governmental agencies had taken 1,811,010 acres of Indian land nationwide for other purposes, including dams, highways, and hydroelectric projects.[26]

During the Indian New Deal, the desperate Oneidas were seeking a life jacket, not self-rule, from outsiders. They incorporated under provisions of the IRA and accepted the Interior Department supervision set out in the act, particularly the key provisions of sections 16 and 17 of the IRA. Section 16 awarded each tribe the "right to organize for its common welfare, and adopt an appropriate constitution and bylaws...." In the spirit of Progressive Era reformers seeking efficiency in management, section 17 aimed to promote business organization by providing a mechanism for incorporation through charters. In both sections, the final approval for constitutions, amendments, bylaws, charters, and elections would be determined by the secretary of the interior and not the Oneidas them-selves.[27] The Oneidas' incorporation meant immediate survival but not the self-determination that was the Wisconsin Oneidas' ultimate goal.

As Loretta Webster brings out in this volume, the Indian New Deal actually increased Wisconsin Oneida dependence on Washington, even to the point of federal officials providing moneys for basic office supplies to the Indian nation. Indeed, eleven of the IRA's eighteen sections — rang-ing from all aspects of land use, business incorporation, constitutions and bylaws, and regulations of hiring Indians for governmental service — required the approval of the secretary of the interior. Hence, a new bureau-cratic tier was now added to the already stultifying administrative struc-ture of federal Indian policy. The Oneidas jumped at the chance to rebuild their nation.[28]

Despite claims to the contrary by federal officials and by some later historians, the operations of the BIA had not radically changed with the IRA. Wisconsin Oneida Robert L. Bennett, who worked for the BIA for many years before being appointed commissioner of Indian affairs by Lyndon Johnson, observed:

> As IRA constitutions were developed, there was not a dramatic shift in terms of the operations at the agency level. Even though tribes ratified constitutions, business went on the same as it always had. When the Bu-reau of Indian Affairs needed something from a tribal government to sanction a particular action, it presented the tribal government with a res-olution in order to get favorable action. This allowed the Bureau to pro-ceed as it had before there was a constitution, bylaws, and a charter. In that early period, there were very few legislative enactments or policy statements enacted by the tribes that were not written by the Bureau of Indian Affairs for the convenience of the federal government.[29]

Under intense criticism, in 1944 Commissioner John Collier admitted that the Indian New Deal had not accomplished many of its stated objec-tives.[30] When Congressman Karl Mundt requested that the commissioner produce a list of Indian nations that could be removed from federal supervision during a hearing of the House Committee on Indian Affairs,

Collier divided Indian nations into three categories: what he claimed was 151,000 "predominantly acculturated," 124,000 "semi-acculturated," and 94,000 predominantly "non-acculturated." Both the Iroquois in the New York agency and all the Indians of Wisconsin, including the Oneidas, were placed in the first category, namely the so-called acculturated Indians ready for termination.[31]

Later, in 1947, Collier's longtime assistant, William Zimmerman Jr., then acting commissioner of Indian affairs, testified before the Senate Civil Service Committee. The senators on the committee had once more demanded a list of Indian nations ready for "release." The Zimmerman plan was more limited in scope than Collier's plan, placing fewer Indian nations in the priority list for termination.[32] In his first category — those he labeled "predominantly acculturated population" — Zimmerman included ten groups, including the Menominees and the Iroquois in New York, whom he claimed could be immediately removed from federal supervision. He placed the Wisconsin Oneidas in a second category labeled "Semi-Acculturated Population" of "Great Lakes (no resources)" that could be released from federal supervision within two to ten years.[33]

During this post–World War II period, Congress was pushing to contain costs and liberate the "captive nations" behind the Iron Curtain, or urging rapid energy development to meet the challenges of the Soviet Union in the cold war. In such a climate, it is little wonder that Washington policy makers became more assertive in pushing for federal withdrawal from Indian affairs. The fallacy of what became known as termination policy is that, because the federal government did not provide moneys for economic development or promote efforts to educate more highly skilled Indian professionals with needed expertise in business and law, in the 1950s many Indian nations lacked the infrastructure to stand on their own. Washington had a fiduciary responsibility to federally recognized Indian nations such as the Wisconsin Oneidas, but it did not meet that responsibility, leaving these and many other tribes unprepared for the new onslaught of termination. Once again, as in the allotment period in the early twentieth century, some state legislators, encouraged by local and corporate interests, also hoped to extend their jurisdiction over the Indian nations. Wisconsin was one of five states that received criminal and civil jurisdiction over its Indian population in P.L. 280, passed by Congress on August 15, 1953. Although some Indian nations pushed for the change in order to address law-and-order problems in their communities, national Indian organizations such as the NCAI saw it as an erosion of tribal sovereignty and a major stumbling block to self-determination.[34]

Congress eventually ended federal recognized status for 109 Indian groups, totaling 13,263 individuals owning 1,365,801 acres of land. They removed restrictions on Indian trust lands to allow for easier leasing and sale; shifted Indian health responsibilities from the BIA to the Department of Health, Education, and Welfare; and established relocation programs to encourage Indian outmigration from reservations to urban areas. Even the creation of the Indian Claims Commission in 1946 became tied in with congressional efforts at "getting the United States out of the Indian business."[35]

In actuality, termination was both a philosophy and a specific legislation applied to the Indians. As a philosophy, the movement encouraged assimilation of Indians as individuals into the mainstream of American society and advocated the end of the federal government's responsibility for Indian affairs. To accomplish these objectives, federal legislation fell into four general categories, all with roots in the Wisconsin past: (1) the end of federal treaty relationships and trust responsibilities with certain specified Indian nations by lump-sum cash commutations of annuities or Indian claims; (2) the repeal of federal laws that set Indians apart from other American citizens; (3) the removal of restrictions of federal guardianship and supervision over certain individual Indians; and (4) the transfer of services provided by the BIA to the states and their localities or to other federal agencies, such as the Department of Health, Education, and Welfare.

Historian Donald Fixico has pointed out that both the philosophy and special legislation initiated by Congress from 1946 to 1961 were rooted well back in American Indian history.[36] Long before the postwar period, Washington policy makers were employing terms such as "emancipation." In the late nineteenth century, white reformers equated their actions with the earlier abolitionist movement, hailed Helen Hunt Jackson as the Indians' Harriet Beecher Stowe, or referred to the Dawes General Allotment Act as the Indians' "Magna Carta."[37] As historian Kenneth Philp has astutely observed, termination legislation also had roots in the rhetoric of the Indian New Deal, with vastly exaggerated claims of furthering Indian self-rule. Philp added that the roots of termination could also be found in nationwide complaints made by Native Americans themselves about the stifling bureaucratic nature of the Interior Department and the overbearing paternalism of Indian service personnel in the BIA.[38]

According to historian R. Warren Metcalf, in the late 1940s and 1950s, Robert L. Bennett, then working for the BIA's Division of Programs, believed that the old paternal relationships most tribes had with the BIA had to be eliminated, and Oneidas back home on the reservation agreed. However, Bennett and others "also believed that the tribes should determine this course of action for themselves rather than succumbing to coercive pressures from Congress or the BIA." Metcalf added that Bennett "felt that tribes should consent to the process before the bureau could terminate the trust relationship."[39] Metcalf has also clearly shown that Congress placed little importance on dealing with Indian nations in the postwar period and that the few advances that did occur had a "serendipitous" quality to them. Consequently, Arthur V. Watkins, the new head of the Senate Subcommittee on Indian Affairs, took advantage of this congressional indifference, as well as divisive Indian politics and local factors associated with his own state of Utah, to lead a small group of congressmen in pushing what he labeled the "Indian freedom program." Presenting Indian "emancipation" as an axiom, one that would inevitably lead to federal withdrawal from administering Indian programs, Watkins and others convinced their colleagues in Congress — and some tribal leaders — that termination could not be stopped. Nevertheless, the Wisconsin Oneidas were not so easily fooled by the rhetoric or by congressional actions.[40]

From 1949 onward, as Karim Tiro details in his analysis in this collection, the Wisconsin Oneida Tribal Business Committee filed a series of cases before the Indian Claims Commission seeking a financial settlement on their New York and Pennsylvania land claims, as "emigrant Indians" to Michigan Territory, and on the loss of their timber resources in Wisconsin. While the federal government saw the possibility of a settlement as a convenient way to extinguish its responsibilities, the Wisconsin Oneidas saw the legal effort in a different light: namely, as a path to assert their legal rights, to deal with outstanding issues that had plagued them for more than a century and a half, and, quite important, to gain some financial assistance to deal with their impoverished state. Once again, the Wisconsin Oneidas' adaptability to changing circumstances characterized their tribal leadership. The experience of bringing cases before this tribunal was both circuitous and frustrating, but Indians such as the Wisconsin Oneidas gained valuable experience and collected information about their history that would aid them in later litigation.[41]

The four-member Wisconsin Oneida Tribal Business Committee pursued this type of legal effort as a means to deal with the realities of poverty on the reservation, but they knew it also meant contending with the excessive restrictions the Interior Department placed on them. By the early 1950s, the BIA once again attempted to buy out the federal government's trust responsibilities under federal treaty. They offered the Wisconsin Oneidas a lump-sum payment as a buyout, one the Indians had already repeatedly rejected. Nevertheless, BIA officials reiterated that the Oneidas would eventually be terminated and their Wisconsin reservation would no longer exist. The reality of termination was made clearer when the Oneida neighbors, the Menominees, were terminated in 1954. Now a vocal group of Oneidas from Milwaukee came to the fore, using antitermination as its rallying cry. To them, treaty rights were not for sale. The result was that in 1956, after a meeting with BIA officials in Des Moines, Iowa, the Oneida Nation of Indians of Wisconsin once again rejected federal efforts at termination.

In addition to the efforts to withdraw federal involvement, end Indian claims, and extend state jurisdiction, other Washington initiatives in the post–World War II period affected the Wisconsin Oneidas. By January 1952, Commissioner of Indian Affairs Dillon S. Myer (formerly the head of the War Relocation Administration, which relocated Japanese Americans to detention camps during World War II) established the Branch of Placement and Relocation. This branch funneled Indians off reservations.[42] Through the placement offices, the BIA deliberately sent Indians to urban areas far from home — a policy echoing the early federal boarding school mandates — as a way to swiftly acculturate them to white mainstream values. Although some Oneidas were relocated to urban areas, many other Wisconsin Oneidas had already moved to urban areas before the federal relocation program began. Nevertheless, the long-standing Oneida community in Milwaukee was affected by Indian newcomers arriving under the auspices of the relocation program. The poor conditions these new arrivals faced and the limited government services provided once they settled into this urban environment spawned red power activism, and some Oneidas became directly involved in Indian militancy.[43]

In 1961, a national convocation of American Indian leaders met in Chicago to discuss a wide range of issues and problems their communities faced. Under the auspices of Sol Tax and Nancy Lurie, this historic meeting — the American Indian Chicago Conference — effectively networked native peoples and encouraged cooperative efforts for tribal improvement. The following year, tribal leaders, including Wisconsin Oneida tribal secretary Eva Danforth, whose memoir is included in this collection, journeyed to the White House for a special meeting with President Kennedy, to present him with the "Declaration of Indian Purpose."[44]

Things were to change in the Kennedy-Johnson years, especially after President Johnson's initiation of his "War on Poverty." But the ideas were initially directed at urban blacks, and helping American Indian communities still remained an afterthought. The programs instituted by the Office of Economic Opportunity's Job Corps and VISTA had significant but "accidental and unintentional consequences for American Indian communities." Historian Thomas Clarkin has written that even Secretary of the Interior Stewart Udall was never involved in the planning of the War on Poverty. "Indian welfare and well-being did not constitute a major area of concern" in Johnson's initiation of his War on Poverty, and few policy makers "knew much about Indians." Programs for so-called culturally deprived populations were, nevertheless, open to American Indians on reservations, and many of these communities took advantage of the programs or the expertise provided.[45] For instance, the Oneida Nation Library originated with these federal programs. The Job Corps and VISTA had a major impact in other areas as well. Tribal leaders saw education as a means of overcoming poverty and began to seek out federal programs to train youth, especially the newly initiated Head Start program. The experience of working in or with outsiders provided skills needed for the Wisconsin Oneida turnaround in the 1970s. Although the 1960s programs were not designed by Native Americans and were excessively paternalistic, a new Wisconsin Oneida tribal leadership, whose roles are described fully in parts 3 and 4 of this book, had the vision to make use of them for Oneida betterment while they lasted. Some of these leaders were Irene Moore, Norbert Hill Sr., and Purcell Powless.

In 1966, President Johnson appointed Robert L. Bennett to be commissioner of Indian affairs, the first Native American to be named to the post since Ely S. Parker during Reconstruction. Although he was hardly radical, according to Clarkin, Bennett "consistently advocated policies and programs that promoted self-determination." Clarkin added that Bennett "used his bureaucratic skills to sidetrack efforts to continue tribal termination." With his "quiet style of leadership," the commissioner helped to slowly sow the seeds for President Johnson's successor, Richard Nixon, to announce the formal repudiation of termination.[46]

In November 1969, a small cadre of idealistic American Indians, working with the leadership of the Oakland–San Francisco Bay council, seized Alcatraz Island, the notorious deserted maximum-security federal penitentiary, and proclaimed it for "Indians of All Nations." Organized by Adam Fortunate Eagle Nordwall, a Red Lake Ojibwe artist and businessman in California, the occupation of Alcatraz immediately drew worldwide attention. The Indians skillfully equated the event with their own tribespeople's "imprisonment" in terrible poverty and federal neglect on reservations and in urban areas. The takeover of Alcatraz predated the more radical direction of Indian politics, most visible later in the rise of the American Indian Movement (AIM). By the summer of 1970, less-committed Indians and hangers-on began to outnumber the original occupiers of Alcatraz, yet the United States Coast Guard did not retake the island until June 11, 1971. This dramatic event had a direct influence on the next three decades. "Veterans" of the Alcatraz takeover included Cherokee tribal chair Wilma Mankiller as well as Gerald L. Hill, former chief attorney of the Oneida Nation of Indians of Wisconsin and former head of the American Indian Trial Lawyers Association. In the midst of the Vietnam War and social upheavals throughout the United States, Native

Americans attempted to focus Americans' attention on issues related to America's forgotten peoples, their poverty, and their dissatisfaction with federal and state policies.[47]

The presidency of Richard Nixon was the turning point in the contemporary history of American Indians. On July 8, 1970, in an important presidential message to Congress, Nixon enunciated a clear shift in federal Indian policy.[48] Calling the American Indians the "most deprived and most isolated minority group in our nation," the president acknowledged that, from first contact, "American Indians have been oppressed and brutalized, deprived of their ancestral lands and denied the opportunity to control their own destiny." He next acknowledged the failures of the United States government's past responses. "Even the federal programs which are intended to meet their needs have frequently proven to be ineffective and demeaning."[49]

Nixon then rejected "forced termination" and turned attention to ending that federal policy. To him, the federal government owed American Indians not a charitable responsibility but a legal obligation. He stressed that through "written treaties and formal and informal agreements," Indians had ceded "claims to vast tracts of land and have accepted life on government reservations" in exchange for American commitments to provide them a "standard of living comparable to that of other Americans." Thus, terminating "this relationship would be no more appropriate than to terminate the citizenship rights of any other American." Besides, Nixon continued, the termination policies of the past decade and a half had failed in their goals and had clearly proved harmful to Indians. President Nixon maintained that the threat of termination had intensified Indians' fears and mistrust of all federal programs, which further weakened the programs' effectiveness. Moreover, termination had increased dependence on the federal bureaucracy rather than fostering independence from it. "Of the Department of the Interior's programs directly serving Indians," the president stressed, "only 1.5 percent are presently under Indian control. Only 2.4 percent of HEW's Indian health programs are run by Indians."[50]

Realizing that he was taking a historic step in reversing policies, Nixon emphasized: "In place of policies which oscillate between the deadly extremes of forced termination and constant paternalism, we suggest a policy in which the federal government and the Indian community play complementary roles." The president concluded: "The Indians of America need federal assistance — this much has long been clear. What has not always been clear, however, is that the federal government needs Indian energies and Indian leadership if its assistance is to be effective in improving the conditions of Indian life. It is a new and balanced relationship between the United States government and the first Americans that is at the heart of our approach to Indian problems. And that is why we now approach these problems with new confidence that they will successfully be overcome."[51]

Meanwhile, Indian activism was growing increasingly potent. In Milwaukee in 1971, AIM had seized an abandoned Coast Guard facility on Lake Michigan and converted it into a school, where they held courses on American Indian traditions. Hundreds of Oneidas had lived in Milwaukee since the 1920s, organizing Indian associations and festivals. Now some of them helped organize protests and lead the AIM chapter in the city.

In October 1972, the "Trail of Broken Treaties" caravan reached Washington, D.C., just before the presidential election and occupied BIA headquarters. The caravan had traveled across the country, bringing Indian treaty rights concerns to the American public's attention. Although the protest was intended to be a peaceful one, some of the activists sacked the building and carried off vital files needed by Indian nations, including the Wisconsin Oneidas, for their litigation. Three months later, members of the American Indian Movement took over the hamlet of Wounded Knee on the Pine Ridge reservation in South Dakota, the site of the massacre of Lakota Indians in 1890. For more than two months, the Indians were in an armed confrontation with federal marshals, the FBI, and American military personnel. As a result, the occupation received worldwide media attention. Before the takeover ended, several Indians and non-Indians were killed and wounded in the showdown.

Though a few Wisconsin Oneidas broke the law to achieve their goals, most sought to use the law to attempt to reclaim land. The two-hundred-year-old Oneida New York land claim was sparked again in the mid- and late 1960s by meetings of three communities — Wisconsin, New York, and Canada. In January 1974, the United States Supreme Court overturned

133 years of case law, allowing the Oneidas legal standing to sue for land in federal courts. Challenging restrictions to sue as set forth in Cherokee Nation v. Georgia (1831), George Shattuck, the Oneidas' attorney, successfully argued that New York state had violated the federal Trade and Intercourse Act of 1790, which required the presence of a federal commissioner in any land dealings made by a federally recognized tribe with a state or individuals.[52] Although this decision has benefited other Indian nations in land settlements with other states, the Wisconsin Oneidas have been thwarted by New York state officials in later federal court decisions in their efforts to gain compensation for lands lost.

With this increasing litigation and intensifying Indian activism, a congressional call went out for a thorough study of American Indian policy. In the first week of 1975, the United States Congress passed two bills that reshaped American Indian policy. The American Indian Policy Review Commission Act and the Indian Self-Determination and Education Assistance Act significantly changed the nature and future direction of the federal government's relationship with American Indian nations.[53] In many ways, these two acts, especially the latter, challenged the overbearing colonial relationship that had existed until then. The changes allowed for a greater tribal voice in decision making, especially in contracting and in educational policies, ones that had often been denied to Native Americans.

On January 2, 1975, Congress created the American Indian Policy Review Commission (AIPRC), also called the Abourezk Commission, to promote the study of the historical and legal status of American Indians and their nations and recommend new legislation to remedy the situation. Sponsored by Senator James Abourezk of South Dakota and coming in the wake of six years of upheavals in Indian country — the Indian takeover of Alcatraz Island (1969), the Indian occupation of the Bureau of Indian Affairs (1972), and the Wounded Knee standoff (1973) — the joint resolution passed by Congress was a bold attempt to conduct a review of policy, the first major study since the Meriam Report conducted by the Institute for Government Research (Brookings Institution) in 1928.[54] Three members of the Senate, three members of the House, five Native American representatives including Wisconsin Oneida Ernest Stevens Sr., and their staffs worked on collecting and disseminating data as well as making extensive recommendations. The result was nine volumes containing vital information and recommendations, including ways to improve reservation economies and health care and potential programs for long-neglected urban Indian communities. The commission also recommended ways to restore federal status to tribes that had been terminated in the 1950s and 1960s. It also suggested changes in the administrative structure within the Bureau of Indian Affairs through which non-federally-funded tribes could seek federal recognition that would allow access to federal courts and to federal funding from the Department of the Interior.[55]

Looking back at the work of the AIPRC more than three decades after the issuance of its final report, one can clearly appreciate its long-term significance. In a reappraisal of federal Indian policy, anthropologist George Castile has concluded that the AIPRC did have a significant impact: "...if nothing else, congressional attention was directed toward Indian affairs." Castile points out that a "small flurry of Indian legislation" was "due at least partly to the issuance of the [AIPRC] report." Castile suggests that the Indian Child Welfare Act (1978), the American Indian Religious Freedom Act (1978), and the creation of the federal acknowledgment process were just a few immediate results of Congress's creation of the AIPRC.[56]

The Indian Self-Determination and Education Assistance Act, passed on January 4, 1975, held even more importance for Wisconsin Oneidas. The legislation provided more Indian control of schools educating Indian children. It amended the Johnson-O'Malley Act of 1934, which had established a contracting relationship between school districts that taught Indian students and the Department of the Interior. In the past, school districts used these Johnson-O'Malley funds for their general student population rather than for educational services for Native American students. Now, for the first time, each contracting school district had to submit a plan with objectives to meet the educational needs of Indian students; where non-Indian students were in programs designed to meet the needs of Indian pupils, "money expended under such contract [would] be prorated to cover the participation of only the Indian students." Moreover, every contracting school district in a district with a minority of Indian students had to have a Native American representative on its school board.[57] Within the first five years of its operation, 370 American Indian nations, including the Wisconsin Oneidas, had "contracted for the operation of $200 million worth of programs" under the act and "$22.3 million was paid to the tribes to cover the overhead in the contracts."[58]

Overall, the act acknowledged both the failure of past federal policies to provide tribal self-rule and, indirectly, the inherent sovereignty of American Indian nations. Section 2 of the act stated, "The Indian people will never surrender their desire to control their relationships both among themselves and with non-Indian governments, organizations and persons...." The act's preamble described its aim:

> ...to provide maximum Indian participation in the Government and education of Indian people; to provide for the full participation of Indian tribes in programs and services conducted by the Federal Government for Indians and to encourage the development of human resources of the Indian people; to establish a program of assistance to upgrade Indian education; to support the right of Indian citizens to control their own educational activities; and for other purposes.[59]

The act acknowledged that the impetus for the legislation came directly from "the strong expression" by the Indian people. It added that the goal was "to permit an orderly transition from federal domination of programs for and services to Indians to effective and meaningful participation by the Indian people in the planning, conduct, and administration of those programs and services."[60]

. . . .

These two acts in 1975 did not create sovereignty in the minds of Wisconsin Oneidas. They merely reinforced what the Oneidas had always known they were: a sovereign nation. The following pages recount the remarkable story of Oneida cultural survival — namely, how this nation was able to maintain its separate existence as native peoples even as it has moved approximately twelve hundred miles from its ancient homeland. Yet this collection is only a beginning. The Oneidas have faced many challenges since 1975, economic survival being only one of them, and they will continue to do so. The Wisconsin Oneida nation — with its expanding population and its division by two counties and five separate school districts — must be ever vigilant about maintaining its unique culture and, with it, its inherent sovereignty as a nation within a nation.

Notes

1. For example, Joseph T. Glatthaar and James Kirby Martin, *Forgotten Allies: The Oneida Indians and the American Revolution* (New York: Hill and Wang, 2006); Carl Benn, *The Iroquois in the War of 1812* (Toronto: University of Toronto Press, 1998), 155–159; Laurence M. Hauptman, *The Iroquois in the Civil War: From Battlefield to Reservation* (Syracuse, NY: Syracuse University Press, 1993), 67–84.

2. Treaty with the Oneidas, Stat. 7 (1838): 566; General Allotment Act, Stat. 24 (1887): 388–391.

3. James W. Oberly, "The Dawes Act and the Oneida Indian Reservation of New York," in Laurence M. Hauptman and L. Gordon McLester III, eds., *The Oneida Indians in the Age of Allotment, 1860–1920* (Norman: University of Oklahoma Press, 2006) 190-193. See also Arlinda Locklear, "The Allotment of the Oneida Reservation and Its Legal Ramifications," in *The Oneida Indian Experience: Two Perspectives*, ed. Jack Campisi and Laurence Hauptman, 83–100 (Syracuse, NY: Syracuse University Press, 1988).

4. "For Benefit of Oneidas," *Brown County Democrat*, February 22, 1901.

5. "[J. C. Hart] Will Petition for Law for Township Rights," *Brown County Democrat*, December 12, 1902.

6. Ida Blackhawk, "Hard Times at Oneida," WPA, Oneida Language and Folklore Project, Oneida Nation of Indians of Wisconsin. For more on these Oneidas, see Hauptman and McLester, *The Oneida Indians in the Age of Allotment, 1860–1920*, 201.

7. Burke Act, Stat. 34 (1906): 182–183.

8. Solomon Wheelock, WPA Story, "How the Oneidas Lost Their Land," in *Oneida Lives: Long-Lost Voices of the Wisconsin Oneidas*, ed. Herbert S. Lewis [with assistance of L. Gordon McLester III], 36 (Lincoln: University of Nebraska Press, 2005).

9. Burke Act, 1,018.

10. Francis Paul Prucha, *The Great Father: The United States Government and the American Indians* (Lincoln: University of Nebraska Press, 1984), 2:876–877.

11. Hauptman and McLester, *The Oneida Indians in the Age of Allotment*, 182.

12. 36 Stat., 855–863 Omnibus Act, June 25, 1910.

13. Jack Campisi, "Ethnic Identity and Boundary Maintenance in Three Oneida Communities" (unpublished PhD dissertation, State University of New York at Albany, 1974): 148–151.

14. Wisc. Stat., ch. 96, secs. 1494-121, 1494-122 (1907).

15. Charles L. Davis, Inspection Report to Commissioner of Indian Affairs, October 16, 1909, #16491-09-312 (Oneida), CCF, 1907–1939, BIA, RG75, NA.

16. See U.S. Congress, House, Oneida Indians. Letter from the Secretary of the Interior Transmitting Report of Negotiations with Oneida Indians for Commutation of Their Perpetual Annuities as Provided by the Act of March 3, 1911, 62nd Cong., 2d sess., 1911, Doc. 251.

17. Caroline W. Andrus, "Changing Indian Conditions," *Southern Workman* 51 (January 1922): 26. For the work of the federal competency commission, see Laurence M. Hauptman, "The Wisconsin Oneidas and the Federal Competency Commission of 1917," in Hauptman and McLester, *The Oneida Indians in the Age of Allotment,* 200–225.

18. Robert Ritzenthaler, "The Oneida Indians in Wisconsin," *Bulletin* (Public Museum of the City of Milwaukee) 19 (November 1950): 23.

19. Anderson Cornelius, interview by Laurence M. Hauptman, October 20, 1978, Oneida, WI; Robert Ritzenthaler, "The Cultural History of the Wisconsin Oneidas" (unpublished master's thesis, University of Wisconsin–Madison, 1940): 10–11; Alfred W. Briggs (Wisconsin director of unemployment relief) to John Collier, May 5, 1934, #14504-1934-723 (Keshena), BIA CCF, RG75, NA.

20. Ralph Fredenberg to commissioner of Indian affairs, April 18, 1935, #803-1934-310 (Keshena), BIA CCF, RG75, NA.

21. Campisi claims that there were 84.8 acres of land held in common by 1934. J. C. Kinney suggests 89 acres of tribal lands and 692 acres of land owned individually by Oneida allottees. Basehart insists that there were 733 acres held individually. See Campisi, "Ethnic Identity and Boundary Maintenance," 158; J. Kinney, *A Continent Lost — A Civilization Won: Indian Land Tenure in America* (Baltimore, MD: Johns Hopkins University Press, 1937): 355–356; Harry Basehart, "Historical Changes in the Kinship System of the Oneida Indians" (unpublished PhD dissertation, Harvard University, 1952): 218.

22. For more detail on this divisive political setting, see Laurence M. Hauptman, *The Iroquois and the New Deal* (Syracuse, NY: Syracuse University Press, 1981), 74–83.

23. Ibid. For the Indian Reorganization Act (IRA) of June 18, 1934, see 48 Stat., 984–988.

24. Hauptman, *The Iroquois and the New Deal,* 74–87, 164–176; Herbert S. Lewis, *Oneida Lives.*

25. Ritzenthaler, "The Oneida Indians in Wisconsin," 25.

26. American Indian Policy Review Commission, Final Report (Washington, D.C.: USGO, 1977), 1: 309–310.

27. 48 Stat., 984–988.

28. For more on this new level of bureaucratic supervision, see Laurence M. Hauptman, "The Indian Reorganization Act," in *Aggressions of Civilization,* ed. Sandra Cadwalader and Vine Deloria Jr., 131–146 (Philadelphia: Temple University Press, 1984). Felix S. Cohen, *On the Drafting of Tribal Constitutions,* ed. David E. Wilkins (Norman: University of Oklahoma Press, 2007). Even Felix Cohen, who had helped draft these model constitutions, as

Wilkins points out in his introduction, opposed the idea of sending "canned constitutions" to be blindly accepted by Indian communities.

29. Quoted in Kenneth R. Philp, ed., *Indian Self-Rule: First-Hand Accounts of Indian-White Relations from Roosevelt to Reagan* (Salt Lake City: Howe Brothers, 1986), 84.

30. House Committee on Indian Affairs, Select Committee to Investigate Indian Affairs and Conditions in the United States, A Bill to Authorize and Direct and Conduct an Investigation to Determine Whether the Changed Status of the Indian Requires a Revision of the Laws and Regulations Affecting the American Indian: Hearings on H.R. 166, Part 1, 78th Cong., 2d sess., 1944, 16–21, 61–63.

31. Kenneth R. Philp, *Termination Revisited: American Indians on the Trail to Self-Determination, 1933-1953* (Lincoln: University of Nebraska Press, 1999), 72–74.

32. Ibid., 75.

33. Ibid., 140–152.

34. Prucha, *The Great Father,* 2:1,013–1,059; Charles F. Wilkinson and Eric R. Biggs, "The Evolution of the Termination Policy," *American Indian Law Review* 5 (1980): 139–184.

35. See note 34.

36. See Donald L. Fixico, *Termination and Relocation: Federal Indian Policy, 1945–1960* (Albuquerque: University of New Mexico Press, 1986), ix–xiv.

37. For the typical rhetoric of the postwar era, see Bess Furman, "Campaign Pushed to 'Free' Indians," *New York Times,* July 22, 1947. For earlier rhetoric on the Dawes Act, see Prucha, *The Great Father,* 2:670–671.

38. Philp, *Termination Revisited,* xi–xiv.

39. R. Warren Metcalf, *Termination's Legacy: The Discarded Indians of Utah* (Lincoln: University of Nebraska Press, 2002), 12–13.

40. Ibid., 11–48.

41. Philp, *Termination Revisited,* 17. See also Harvey D. Rosenthal, *Their Day in Court: A History of the Indian Claims Commission* (New York: Garland, 1990).

42. Prucha, *The Great Father,* 2:1,081.

43. American Indian Policy Review Commission, Task Force Eight, Final Report: Report on Urban and Rural Non-Reservation Indians (Washington, D.C.: USGO, 1976), 23–43.

44. Nancy O. Lurie, "The Voice of the American Indian: Report on the American Indian Chicago Conference," *Current Anthropology* 2 (December 1961): 478–500; Laurence M. Hauptman and Jack Campisi, "The Voice of Eastern Indians: The American Indian Chicago Conference and the Movement for Federal Recognition," Proceedings of the American Philosophical Society 132 (December 1988): 316–329.

45. Thomas Clarkin, *Federal Indian Policy in the Kennedy and Johnson Administrations, 1961–1969* (Albuquerque: University of New Mexico Press, 2001), 111–112.

46. Ibid., 228–230.

47. For a firsthand account of the Alcatraz occupation, see Adam Fortunate Eagle Nordwall, *Heart of the Rock: The Indian Invasion of Alcatraz* (Norman: University of Oklahoma Press, 2002).

48. George Pierre Castile, *To Show Heart: Native American Self-Determination and Federal Indian Policy, 1960–1975* (Tucson: University of Arizona Press, 1998), 158–160; Joan Hoff, *Nixon Reconsidered* (New York: Basic Books, 1994), 44; Laurence M. Hauptman, "Finally Acknowledging Native Peoples: American Indian Policies Since the Nixon Administration," in *"They Made Us Many Promises": The American Indian Experience, 1524 to the Present*, 2nd ed., ed. Philip Weeks (Wheeling, IL: Harlan Davidson, 2002), 220–228.

49. Richard Nixon, Public Papers of the Presidents of the United States: Richard Nixon, 1970 (Washington, D.C.: USGO, 1971), 564–576.

50. Ibid.

51. Ibid.

52. Oneida Indian Nation v. County of Oneida, 414 U.S. 661 (January 21, 1974); George Shattuck, *The Oneida Land Claims: A Legal History* (Syracuse, NY: Syracuse University Press, 1991); Jack Campisi, "New York–Oneida Treaty of 1795: A Finding of Fact," *American Indian Law Review 4* (Summer 1976): 71–82.

53. Establishment of the American Indian Policy Review Commission, (January 2, 1975): Stat. 88 Stat.: 1,910–1,913; Indian Self-Determination and Education Assistance Act, Stat. 88 (January 4, 1975): 88 stat. 2,203-14.

54. Lewis Meriam et al., *The Problem of Indian Administration* (Baltimore, MD: Johns Hopkins University Press, 1928).

55. For a summary of the commission's findings, see American Indian Policy Review Commission, Final Report, 2 vols. (Washington, D.C.: USGO, 1977).

56. George Pierre Castile, *Taking Charge: Self-Determination and Federal Indian Policy, 1975–1993* (Tucson: University of Arizona Press, 2006), 36, 47–48.

57. 88 Stat., 2,203–2,214.

58. Prucha, *The Great Father*, 2:1,162.

59. 88 Stat., 2,203–2,214.

60. Ibid.

A Nation
within
a Nation

Voices of the
Oneidas in Wisconsin

Part 1

Maintaining Wisconsin Oneida Community Life

Reservation and City

Introduction

T HE WISCONSIN ONEIDAS HAVE MANAGED to maintain their community life and separate existence, even in the face of threatening federal Indian policies and state and local efforts to reduce their landbase and restrict their jurisdiction. In the first essay in Part I, Dr. Jack Campisi, emeritus professor of anthropology at Wellesley College and former project director of the Mashantucket Pequot Tribal Nation Museum, shares his insights on Wisconsin's Oneida community in the 1970s. Based on his forty-year fieldwork experiences among the Wisconsin Oneidas, Campisi describes how the Wisconsin Oneidas maintained a separate way of life from their non-Indian neighbors, held fast to their kinship networks, and built community institutions separate from those of the non-Indians of Brown and Outagamie counties.

The remaining essays in Part I support Campisi's description of a distinct Indian existence by elaborating on the different aspects of this separate community. Loretta Metoxen, former vice chair of the Wisconsin Oneidas and presently tribal historian, and Dr. Carol Cornelius, the head of the Oneida Cultural Heritage Department, explain the importance of the current reservation lands to the Wisconsin Oneidas, past and present. After migrating from their New York homeland in the 1820s and 1830s, the Oneidas developed a special reciprocal relationship with their new environs and the natural world of Duck Creek, where they have now lived for seven generations.

Much of Oneida life centered around the two major churches, as Evelyn Smith-Elm explains in her essay on the Christian traditions the Oneidas brought from New York. The reservation's Methodist and Episcopal churches had their beginnings in New York during the second half of the eighteenth and early nineteenth centuries. Oneidas who migrated in the 1820s established the Hobart church, later the Holy Apostles Church, which is the oldest Episcopal congregation in Wisconsin.[1]

The Hobart church, according to Smith-Elm, served a larger population and was more documented than that of the Oneida Methodists. The Methodists were the minority of Oneidas, descended from Indians who migrated in the early 1830s under the leadership of Chief Jacob Cornelius, but they, too, have played a key role in the history of the community. In the early 1970s, the Oneidas gained another spiritual asset as well: an Iroquois longhouse was established for the first time in Wisconsin. It continues, along with the Methodist, Episcopal, and other denomination churches, to serve the spiritual needs of the community.

Also in Part I, two authors focus on Oneida education through the years. After World War II, Oneida tribal leadership faced a crisis in education stemming from the nation's impoverished state. In the 1950s and 1960s, a new tribal leadership emerged that saw that the cycle of poverty could be broken only by encouraging new directions in education. Thelma McLester, director of the Oneida Nation Education Department, describes the crisis — focusing on two outside reports made in the 1950s — and the subsequent turnaround. Judy Cornelius, who for eight years headed the Oneida Nation Library, a vital part of the education of children and adults on the reservation, shows the early precedents for the library and how the Lyndon Johnson–initiated programs of the 1960s, CETA and VISTA, contributed to the formal establishment of the community library.

Another essay discusses the years from 1898 into the post–World War II period, when Wisconsin Oneida women established a guildlike enterprise that allowed them to achieve national and international recognition as artists; at the same time, it provided some supplemental money for their households. This "self-help" project was inspired by the arts and crafts movement of the late nineteenth and early twentieth centuries. Dr. Patricia Matteson describes the life and influence of Sybil Carter, a Southern white reformer-missionary, who founded, organized, and administered a northern European lacemaking enterprise among the Wisconsin Oneidas. Led by Josephine Webster, the daughter of Chief Cornelius Hill, the venture included well more than one hundred Oneida women. Some made lace, others did the packing and mailing, while still others traveled to regional gatherings, world's fairs, and national and international expositions to display and sell the award-winning lace. Their most famous artistry is housed at one of New York City's architectural gems, the Cathedral of St. John the Divine; the Oneida lace served as the altar pieces when the cathedral was dedicated in 1911. Although Carter's association formally ended in 1926, Webster and the Oneida women continued this tradition until well after World War II.[2]

Debra Jenny and Betty McLester also discuss how this earlier project motivates Oneida women today to try to revive the great artistic tradition of their mothers' and grandmothers' generations.

Next, an essay by Oscar Archiquette, a nationally prominent Wisconsin Oneida who pushed for the acceptance of the Indian Reorganization Act and continued to be active in tribal politics until his death in 1971, recounts the positive changes in the community during the Indian New Deal. One of the leading promoters of the Oneida language throughout his life, Archiquette was a key figure who worked with anthropologists on the WPA Oneida Language and Folklore Project from 1938 to 1942. This project resulted in the publication of a modern orthography of the Oneida language, a hymnal in the Oneida language, and thousands of pages of language texts containing every aspect of Oneida culture and history from the 1820s to the New Deal.

The WPA Oneida Language and Folklore Project of the 1930s has special meaning to the community. In contrast to the WPA Indian-Pioneer History of Oklahoma and other Native American oral history projects of the time, these WPA interviewers were all Oneida tribal members who collected stories about events, foods, language, medicine, personalities, and traditions in the Oneida language.[3] The project, administered for the WPA by the University of Wisconsin Anthropology Department — Morris Swadesh, Floyd Lounsbury, and Harry Basehart — amassed a unique collection that has been used to educate and inspire several generations of Oneidas.[4]

Dr. Clifford Abbott, professor of anthropology at the University of Wisconsin at Green Bay, has worked with Oneida elders for more than thirty years in efforts to preserve this Indian language. He describes one of the lesser-known legacies of the WPA project: codeswitching. Abbott's analysis is followed by Lewis Webster's WPA story describing one aspect of Oneida economic survival in hard times: work as itinerant cherry pickers in northern Wisconsin. After Webster's story, Ernest Stevens Jr. describes tribal efforts to teach the Oneida language in the early 1970s.

Stevens also tells the remarkable story of his grandmother, Maria Hinton, who, along with Dr. Abbott and Hinton's late brother Amos Christjohn, compiled the first modern dictionary of the Oneida language.

Finally, Part I concludes with a contribution by Opal Skenandore — whose family was among the first Oneidas to settle in Milwaukee — showing the significance of city life to tribal existence. Even before the construction of interstate highways, the Milwaukee community was never completely isolated from the Oneidas in Brown and Outagamie counties. Skenandore describes Alpheus Smith's important role in establishing the Consolidated Tribes, the first Native organization in the city. She also evokes the Milwaukee Oneidas' attempts at collaborative efforts to develop cultural events and activities and describes the city's gathering places, the visits back home to Oneida, and the changing political climate that led to red power militancy. As will be shown in Part 3, these particular Milwaukee Oneidas were to significantly shape tribal politics from 1933 to 1970.[5]

Notes

1. See, for example, the numerous references to the history of the Episcopal Church among the Oneidas in Laurence M. Hauptman and L. Gordon McLester III, *Chief Daniel Bread and the Oneida Nation of Indians of Wisconsin* (Norman: University of Oklahoma Press, 2002), chapter 10. The Episcopal Church among the Oneidas is the focus of much of Julia Bloomfield's *The Oneidas*, 2nd ed. (New York: Alden Bros., 1907) and the pamphlet published by the Episcopal Church Mission to the Oneidas, *Oneida: The People of the Stone: The Church's Mission to the Oneidas* (Oneida, WI: Episcopal Church of the Holy Apostles, 1899).

2. Sybil Carter Lace Association, Annual Reports, 1911 and 1912; Josephine Webster, *The Oneida Indian Lace Makers of Oneida, Wisconsin* (Oneida Indian Reservation, 1943) — sales brochure, found in (Smithsonian) Cooper-Hewitt Museum, New York City. See also Laurence M. Hauptman and L. Gordon McLester III, eds., *The Oneida Indians in the Age of Allotment, 1860–1920* (Norman: University of Oklahoma Press, 2006), 92–95, 109–111; Thelma McLester, "Josephine Hill Webster, 1883–1978: Supervisor of Oneida Lace Industry and First Woman Postmaster," in *The Oneida Indian Experience: Two Perspectives*, ed. Jack Campisi and Laurence M. Hauptman, 116–118 (Syracuse, NY: Syracuse University Press, 1988).

3. For books that draw from WPA Oklahoma Indian-Pioneer series administered by Grant and Carolyn Foreman, see Theda Perdue, *Nations Remembered: An Oral History of the Cherokees, Chickasaws, Choctaws and Seminoles in Oklahoma, 1865–1907* (Norman: University of Oklahoma Press, 1980) and David La Vere, *Life Among the Texas Indians: The WPA Narratives* (College Station: Texas A&M University Press, 1998).

4. Herbert S. Lewis, ed., *Oneida Lives: Long-Lost Voices of the Wisconsin Oneidas* (Lincoln: University of Nebraska Press, 2005), xvii–xxxviii. See also Jack Campisi and Laurence M. Hauptman, "Talking Back: The Oneida Language and Folklore Project," Proceedings of the American Philosophical Society 125 (December 1981): 441–448.

5. For the Oneidas in Milwaukee, see Nancy O. Lurie, "Recollections of an Urban Indian Community," in Campisi and Hauptman, *The Oneida Indian Experience*, 101–107; Robert E. Ritzenthaler and Mary Sellers, "Indians in an Urban Setting," *Wisconsin Archaeologist* 36 (1955): 147–161.

Looking Back

The Oneida Nation of Indians of Wisconsin in the Early 1970s

by Jack Campisi

ARRIVING AT AUSTIN STRAUBEL INTERNATIONAL AIRPORT in Green Bay, Wisconsin, one cannot help but be aware of the presence of the Oneida Nation. Directly across from the airport are a hotel, casino, and bingo hall owned by the nation. Traveling west on Airport Road one sees some of the Oneidas' administrative buildings identified in the Oneida language. In addition, there are other obvious markers: street names, billboards, radio and television spots. These are more than ads. They identify the locations of Oneida tribal buildings. This is a far cry from what I had seen of the community in the early 1970s.

My first meeting with the Wisconsin Oneidas came on a clear, windy, bitterly cold day in the first week of January 1972. I landed at Austin Straubel and was met by Bill Gollnick, an Oneida and a student at the University of Wisconsin–Green Bay. He had been sent to pick me up by James Clifton, anthropologist of note and dean at the university. We piled into Gollnick's car, which I recall had a nonfunctioning heater, and headed off not to the university but to his mother's house in a development on the outskirts of Green Bay. It seemed to me that the area was tabletop flat, but it was hard to make out geographic features because of the blowing snow. At the house I met a contingent of Oneidas, among them Gordon McLester, Myron Smith, and of course Gollnick's mother, Josephine. Much of the meeting is a blur now, partly because of the lapse of time and partly because upon coming into the very warm house from the frigid outdoors, my glasses frosted up, and I was never quite able to see clearly through them or without them. My hosts asked some questions about the purpose of my visit, and I explained that I was working on a dissertation on the three Oneida communities in Wisconsin, Ontario, and New York. However, a serious, unanticipated problem soon became eminently clear. When I told them that I had come to work with Oscar Archiquette, there was a long pause. They informed me that he had died a week or so before.

We exchanged a few more pleasantries, and then Gollnick and I left for the university. There Bill guided me through the semisubterranean labyrinth that was the university, and again I struggled to clear my glasses. He delivered me to Dean Clifton's office and left. Clifton and I went over my teaching assignments for the intersession, and then I informed him of the death of Oscar Archiquette. From the expression on his face I knew immediately that this was a serious turn of events. For one thing, I was to have stayed with and worked with Archiquette. Clifton made arrangements for me to stay at a local motel while he worked on getting other accommodations. In a few days, Gordon and Betty McLester graciously opened their door to me.

The very inception of the trip to Green Bay had been serendipitous. The previous October, Dr. William Fenton, who was the senior professor on my dissertation committee, a research professor of anthropology at the State University of New York at Albany, and the acknowledged "dean of Iroquois studies," had received a call from Clifton, asking if he had any students who would be interested in doing research with the Wisconsin Oneidas. I happened to be in Fenton's office, and he handed me the telephone. A day or so before, Clifton explained, Oscar Archiquette had walked into Clifton's office and demanded to know why he and the university were expending so much time and energy on the Menominees and ignoring the Oneidas. He wanted Clifton to find someone to write the Wisconsin Oneidas' history, which initiated a quick call to Fenton. (Clifton once told me that he did not allow a paper to remain on his desk at the end of the day.)

A second, earlier, serendipitous event had set me on the research topic in the first place. By chance, one of my neighbors in my home town of Milan, New York, was an Oneida, originally from Ontario, Canada. His name was Richard Chrisjohn, and we had met several summers before while we were doing construction work. Chrisjohn had complained to me on a number of occasions that no one seemed to be interested in the history of his tribe. At that time I was teaching social studies in a local public school and making ends meet by working on construction during the summer. At age thirty-eight, I decided to go for a doctorate in anthropology, and Chrisjohn's complaint offered an opportunity for research.

I spoke with him about my plans, and he agreed to help me. I could not have had a better friend. He introduced me to people on his reservation at Southwold, Ontario, and at the thirty-two acres remaining to the Oneidas in New York at the time. We also visited Oneidas living on Onondaga reservation south of Syracuse and elsewhere in the state. During the two years prior to my Wisconsin visit, we traveled together to visit Oneidas, and I spent many hours at Chrisjohn's home in Milan, talking about his experiences growing up in Canada and later New York, while he carved condolence canes, masks, tables, and a range of other items for sale. He provided me with details on the culture of the Oneidas as he understood it. Through him I made valuable contacts in New York and Ontario, and through me, he first met his fellow Oneidas in Wisconsin. It was a natural symbiosis.

I returned to Green Bay with my family in the summer of 1972 to teach and to continue my research. By this time I had blocked out the main areas of research and had received approval from my committee for the dissertation topic. I was to do a longitudinal study of the Oneidas, with particular attention to the culture, histories, and contemporary societies of the three Oneida communities. The objective was to understand the means by which the three communities adjusted to the changing conditions they faced over the three centuries of interaction with Euro-Americans.

The prevalent view at the time, held by the national government and by the social sciences, was that assimilation was inevitable and once completed would result in the disappearance of ethnic groups, including Indian tribes. Many anthropologists accepted this so-called melting pot view and, as a result, expended their research efforts on what was termed "salvage anthropology." As late as the 1960s, researchers were predicting the end to ethnic differences:

> In virtually all instances of inter-ethnic contact, no matter how great the initial differences between the groups, people sooner or later become integrated into a single unit and convinced of their descent from common ancestors; the only exceptions are those few cases in which one group has been completely exterminated.[1]

This viewpoint portrayed the dominant society (e.g., American) as the independent variable. As ethnic groups (including tribes) were drawn into the dominant society's economic system, and as individuals in ethnic groups become acculturated, the social distance between them and the dominant group diminished and they identified themselves more with the social system of the dominant group. In the end, the distinctive ethnic markers would be replaced by identity with and assimilation into the dominant group. Differences would continue to exist, but they would be the product of social class (or caste) and not based on ethnicity.

The problem with this model, when applied to American Indian tribes, was that despite two hundred years of national and state efforts, Indian communities continued to exist throughout the United States. For assimilationists the explanation was simple: reservations did not represent Indian communities. They were not ethnic entities at all — the products of traditional patterns, values, beliefs, symbols, and behaviors. Instead, they were "poor white" type communities.[2] "Indian behaviors" were seen as adjustments to the conditions of poverty and not due to the adaptations of aboriginal structures.

This approach had serious policy ramifications, as Bernard James was quick to point out:

> Policy implications for the conduct of American reservations flow from the interpretations of the Indian subculture I have advanced. I cannot explore these here. But if it is correct to conclude that native cultures have been replaced by reservation subcultures of a "poor white" type, and an essential functional requirement for their existence as we know them, is an extreme socioeconomic status differential, prescriptions that attempt to perpetuate this "Indian way of life" may be both unwise and inhumane.[3]

In contrast, other anthropologists pointed to the persistence of uniquely "Indian ways" that were neither the product of socioeconomic conditions nor replications of "poor white" structures in Indian garb.[4] As Nancy Lurie explained:

> In their difficult dealings with Whites, Indian communities have something more than misery seeking company holding them together. Indian people are aware of being different from Whites, and in the matters that

count to themselves the differences are not equated with inferiority but with meaningful social identity. Their humor is different; their decision-making processes are different; their religious attitudes are different, even if based on Christianity and church membership; their attitudes toward land and material wealth are different; and their expectations of one another are different.[5]

Accordingly, the differences between Indians and whites were not solely the product of the exclusion of Indians from a full participation in the white socioeconomy, although such exclusion was generally the case. For the dominant society, "Indians" existed as a statistical category, but as such the category provided little insight into the ethnic makeup of its component groups. Each tribe shared in common with its members attitudes, values, behavioral patterns, and structured relationships, which not only differed in some or many respects from the dominant society but also differed from other Indian tribes. The difference among tribes was as great as their difference from American society. As Lurie suggested:

> ... there is more involved than just Indian ways as opposed to American ways. Ojibwa sub-culture differs subtly from Winnebago sub-culture and Winnebago sub-culture from Ottawa sub-culture and so on. The differences may not be readily apparent or appear important to the non-Indian observer, but Indian people talk about the tribal differences among themselves as they talk about general Indian similarities in comparison to the White world in general. Some of the differences between tribes today relate to the fact that given groups felt a need to retain more recognizable "aboriginal" traits than others to preserve their identity.[6]

This was the research quandary I faced in the summer of 1972. The assimilationists' position failed to explain the persistence of tribes over long periods of time. Their position was that either (1) tribes would disappear when the dominant society removed its barriers to total assimilation; or (2) the distinctions that existed were not ethnic at all but were the results of social stratification and were distinctions shared by all poor. In effect, this approach sought to resolve the problem of ethnic persistence by either arguing that the dominant society was not ready to eliminate it or by defining it away.

The argument based on the persistence of cultural traditions also had its failings. It suggested that for tribal identity, maintenance of tradition was an enduring cultural phenomenon with little relation to the surrounding society. It was static in that it did not allow for innovation, new ideas, or new cultural processes. It bound the tribe's identity to what were deemed to be aboriginal cultural patterns.

By the time I was ready to return to Wisconsin to continue fieldwork, I was convinced that the data I had collected did not support either research model. Both positions failed to take into account the tribes' adjustments made in response to the actions of state and nation governments. My conclusion was reinforced during the summer's research, as well as by discussions I had with Clifton, Robert Ritzenthaler, Lurie, and others. Clifton, for example, argued "that stable structural forms have obviously developed out of the accumulative experience of American Indians; that these forms are quite different from aboriginal and American forms."[7] With this in mind, I began looking at other scholars for research direction, and one in particular, Frederik Barth, seemed to hold promise. According to Barth, ethnic identity is by ascription and marked by differential interaction between group members and nonmembers. To survive, an ethnic group must circumscribe certain behavioral patterns that are shared and that permit identification of membership and dictate proper responses to members and nonmembers; they must delineate and maintain the social boundaries.[8]

The focus on the role of boundary maintenance assisted me in understanding two aspects of ethnic identification. First, ethnic groups are defined in the context of the relationships between themselves and others. The characteristics of these relationships are definable by culturally distinct attributes reflecting significant differences in the structuring of the social system. This gives definition, dimension, and scope to the boundary system. It is not by objective criteria that groups are identified but rather by the distinctions made by and among the participants.

Second, shifts in the cultural content of a group are of less importance than corresponding shifts in the boundary-maintaining mechanisms — those interactions that sustain the group's viability. According to Barth:

> The cultural features that signal the boundary may change, and the cultural characteristics of the members may likewise be transformed, indeed, even the organizational form of the group may change — yet the fact of continuing dichotomization between members and outsiders allows us to specify the nature of continuity; and investigate the changing cultural form and content.[9]

The "cultural features that signal the boundary" are significant in that they provide a means by which to identify the in-group. Changes in these features may reflect adjustments to ecological shifts or internal group dynamics. While ethnic group membership is by ascription and identification an intra- and intergroup matter, changes in cultural features reflect more the influence of external factors. Thus there is a continual process of adaptation of identity symbols used to support the necessary constancy of social boundaries. Ethnic groups consciously maintain their boundaries, adjusting relationships and symbols to meet internal and external factors. They are not passive entities awaiting absorption. Indeed, their actions to maintain identity precipitate adjustments in the dominant society. It was this model that informed my research with the three Oneida communities.

During the summer of 1972, my family and I lived in Green Bay, but nearly every day I made the thirteen-mile trip to the Oneida community. Traveling west along State Route 54, I soon crossed the 1838 boundary line of the Oneida reservation. Except for a sign identifying the unincorporated village of Oneida, there was nothing to indicate the presence of the Oneida tribe. Farmland stretched on either side, with occasional groupings of three or four houses. Signs gave directions to Green Bay, De Pere, Black Creek, Seymour, or more distant places such as Stevens Point and Madison. Yet in this area lived more than two thousand Oneidas with a separate social and political existence. The community I visited was scattered over the 65,428 acres of its former reservation on 2,106 acres of tribal land, almost all of which was purchased as part of the Indian Reorganization Act of 1934 (IRA). Prior to these purchases by the United States, tribal lands consisted of an 84.8-acre parcel reserved for school use. This land was located in the southwest corner of the former reservation, a place called Chicago Corners. In 1972 the school building was being used as the tribal offices. In addition to trust land, there were 466 acres classified as heirship, as well as other land owned by individual Oneidas in fee simple.[10]

In 1965, the Oneida Business Committee, the tribe's day-to-day governing body under its IRA charter, commissioned an economic study. The study found that 52.6 percent of the reservation population was younger than eighteen and another 8.4 percent was sixty-five or older, leaving just 39 percent within the income-producing age group. There was an established pattern that saw young adults, single and married, leaving the reservation, generally seeking employment opportunities, and returning around age forty. This pattern, which had been going on at least since 1940, was exacerbated by the federal government policy of relocation started in the 1950s.[11]

The same survey found that of the 298 households surveyed, more than half had an annual household income of less than three thousand dollars. [According to the U.S. Census, the 1972 median money income of households in the United States was $9,700.[12] — Ed.] The survey also found that most of the existing housing was inadequate. More than half lacked indoor plumbing, and nearly all needed some level of repair. The unemployment rate, according to a 1972 Bureau of Indian Affairs survey, was 21.6 percent. Those who found employment generally found it off reservation. Approximately half worked in Green Bay in construction, or in the paper mills, or in the canning and packing plants. Many "shaped up" as stevedores, while others worked as farm laborers in the area. A few had their own businesses, generally as subcontractors to the larger mills in the Green Bay–De Pere area. It was common for both husbands and wives to work, when work was available.[13]

As I reflected on these numbers, it struck me that they could have been from almost any rural community across Wisconsin, indeed across the nation. For example, the need or desire for young adults to leave the community to find employment was not unique, although in the case of the Oneidas, the desire to return was. As part of my research I visited with Oneidas living in Milwaukee, Chicago, Detroit, and other locations, and they almost universally spoke of returning to the reservation, even though some had been away for decades.

Even the one residential center — the unincorporated village — was on the surface indistinguishable from a thousand others across the country. It was located near Duck Creek in the northeast section of the 1838 reservation. The bulk of the settlement lived on one main and a few side streets. Besides the residences, the village contained two grocery stores, a garage, a post office, a diner, and four taverns, two at each end of the village as if to bracket the settlement. It had no central water or sewage system; no separate fire, police, or highway department; no hospital, doctor, dentist, attorney, or pharmacist. There were no factories or other commercial concerns located in or near the village, but it did have two small housing projects.

Once I became acquainted with the Oneida community, the boundaries became clearer. Some manifested themselves internally, while others overtly marked the differences between Oneidas and outsiders. Although the list is quite long, I will limit my comments to the most general.

Outsiders perceived the Oneidas in a number of ways but most commonly as clannish, meaning that Oneidas tended to stick together in social situations. What outsiders took as clannish behavior was in fact the operation of kin networks within the tribe. While the Oneida kinship system in most ways mirrored that of the surrounding communities, it differed significantly in the emphasis placed by Oneidas on particular kin relationships. There were, for example, close ties between grandparents and grandchildren. Grandparents were the first to assume parental responsibilities in times of crisis. Occasionally grandchildren were raised by grandparents, and extended "visits" with grandparents were a common occurrence. During the research I was struck by the genuine feeling of affection apparent between the two.[14]

Most Oneidas exhibited an expansive knowledge of kin relations that covered nearly every community member, including members living away. The most common term applied to others was *cousin* (in Oneida, **yuk-yalá·se?**, meaning, "we are cousins").[15] Referring to someone as *cousin* was by no means an honorary designation or fictive kin appellation. Rather, it demonstrated an intimate knowledge of the kin relationship between individuals. It also served to identify the individuals as members of the community.[16]

In addition to the extended family ties, there were a number of Oneida organizations that brought community members together. Paramount among these were the churches: Episcopal, Methodist, Mormon, Catholic, Assembly of God, Church of Christ, and Lutheran. Among these, the Episcopal and Methodist were the largest.[17] These two faiths had accompanied the Oneidas in their movement to Wisconsin from New York in the 1820s and remained the dominant religious institutions throughout the centuries.

The churches provided more than spiritual support. They offered a range of social programs for members: youth programs, bible classes, Sunday school teaching, senior citizens programs, choirs, retreats, etc. Of particular importance was the Oneida Singers, an Episcopal group that sang hymns in Oneida. Some of these hymns dated to the late eighteenth century and were sung in a unique contrapuntal way, with the male voices singing bass and the female singing soprano.[18]

Friendship circles, particularly among older women, were closely aligned with church affiliation. Older women were active in church affairs, exerting their influence through the church's organizations. The ministers were outsiders who carried out their religious duties and offered advice, guidance, and assistance, but they did not form or direct public opinion. The church councils, made up of Oneidas, provided the mechanisms to bring to bear approbation or condemnation on community members.[19]

While religion did not exert the level of control among Oneidas that it had a century before, it was one of the most important factors in the social and political activities of the tribe. First, it provided a network of relationships linking the elderly and influential members of most of the reservation families to each other. Second, while differences among the Protestant faiths to some extent divided the community, they never obscured two important facts: the Oneidas were generally an enclave of Protestants in a Catholic region and a settlement of Indian people surrounded by white communities. Third, and as a consequence of the second factor, church activities acted to integrate and bind Oneidas, making explicit the differences between them and the outside world. Weddings, baptisms, and funerals drew together sectors of Oneida society, crossing religious lines and reinforcing the exclusivity of the community. The checkerboard nature of the reservation served to make the differences apparent to the nontribal residents who lived within the 1838 reservation boundaries.[20]

Besides church-affiliated organizations, the Oneida community had a large number of other voluntary associations. While they appeared superficially similar to their white counterparts, they differed in their dynamics of action and decision making because of the interplay of kinship, religion, reservation neighborhoods, and family statuses. They crossed age, family, geographic, and religious boundaries.[21]

The oldest of these was the mutual aid society known as the Oneida Helpers. It had some thirty members who paid ten dollars a year into a burial fund. Additional money was raised by raffling items at their monthly supper meetings. When a member died, the society contributed two hundred dollars toward the burial. During the 1920s there were more than twenty-five such organizations. With no religious or geographical limitation on membership, the Oneida Helpers' membership included individuals from all segments of Oneida society. Monthly meetings were social events that provided an opportunity for members to discuss issues facing the tribe and community. Prior to the 1930s, these organizations acted as part of the tribal government. The members raised and discussed issues and, when a consensus or decision was reached, appointed a spokesperson to bring the issues to the attention of the Indian agent. With the formation of the Business Committee under the Indian Reorganization Act, the concerns of the societies were expressed to and through the tribal government.[22]

Visiting the weekly senior lunch and craft program at the Methodist church gave me an opportunity to meet with and enjoy the company of many of the elders. The program brought together elders from all parts of the reservation. These weekly meetings were the one place I was certain to hear Oneida spoken. The women were more willing to converse in Oneida at the meetings than were the men, although both offered information on other occasions.[23]

Language was one of the key boundary markers for both tribal members and the outside society. There were around two hundred speakers of Oneida in the community when I was conducting field research, and despite the relatively small number of speakers, facility with the Oneida language loomed large in the identity consciousness of tribal members; its preservation was a primary concern to many. For the older speakers, its use gave a high degree of prestige, more than that due to age alone. They were a part of that heritage that many younger Oneidas expressed the desire to preserve and perpetuate. Many younger Oneidas with whom I spoke lamented the loss of language, due in large part to the efforts of the federal government to discourage its use.[24]

For the speakers, Oneida was much more than a curiosity from the past. Its use gave privacy to conversation, while its vocabulary, structure, grammar, and syntax permitted expression difficult to replicate in English and humor that was untranslatable. Speakers enjoyed playing word games, juxtaposing morphemes to create complex and subtle meanings. Often these games would begin with someone (like me) asking how one would say some commonplace English word or term for which there was no literal Oneida equivalent. I recall once asking how one would say "ceiling," which resulted in several discussions and a great deal of laughter (most of which I had difficulty understanding).[25]

Along with the importance of language preservation went a strong interest in the tribe's history and cultural heritage. This manifested itself in groups of Oneidas taking trips to visit other Iroquois reservations in New York and Canada and visiting museums, libraries, and archives to collect information. There was a widespread sense of injustice resulting from the manner in which the tribe had lost its lands in New York and the failure of the state and the federal government to redress these wrongs. During the time of my research, a regular topic of conversation at tribal meetings was the delay in settling the Indian Claims Commission case that the Oneidas and other Six Nation tribes had brought against the United States. (I vividly recall the rustling of paper bags — brought to hold the award — at one tribal meeting, and the look on Chairman Purcell Powless's face as he attempted to preside. There was no mistaking the object of the rustling bags: they expressed the frustration of the members, particularly the elderly ones, with the failure of the United States to honor the court decision and the justifiable doubt that they would ever see their claims resolved.)[26]

To emphasize their Oneida identity and to encourage pride in their Iroquois heritage, a group of Oneida men formed the "Indian dancers." Members of this group also made trips to Canada and New York to experience and learn songs and dances. While there was no Code of Handsome Lake Longhouse when I began fieldwork in Wisconsin, the elements for its development were there. The impetus for cultural regeneration centered in the middle-generation Oneidas. Their concern was the recovery of more traditional aspects of Oneida culture — its language, social system, material skills, and belief system. Younger Oneidas, particularly those of college age, were more oriented to pan-Indian political movements, and for good reasons. The failures of the termination policy had led to a mass movement for restoration among the Menominee, and controversies over federal treaty fishing rights and the deplorable living conditions on some reservations, as well as in urban centers where Indian people had been shipped in the previous decades, had resulted in militant actions such as the takeover of Alcatraz in 1968, the formation of the American Indian Movement in 1968, and the Trail of Broken Treaties and the takeover of the Department of Interior building in Washington in 1972. Also, Indians in this age group increasingly identified with the issues that had preoccupied the previous generation, which may have been partly due to informal cultural programs within the tribe and university programs emphasizing Native American culture.[27]

Athletics was another focal point of identity. Playing baseball was a major preoccupation of both youths and adults and a source of interest and conversation among all age groups. The Oneidas supported several youth teams as well as adult teams that competed against teams from neighboring white communities. In the winter, basketball generated the same interest and participation. Football occupied the fall, but the more traditional Iroquois game of lacrosse was largely unknown. Older tribal members recalled lacrosse being played on the reservation; some remembered a children's game similar to lacrosse played with a hooked stick, the object of which was to toss two short sticks, tied together in the form of a cross, over an opponent's goal. To coordinate the many sports activities, the tribe had formed the Oneida Athletic Association to schedule games and the use of the facilities and to provide personnel from which to draw the leadership for the various teams. Leaders of the association periodically attended tribal governmental meetings to give reports and request support and services.[28]

While whites and Oneidas occasionally met in the course of these pursuits, in two particular areas of social interaction their meetings were direct, overt, and often confrontational. The first was education. There was a general feeling that the education being received by tribal children in the public schools was inferior and that the school boards were insensitive to the Oneida students' needs and the Oneida community's interests. To combat these perceived inequities in education, the community formed a parents group "to discuss the problems of area students and the community in general." *Community* was defined by the organizers so as to limit membership to Oneidas, because, although the non-Oneida residents on the 1838 reservation may have had similar concerns, they did not share the political institution for action and resolution. The parents group operated as a pressure group to implement change in the four public school systems that served Oneida. The points of contention revolved around the group's proposals that school authorities viewed as contradictory to the values of the wider communities they represented. These suggestions often focused on efforts to increase the self-esteem of tribal youths, actions to eliminate perceived discrimination and unequal treatment, and programs to enhance Oneida identity and pride. In this manner the concerns of Oneida parents in one school district became the concerns of Oneida parents in the other districts.[29]

This is not to say that the Oneidas and non-Oneidas did not share any educational concerns — of course they did — yet no joint parent group emerged. The failure of cross-community organizations to form was due in part to the more parochial view held by whites, who focused their attention on their particular school system, and in part to their unwillingness to associate with Oneidas. Sociologist John A. Dowling succinctly summed up the situation in 1968:

There are, in fact, two communities in the same geographical area, one white and the other Indian. There is little communication of any kind between them. Even when Indians and whites are in the same store or tavern they typically ignore one another. Similarly, neighbors generally ignore one another if they are of different races. Both populations are largely endogamous.[30]

Oneidas recognized white hostility and normally reacted to it with diffidence. Many white leaders were aware of its existence, its economic effect, and its social ramifications, but little was done to alter the relationships. The hostility took many forms. Oneida parents reported that their children were occasionally invited to play in the homes of white neighbors; white children were not permitted to accept reciprocal invitations. In another example, an Oneida parent told me that he had enrolled his son in the local Boy Scout troop. Additional openings occurred and more Oneidas enrolled. When the white scout master dropped out, an Oneida took over the troop. The following year no whites enrolled, and shortly thereafter, a second all-white troop was formed.[31]

In some cases, Oneidas claimed the whites discouraged membership in voluntary associations by making Oneidas feel "uncomfortable." An Oneida woman with a non-Oneida surname was invited to join a newly formed neighborhood club. When she arrived and was recognized as Oneida, she noted:

> They began making remarks about Indians although they never let on they knew I was Indian. One suggested that they call the club "The Squatters" [an allusion to the Oneida claim that whites had seized much of their land illegally]. Others made remarks about people I knew. I knew what they were doing so when it was over I just left and never went back, and they never invited me again.[32]

These were not isolated instances, nor were they misinterpretations of white behaviors. I held many conversations during my research trips with local residents that confirmed what Oneidas told me.[33]

When I spoke with non-Oneida individuals living in the surrounding communities, they were often quick to say that the Oneidas, generally speaking, had no sense of or interest in town or county affairs. The Oneida 1838 reservation straddles two counties — Brown and Outagamie — and is part of four towns — Hobart, Oneida, the city of Green Bay, and the village of Ashwaubenon — but except for school issues, Oneidas turned their political attention to tribal government. The outside public failed to recognize and appreciate that the Oneida tribe in Wisconsin was a federally recognized tribe, chartered under the provisions of the IRA of 1934. Outsiders saw this government as a needless relic of the past, interfering with the ability of tribal members to assimilate into American society.[34]

Individual whites saw the presence of a federally recognized tribal government as antithetical to their understanding of equality. When informed that the Oneidas had a long history of federal treaty relations, the common response was to see this as some historical anomaly. Individuals with whom I spoke could not understand how the Oneidas could now file suit for lands they had sold a hundred years before. One person asked, "Weren't they paid?" and when I said that the payment was well below the value and that the federal government should have protected the tribe, the individual took the position that they made a deal and now wanted to go back on it. Finally, whites constantly objected to the fact that tribal land was held in trust by the United States and therefore was not taxable.

. . . .

FREDERIK BARTH NOTED that the important features in ethnic identity are those selected by the members of the ethnic group as marking their distinctiveness. These features may or may not encompass all of the "objective" differences among groups, and there is no need that there be agreement among groups on the relative value of specific differences as boundary markers. Social boundaries denote differentials in interactions among members of the in-group and between them and outsiders. The distinctive features that identify boundaries may include dress, language, music, and what Barth has called "basic value orientations: that standard of morality by which performance is judged."[35] I refer to this collection of valued attributes, which establish, delineate, and limit the boundaries of an ethnic group and its estate.

Part of the difficulty in understanding Oneida ethnicity results from what is generally referred to as "behavioral assimilation." To a casual observer in the third quarter of the twentieth century, many Oneidas were indistinguishable from their non-Indian neighbors. But, as I have argued here, even assuming an apparent behavioral assimilation, it soon became clear that Oneidas were institutionally distinct, that their primary group relations were almost exclusively Oneida and were ordered on distinctly different premises. They articulated a different value system, one that influenced their political processes as well as the way they viewed the social and political processes of the dominant society. Finally, it should be understood that the ethnic boundaries of a group may change as social conditions change. Ethnic groups invent traditions that define them; they modify existing traditions and even eliminate particular attributes when they no longer serve to mark the group. It is axiomatic that every tradition started out as an innovation, and few traditions remain unchanged over time.

In this essay, I have not sought to describe the full extent of the boundaries I saw during my research with the Oneidas. Nor have I sought to compare those elements of the Wisconsin Oneidas' estate with those of the other two Oneida communities. That task was beyond the limits set for me. A researcher studying with the Oneidas in Wisconsin would, in all likelihood, find some of the same boundaries I have described, but he or she would almost certainly see others not part of the estate that I saw. I would suggest the underlying values of the Oneidas in Wisconsin have remained fairly constant, although their expression may have changed. But that is a study for another time.[36]

I have visited the Oneida reservation in Wisconsin many times over the nearly four decades since that frigid arrival in the winter of 1972. When I first visited there were virtually no physical markers of the tribe's presence. This has changed over the years, but these markers are literally on the surface. The underlying Oneida values have remained fairly constant, as have the ethnic boundaries that mark the tribe's presence and serve to separate the Oneidas from other groups — Native and non-Native. Family, religions, tribal governance, a unique history, a relationship with the United States bound to treaties, and, of course, land, in both Wisconsin and New York, all act as defining aspects of Oneida identity.

Notes

1. T. Shubitani and K. W. Kwan. *Ethnic Stratification: A Comparative Approach* (New York: Macmillan, 1965), 571.

2. Bernard James, "Social-Psychological Dimensions of Ojibwa Acculturation," *American Anthropologist* 63 (1961): 721–746; Bernard James "Continuity and Emergence in Indian Poverty Culture," *Cultural Anthropology* 11 (1970): 435–452. See also John A. Dowling, "A 'Rural' Indian Community in an Urban Setting," *Human Organization* 27 (1968): 236–240.

3. James, "Social-Psychological Dimensions of Ojibwa Acculturation," 744.

4. Alexander Lesser, "Education and the Future of Tribalism in the United States: The Case of the American Indian," *Social Science Review* 35 (1961): 1–9; James Clifton, "The Southern Ute Tribe as a Fixed Membership Group," *Human Organization* 24 (1965): 319–327; Nancy O. Lurie, "Comments on Bernard J. James' Analysis of Ojibwa Acculturation," *American Anthropologist* 64 (1962): 826–833; and Nancy O. Lurie, "The Contemporary American Indian Scene," in *North American Indians in Historical Perspective*, ed. Eleanor B. Leacock and Nancy O. Lurie, 418–480 (New York: Random House, 1971).

5. Lurie, "Comments on Bernard J. James' Analysis of Ojibwa Acculturation," 829.

6. Ibid., 829–830.

7. Clifton, "The Southern Ute Tribe as a Fixed Membership Group," 320.

8. See Frederik Barth, Ed., *Ethnic Groups and Boundaries* (Boston: Little, Brown, 1969).

9. Ibid., 14.

10. Jack Campisi, Wisconsin Oneida field note, 1972–1974.

11. Ibid.

12. Source: U.S. Bureau of Census, Current Population Reports, Series P-60, No. 89, "Household Money Income in 1972 and Selected Social and Economic Characteristics of Households." U.S. Government Printing Office, Washington, D.C., 1973.

13. Campisi, Wisconsin Oneida field note.

14. Ibid.

15. Amos Christjohn and Maria Hinton, *An Oneida Dictionary.* ed. Clifford Abbott, 28 (Oneida, WI: privately printed, 1996).

16. Campisi, Wisconsin Oneida field note.

17. Ibid.

18. Ibid.

19. Ibid.

20. Ibid.

21. Ibid.

22. Ibid.

23. Ibid.

24. Ibid.

25. Ibid.

26. Ibid.

27. Ibid.

28. Ibid.

29. Ibid.

30. Dowling, "A 'Rural' Indian Community in an Urban Setting," 237.

31. Campisi, Wisconsin Oneida field note.

32. Ibid.

33. Ibid.

34. Ibid.

35. Barth, *Ethnic Groups and Boundaries*, 14.

36. For further analysis that also focuses on two other Oneida communities (Southwold, Ontario, and New York), see Jack Campisi, "Ethnic Identity and Boundary Maintenance in Three Oneida Communities" (PhD dissertation, SUNY Albany, 1974).

An Environmental History
of Oneida Life at Duck Creek

Then and Now

by Carol Cornelius and Loretta Metoxen

IN 1997, AN ONEIDA TEENAGER OVERHEARD two older men talking about fishing in Duck Creek. He said to them, "Wow, you actually know someone who can remember fishing in Duck Creek?"

But back in 1822, when the Oneida people who moved to Wisconsin settled in the Duck Creek area, they found a region alive with vital natural resources including timber, the clean water and fishing potential of Duck Creek, and a wide variety of birds, animals, and plants.[1] The Oneidas found a plentiful supply of berries — blackberries, blackcaps, blueberries, wild highbush cranberries, and raspberries. One Oneida, Jefferson Baird, noted, "They saw also all kinds of birds — partridge, bobwhite and pigeons. They did not delay in returning to tell how cheaply they could live at Duck Creek."[2] Gathering edible plants such as pigweed, dandelion, cowslip, and milkweed was a common activity that supplemented the hunting, fishing, and corn-agriculture diet.

Many of our ancestors have talked about the good times in the 1800s when the Oneida reservation was whole and there was an abundance of fish, game, berries, nuts, and medicine. Recently, Oneida elder Earl Jordan, who has lived on the Oneida reservation all of his life, recalled the conditions of the environment when he was a child. Back then, he remembered, they hunted and fished a great deal: "We ate 'em: northern, suckers, bass, sunfish, blue gills, and perch...." Jordan also described hunting fox, badger, weasel, raccoon, and mink for its hide.[3] Many Oneida families grew white corn and beans, Jordan noted, kept milk cows — he hated milking — and raised pigs. They fished and hunted rabbits and squirrels as well as wild turkeys, ruffed grouse, and Hungarian partridge.[4] They also relied for subsistence on nut trees — hazelnuts, butternuts, and hickory nuts — and on berry picking — elderberries, chokeberries, blackberries, raspberries, and June berries.

The Oneidas understood the interaction and reciprocity of all these things with the main waterway of Duck Creek. They depended on the vast forest that surrounded them. Their pigs grew fat from the acorns of the red and white oak. They built their houses from the pine and wove baskets from the black ash. They prepared hoop poles by the thousands for barrel making in social affairs with the participation of all family members — or even entire neighborhoods. The Oneidas harvested huge quantities of maple syrup and sugar from various "sugar bushes," again using family gatherings where everyone had a certain responsibility. Subsistence farming and gathering from the environment provided the Oneidas with the means to sustain their community, and they thanked the Creator every day for all of these things.

From 1860 to 1970, however, the natural environment began to deteriorate. As the natural resources dwindled due to logging, dams, and pollution, the Oneida peoples' way of life also changed. Before the Dawes Allotment Act was implemented on the Oneida reservation, timber barons and lumber merchants strove relentlessly to get their hands on the Oneidas' superior white pine timber, motivated by the need for building material for the rapidly expanding state population and for the rebuilding after the Chicago and Peshtigo fires. Prior to the Dawes Act, only the Indian agent could contract for the sale of timber, and the proceeds would go into the United States Treasury to be used at the discretion of the same agent for the benefit of the Oneida Nation.

But after allotment, individual allottees could and did make arrangements of various kinds with the sawmills, both on and off the reservation. The timber and the individual allotments soon fell into the hands of farmers, often European immigrants, seeking cheap farmland. The farmers finished clearing most of the land, using much of the hardwoods for heating purposes and selling the remainder for saw logs or to the newly established paper mills.

Between 1900 and 1925, the entire ecosystem of the Oneida reservation was severely altered from what it had been one hundred years earlier, when the Oneidas had first arrived along Duck Creek. Now fencing was common, and every farmer pastured cattle and horses adjacent to Duck Creek or its tributaries. These domestic animals ate the young wild berry plants, including the blackberry and red and black raspberry bushes, and they roamed the entire territory of their confinement, trampling the young shoots of the blueberry bushes and hazelnut trees. There ceased to be any underbrush in the pastured areas, which caused a major shift in the wild animal habitat that had existed there for centuries. Now, with the earth lacking tree roots to retain water, the water table dropped significantly. Free-flowing springs diminished or ceased to flow altogether. The black ash trees that had grown on the banks of Duck Creek started to disappear. Consequently, families no longer drew income from homemade Oneida black ash baskets. Butternut trees became virtually nonexistent.

Perhaps one of the most significant losses was the deer. Oneida people no longer saw deer on the Oneida reservation in the 1940s through the 1960s, though deer had been a basic food staple well into the early 1900s. Moreover, the farmers at that time were not aware of steps to prevent erosion, nor were they cognizant of any damages from animal manure reaching the streams through pasturing or through runoff from the manure-fertilized fields. With the demand for increased production, especially during World War II, commercial fertilizers came into heavy use, as did chemical pesticides. Neither farmers nor their advisers in the United States Department of Agriculture were cautious about the immediate or long-range effects either in commercial fertilizer application or in the use of chemical pesticides. The streams filled with loam, clay sediment, and chemical pollution. Where once there had been a variety of edible fish there was now a complete absence. The bird and animal populations dependent on such fish also decreased and disappeared.

No longer could Oneidas go onto neighboring farms owned by non-Indians (formerly part of the reservation until the allotment era) to collect medicinal plants that grew wild in the fields, as Earl Jordan lamented. Jordan was also disturbed by the runoff pollution caused by fertilizers used on golf courses and farms in the area, and he, too, witnessed the sharp decline of fish from the 1950s to the 1970s, when the water was no longer clear and fertilizer would run off into the ditch and drain into the creek.[5]

In 1980, the Oneida Nation enacted the Shoreline Protection Ordinance as a proactive, responsible approach to clean up and restore Duck Creek to a healthy condition.[6] Although nontribal farmers owned and operated most of the lands adjacent to Duck Creek and its tributaries, the Oneida Nation took steps to work cooperatively with them for everyone's benefit.

Since then, Jordan has noted some improvement:

[Around 1990] it got better. Today there's trout and salmon in the creek when there never used to be. People hunt rabbits now. There would be a lot of trout but the Pamperin Park dam stops the fish. Hunting is good. The coyote is coming back [indicating that small animals are plentiful]. The water is way better than it used to be. I can see the bottom now through the ice.[7]

Now the Oneida Nation has an environmental department that continuously monitors and tests the waters of Duck Creek. There is additional reason to hope as well. During the past twenty years the deer population has returned and flourished because of the improving environment. In 1998, eagles returned to nest on the Oneida reservation.

Notes

1. The following stories in the WPA Oneida Language and Folklore Project (OLFP) (1938–1942) describe the Duck Creek environment: Oscar Archiquette, Z-15; Ida Baird, J-30; Andrew Beechtree, A-44; Mrs. Nelson B. Cornelius, D-90; Lavina Elm, G-33; Tom Elm, G-50, S-20; LaFront King, F-4; Jessie Peters, D-83, S-23; John A. Skenandore, J-34; Sara Summers, S-41; Martin Williams, S-30, Oneida Nation of Indians of Wisconsin (ONIW), Oneida Cultural Heritage Department (OCHD), Oneida, WI.

2. Jefferson Baird story, D-29, WPA OLFP, ONIW, OCHD, Oneida, WI.

3. Earl Jordan, interview by Loretta Metoxen and Carol Cornelius, December 26, 1997, Oneida, WI.

4. Ibid.

5. Ibid.

6. ONIW, Oneida Business Committee, Shoreline Protection Ordinance (1980), copy on file in ONIW, OCHD, Oneida, WI.

7. Earl Jordan, interview by Metoxen and Cornelius.

The Oneida Methodist Church, 1816–1975

by Evelyn E. (Schuyler) Smith-Elm

I am a lifelong member of the Oneida United Methodist Church in Oneida, Wisconsin. Here I attempt to chronicle the history of the church, through research and my own recollections from a life of participation in the church. — Evelyn (Schuyler) Smith-Elm

LONG BEFORE THE ONEIDAS CAME TO WISCONSIN, Christianity played a role in Oneida life.[1] Missionaries had worked among the Oneidas in their homeland in New York, and by 1816 a Methodist church had been built near New Castle, New York. When the Oneidas arrived in Wisconsin, most had already converted to Christianity. A group called the Orchard Party, who had split off from the Second Christian Party, converted to Methodism and settled on the south end of the Duck Creek Settlement.[2] According to one account:

> In 1830 there came to the Territory of Wisconsin from New York State, a group of Oneida Indians known as the Orchard Party. They made their first settlement at what is now Kimberly and called it Smithfield. Having been taught in the ways of law and order while in the Iroquois Confederacy and also in the teachings of Christianity by early missionaries, one of their first plans was to build a church and school, so they built a place to serve both purposes. This was the first Methodist Church between Lake Michigan and the Pacific Ocean. To their aid, missionaries came and went, and according to the records, they were very strict in their rulings.[3]

The Methodist clergy have always been an itinerant type of ministry. Therefore, not until 1928 was there a missionary minister with the Oneida Methodists for a lengthy period.

Around 1833–1834, the Oneida people constructed a log building near Smithfield to serve as the Methodist church and school. In 1838, a larger, more beautiful church was built across the road from the present location of the church; it was dedicated on January 4, 1840, as the Methodist Episcopal church on land granted by the Oneida Nation. The founders of the church were Chief Jacob Cornelius and other Oneidas — John and Moses Cornelius, Thomas Lorick, John Cooper, Isaac Johnson, Homer Smith — as well as Julius Field, a representative of the Methodist missionary society. A brief time after that, a parsonage/school was built south of the church.

Most of the work of the early Methodist missionaries was directed toward establishing the mission. Besides preaching the gospel and "saving the heathens," the missionaries assisted the people in becoming more self-sufficient farmers and in building homes. The missionaries felt great compassion for their converts and accepted responsibility for their well-being, though their methods focused on assimilation. They kept their "new Christians" closely gathered in the church for nurture and discipline, setting up programs to transform the people into members of the dominant society. In 1895, Epworth Hall was built to accommodate the parishioners for social functions, youth activities, dinners, and so forth.[4] The hall is still in use today.

One missionary was noticeably different from the others. J. H. Wenberg became the pastor of the Oneida Methodist Church in 1928, and his unpublished writings illuminate much about Oneida life from 1928 to 1950.[5] Beloved in the community, Wenberg and his wife, Edna, were staunch supporters of the Oneidas throughout the pastor's tenure. Wenberg not only served as a preacher but lobbied on behalf of the Oneidas before local, state, and federal officials for twenty-two years. Unlike earlier clergy who hoped to take the "heathenism" out of the Indian and force change in traditional clothing, language, and cultural and religious practices, Wenberg served as an advocate for the Oneidas.

The Wenbergs helped the Oneidas through some difficult times. In 1943, as the Methodist congregation was rejoicing in the refurbishing of the church, a bolt of lightning hit the bell tower. The bell fell, and the church slowly burned to the ground. Neighbors saved most of the furnishings and relocated them to Epworth Hall, where the congregation worshipped the following Sunday and for the next ten years.

Wenberg's successor, Pastor John Thompson, oversaw several building projects during his tenure from 1950 to 1957, including obtaining a loan to build a new church and replace the one that had burned. Epworth Hall was also vastly improved during his time. Lifted from its base and moved back from its former close proximity to Ridge Road, Epworth Hall literally stood on stilts while a new foundation was built under it. Thompson was also a staunch and persistent leader in addressing the needs of the community, especially concerning Oneida youth. The volleyball court behind the parsonage provided an outlet for the young to gather and develop teamwork. The Methodist Church sponsored Christmas plays, youth performances and meetings, and choir practice, keeping the congregation quite busy during Pastor Thompson's leadership.

In 1958, Lynn Paughty, a Kiowa Indian from Oklahoma, succeeded Thompson, who had moved to a parish in Green Bay. With a southern drawl, fire and brimstone preaching style, and gift for gospel music, Paughty's approach shook the rafters of the church. Because of the Oneidas' long tradition of and talent in singing hymns, they greatly appreciated Paughty's style. By the time he left in 1960, the congregation had grown so much that the elders realized that there was a need for a new parsonage.

In 1960, Fred Thomas and his wife, Ilda, came to Oneida and became the first family to live in the new parsonage. (Thomas also shared his preaching with the Moravian Church in Freedom, Wisconsin.) As a young minister with children, Thomas fit in nicely with the many young families in the congregation. By this time, I had married and was raising four children. I was also involved in church service programs, and I remember that Reverend Thomas was also an excellent plumber and worked with us to repair and improve Epworth Hall, where many of our meetings and social events were held.

By the late 1960s, America had become quite aware of the plight of the American Indian. In 1967, Eldon Riggs was appointed to serve the Oneida Methodist church. He was to spend the next eighteen years as our pastor. The nation's climate was changing as Indian efforts at self-determination strengthened, and we were not left behind. Pastor Riggs worked to assist people in developing leadership skills (many of the tribal leaders were members of the church). He also worked diligently with the Oneida Business Committee and achieved a great deal during this period. Among these accomplishments were the repair of the Epworth Hall roof and the sponsorship of the "Tarnished Angels," an Oneida children/youth choir and their guitar-playing pastor, who performed throughout Wisconsin. The Oneida Methodists also developed and trained their leadership: they improved grant writing, hosted a major ecumenical crusade at the Norbert Hill Center, established an annual women's retreat at Camp Byron, and reactivated the Oneida Hymn Singers at Sunday worship. And the church's men's club did extensive work on behalf of the Oneida community. The Oneida Methodist Church has continued to make great strides under the leadership of the pastors who followed Reverend Riggs: Carson Timlin (1986–1989); Walter Moffett (1989–1992); Mark Klaisner, Harriet Alicia, and Charles Munson (1993–2001); and Im Jung (2001–present).

. . .

AS I REFLECT ON THE EFFECT of the Methodist missionaries who brought the message of the Christian religion to our people, I feel that, had they come with only the message of Jesus Christ, the outcome may have been better than it is today. Because the church and the federal government worked as one unit at the time, the goal became to change the "heathen Indians" into a white European culture. Today, the Oneida people have finally recaptured their roots, and we experience a conflicted culture with mixed emotions about the replacement of the old "Longhouse religion" with Christianity. Most of us today grew up knowing no other religion but Christianity.

The Methodist Church in Oneida has undergone some denominational changes over the past 50 years. From a group of 25 to 30 people 175 years ago, we now boast 275 congregants. The Methodist Church today still serves as a major place of worship in the community, and throughout its long history, the mission remains the same: to provide a place to worship, preach the gospel of Jesus Christ, and nurture and care for the people of the community and mankind. Over the years it has developed leaders, at the church and at the community level, in education and in government. There are several families who have devoted themselves to the Methodist church throughout its history: the Baker, Benson, Cornelius, Doxtator, Hill, John, Johnson, King, Metoxen, Moore, Nickolas, Parker, Parr, Polzin, Schuyler, Silas, Skenandore, Stevens, Summers, and Wheelock families. The culture of the people has always been not to single out and give credit to individuals in the tribe, except in choosing spiritual leaders. We share jointly in the success and shortcomings of the congregation.

Notes

1. The research for this article is largely derived from the records held by the Oneida Methodist Church and the Oneida Cultural Heritage Department, Oneida, WI.

2. The early history of Oneida Methodism in Wisconsin can be found in Henry Coleman, "Recollections of Oneida Indians, 1840–1845," in *Proceedings of the State Historical Society of Wisconsin at Its Fifty-Ninth Annual Meeting* (Madison: State Historical Society of Wisconsin, 1912): 152–159. See also Reginald Horsman, "The Wisconsin Oneidas in the Preallotment Years," in *The Oneida Indian Experience*, ed. Jack Campisi and Laurence M. Hauptman, 67–75 (Syracuse, NY: Syracuse University Press, 1988); and Laurence M. Hauptman and L. Gordon McLester III, *Chief Daniel Bread and the Oneida Nation of Indians of Wisconsin* (Norman: University of Oklahoma Press, 2002), 102–103, 112–115, 118–119, 129, 143, 181 n 29.

3. Episcopal Church Mission to the Oneidas. *Oneida: The People of the Stone: The Church's Mission to the Oneidas* (Oneida, WI: Episcopal Church of the Holy Apostles, 1899), 52.

4. Ibid.

5. Reverend J. H. Wenberg's unpublished writings can be found in the records of the Oneida Indian Historical Society, Oneida, WI. For other important information about the Methodist Church, see Thelma McLester, "Oneida Women Leaders," in *The Oneida Indian Experience*, 112–114, 119–120, 122–123.

The Indian New Deal at Oneida

by Oscar Archiquette

Oscar Archiquette was a well-known Oneida linguist, storyteller, and politician from the 1930s to his death in 1971. He was instrumental in working with Drs. Floyd Lounsbury and Harry Basehart in the development and success of the Wisconsin Oneida Language and Folklore Project, 1938 to 1942. This interview was conducted by Robert W. Venables at Shell Lake, Wisconsin, July 14, 1971, and is reprinted by permission of Dr. Venables. — The Editors

WE CAME HOME IN LATE 1932 and managed to live by getting work here and there in Oneida. We were then checkerboarded with whites, as we had been since 1920. My teenage stepdaughter was in U.S. Indian school and the boy in a Civilian Conservation Corps camp. In 1933 I planted a garden, which helped out a lot on groceries. In the fall my wife and I would go out husking for farmers at five cents a bushel. In a way this was fun for us. In the spring we took a job cutting brush by the acre.

I worked on a WPA project near Duck Creek, where we were doing some grading, shouldering, and culvert work. There was a culvert to be walled with limestone on each side. I jumped in and started laying stone as if I were experienced, and I was not; this really was my first experience in laying stone. The boss saw my work and was well satisfied, and he reclassified me as a stonemason.

I soon became a grade foreman under WPA. The only reason why I was selected to be a foreman was my past experience in construction work. Here again, I could have held a higher-paid position if I did not use liquor.

Jobs were hard to get. Many Oneidas went up north, where they found work in the woods, such as cutting pulp, logs, and cordwood. The Oneidas were 99 percent landless, but my wife [Esther House Archiquette] had a home, and somehow I managed to make a living at home [in Oneida].

During the Depression I started to build a three-room house. The first thing I did was to dig a basement on a side hill; then I set forms for concrete. I then put on the first floor and we lived in the basement that year. And finally I finished it by piecemeal. I used to mix mortar for an old Indian who used to do a little mason work now and then. Since I laid limestone I was interested in mason work. He did show me how to lay cement blocks the right way. I used to help him lay blocks every chance I had. He also made a number of brick chimneys and a couple of glass block windows.

The Indian Reorganization Act came into being in 1934, and the Bureau of Indian Affairs employees started to explain the act to various tribes of Indians. Since the Oneida chiefs were not recognized as legal representatives for the Wisconsin Oneida tribe, the Ashland Indian Agency did not know just whom to contact for a meeting in regard to the Reorganization Act. But they started out with the self-appointed chief. I finally did get a copy of the act, and I read it. I thought it was a good thing for my people, and I started talking about it to friends, and we had a number of Oneidas who had fair education and were not followers of the self-appointed chief; they also favored the act.

Somebody called a meeting in a private home where I was called to explain about the Wheeler-Howard Act, as it was called. The small log home where the meeting was held was back in the bush. I spoke in Oneida language all the way through, and when I finished everybody applauded. One Oneida man stood up and he said, "This cousin of mine has no business talking back here in the brush; he belongs in some big hall where he should talk about these good things he told us here tonight." It was not long before arrangements were made for me to explain about the act at the Methodist Church hall. Again I made a great speech concerning the act.

The people were really interested now and wanted to know more about it. And of course my background was considered, my father [John Archiquette] being a former captain of the U.S. Indian Oneida Police for twenty-four years, judge of Indian court, interpreter, and more or less legal adviser. And honest. At this meeting a committee was selected to work with me.

In the meantime, the self-appointed chief was busy telling his few followers that if the federal government purchased any land under this act, it would be way up north where there are rattlesnakes and stones. I wrote to the BIA in Washington, D.C., about this, and the answer was that the government would buy land wherever the groups of Indians wanted to live. My committee contacted an attorney who was part Menominee to be a legal representative for the Wisconsin Oneidas.

We were told to organize under the state law, which we did. Next, officers were chosen; first was chairman. They said I should be the one. I said no, I was not qualified. One said, "You were the first one to go against the self-appointed chief, and it is no more than right that you be the first chairman." So I was elected.

The chief had called a meeting at the Parish Hall and even had a police officer present from Green Bay, since there were a great number of Oneidas who now hated him. Anyway, the hall was full; he acted as chairman and had an Oneida man to explain the act in Oneida. Then people could ask questions.

Every time I tried to get the floor he would ignore me, till the people started to stomp their feet on the floor, telling him to give me a chance, which he did. I thanked the man who explained the act as written. Then I said, "You have been told the government will buy the land elsewhere." I told them I had a letter with me from Washington, D.C., and I pulled out the letter and read it. I am sure most of the Oneidas applauded.

The agency was then dealing with my committee. An election date was set in 1936, at which time the majority voted in favor of the Indian Reorganization Act. Some time after, the chief left for Chicago to live, where he died.

We were operating under a constitution and bylaws under state law. Since we [had] adopted the Indian Reorganization Act, it was then necessary to come under federal law, so we drew up a new constitution and bylaws. Election of tribal officers known as the Executive Committee took place once a year, and there was a general tribal council meeting every six months, in January and July.

About 1937 and 1938 I went among the white farmers on the former Oneida reservation, taking options on land for the government, from which the government purchased 2,400 acres for the Oneida Indians of Wisconsin. Land was held in trust by the federal government. Since I did not have a car, I walked most of the time. My time was free of charge. The

Executive Committee attended meetings once a month regarding tribal affairs.

When we organized under state law, only those born on the original reservation were eligible for enrollment, and we were operating under the four-person Executive Committee. When we switched to federal charter, we changed the membership rule, so that any Oneida who could prove one-quarter Oneida blood would be eligible for enrollment, and of late our constitution was amended to have nine members of a tribal council — four officers and five councilmen. The officers are now paid ten dollars per meeting, and they meet at least once a month. I don't know how many years some of us served without pay.

There were some fees promised in the Reorganization Act that never materialized. We were informed that there was a grant of thirty-six thousand dollars as a revolving fund for the Oneidas. In the start the agency handled all loans made to Oneidas for lumber (and I know of one family that borrowed money to buy one milk cow). After a while, the revolving money of supposedly twenty-six thousand dollars was turned over to the tribal treasurer. Our revolving fund had dwindled down to sixteen thousand dollars. This could be due to bad loan agreements.

As for the 2,400 acres purchased under the Reorganization Act, this land was to be held in trust for us; now we are forced to pay for every inch of it, whether we approve of it or not. We are treated like orphans. We paid sixty dollars to eighty dollars an acre to the government, and it paid us eighty cents an acre for the same land in 1962. We are still waiting for a per capita payment. There has been 15 percent set aside for reservation improvement from the tribe's share of the judgment fund.

In [1938] an Indian folklore project was set up in Oneida under the Works Project Administration, under the sponsorship of the University of Wisconsin at Madison. I was one of the first Indians to be contacted by a linguist [Floyd Lounsbury] to help set up the vowels of our language. I was recommended because I speak both English and Oneida languages fluently.

After the vowels were set up, then the linguist taught us the phonetic alphabet, which I mastered in four days. On the fifth day I went out in the field writing stories in Oneida. There were two of us who were considered the best spellers in a class of fifteen. I was chosen to do proofreading, and I could read the hand-copied hymnbook written in Mohawk sounds. I was asked to make the transliteration into the new alphabet. Since then I have been recommended as capable of teaching the Oneida language by a linguist....

Codeswitching in the Oneida WPA Texts

by Clifford Abbott

THE REMARKABLE WPA ONEIDA LANGUAGE AND FOLKLORE PROJECT of the late 1930s and early 1940s produced a document collection that has had many uses.[1] The project was unique in having speakers of an indigenous language collect and preserve examples of their language.

One use of the collection is that the English translations have become an important primary source for scholars of Oneida history. They provide information about daily life, memories, political events and attitudes, jokes, recipes, and knowledge of local customs for that time.

Another use of the collection is in what it has added to the efforts to preserve the highly endangered Oneida language. The efforts of language revitalization today can be traced directly back to the WPA project. Floyd Lounsbury was a director of the project as an undergraduate student, and he went on to a distinguished academic career. He provided grammatical analysis and a standardized writing system. His students have continued that work and have consulted for the revitalization efforts to this day.[2] Oscar Archiquette was one of the speakers employed by the project, and he went on to be an influential leader. He was also deeply committed to the language and provided community language instruction on his own throughout the 1950s and 1960s. His students continued that commitment and were largely responsible for securing the resources and structures for later language programs, again continuing to this day. The material itself from the collection has been worked into curriculum materials for learning both language and culture. Oneida speakers in the 1970s and 1980s read many of the documents in the Oneida language, providing an audio record to accompany the written record; currently there are efforts to archive these records so they can be useful to future generations. The materials from the collection formed the basis of a dictionary as well. Lounsbury began this effort, and I have worked on it since the 1970s. Many speakers of the language contributed, and Amos Christjohn and Maria Hinton spearheaded the effort to get it into print in 1996. Since then Maria Hinton has continued her commitment and has read the dictionary onto digital tape so that a talking dictionary can be made available online.[3]

There is another use of the collection that has not been tapped and is worth exploration. The dozen or so Oneida speakers who worked for the WPA project were bilingual, speaking both Oneida and English. Not often, but every now and then, these speakers would use some English in their Oneida stories. This is something linguists call "codeswitching," and the question is why people do this. The answer may reveal some attitudes held at the time about the two languages and cultures. In general, native languages in this country have resisted borrowing too much vocabulary from the English language that surrounds them. Given that speakers of native languages are in such a minority and given that most of them also know English these days, it is remarkable that native languages are not overwhelmed with English vocabulary. So the few examples that do occur in the WPA collection are noteworthy.

There are several possible reasons why someone might switch and include an English expression while speaking Oneida. Maria Hinton has suggested that back in the times when fewer people were as comfortable with English as they were with Oneida (this is likely in the early part of the twentieth century), using some English might have been a way to show off a bit. This makes sense but probably does not explain too much of the use of English in the WPA collection. After all, the whole point of the collection was to provide examples of the Oneida language and to stay in that language as much as possible. Another possible explanation for the English may be that an English expression is shorter, more efficient, or easier in some sense than the corresponding Oneida expression. This too makes sense, but there are certainly many counterexamples. The words for "table" or "chair" are considerably longer in Oneida ("**atekhwahlákhwaʔ**" and "**anitskwahlákhwaʔ**"), but there are no instances of those English words in the collection. Dates also are far easier in English. The date 1939 has five syllables in English but twenty-three in Oneida: "**wá·tlu yawn·lé tewʌʔnyáwelu ok áhsʌ niwáhsʌ wá·tlu tshiyohslashe·tás.**" Still, all the dates in the collection are either numerals or written out in Oneida words, not English.

Certainly one compelling reason to slip into English is when there simply is no Oneida equivalent. One can certainly describe a tenor saxophone in Oneida, but unlike a term such as "tape recorder," for example, for which Oneidas have standardized a description ("it catches words") into a single word ("**kawʌnaye·nás**"), the closest one could get with a tenor saxophone is to call it a horn. Many names offer a similar reason to codeswitch into English. Oneidas have their own names for many local places, but places less commonly visited or farther away might not have an Oneida name, and there is no alternative to using the English name. Even so, many of the WPA speakers often spelled out the English names with an Oneida pronunciation. The same is true of personal names. A better explanation for much of the codeswitching in the collection might be that the English term has an exactness or precision that the speaker feels is important. It is common for languages to differ in how specific or general their words are. Oneida, for example, has a root element that is often translated as "settlement" but in various contexts might be as specific as "homestead" or "estate" or as general as "town" or "city." We can look at a sampling of the English used in the Oneida stories and see if this search for more precision explains the codeswitching. The examples used here are taken from a sampling of the WPA collection — the works of three of the contributors: Dennison Hill, Guy Elm, and Oscar Archiquette. There are two main ways English can be brought into Oneida. One is simply to use whole English words or expressions. The other is to mix Oneida and English elements within the same word. Oneida differs from English in that most of its words contain multiple parts, prefixes and suffixes, which often pack much more into the Oneida words. Oneida words end up often being closer to whole sentences in English. Dennison Hill used the word "**yukwabás**," which contains a common Oneida prefix "**yukwa-**" meaning "our" and "**bás**," which is his Oneida spelling of the English word "boss." He chose not to use an Oneida term for "boss," perhaps because that term, "**tyohʌ·tú**," has a less specific meaning. It can mean a leader more generally as well as a boss. Instead, he Oneidacized the English word by using Oneida elements as well.

Table 1 contains the whole English expressions that three of the WPA workers used in their sections of the collection. Table 2 contains the English expressions that the same workers made part of Oneida words. What patterns can we see here? Some things are certainly not surprising. In the earlier twentieth century, some aspects of Euro-American culture were still new to Oneida people. The Oneida language thus would not have had traditional vocabulary for newer technology such as machines, steel forms, airplanes, or saxophones or for social practices such as childhood games or entertainments. Still, some elements in the tables are surprising. Two of the three speakers use the English word "job," actively incorporating it into Oneida forms. There exists a perfectly good Oneida root for work ("-yoʔt-"), and Dennison Hill does use it (see his final item in Table 2), but something is pushing him to use the English word "job." It may be because the English conception of a job with a boss, regular hours, and a paycheck is distinct enough from the Oneida conception of work that he needs a more specific word. So here the codeswitching may tell us something about Oneida attitudes toward work and the experience of work for Oneida people at that time. Two of the speakers use the English word "chief"; Guy Elm uses the word by itself, and Oscar Archiquette uses it with an Oneida suffix. The Oneida language has many traditional terms for leaders, most of them more specific than the English word "chief." For a generation experiencing different kinds of both traditional and newer types of leadership, the more generic English term may have made more sense than any specific traditional terms from the Oneida language. Again, we may be able to read something of the attitudes of the day in the codeswitching.

One more example is the word "farm." Oneidas have an ancient tradition as an agricultural people, and the language is rich in vocabulary for planting practices. So it seems odd for the English terms "farm" and "farmer" to be borrowed into Oneida. It would be less odd, however, if the English concept of farming didn't quite correspond to anything in the native vocabulary, and that may well be the case. The individual family farm on an allotted parcel of land is not the tradition for Oneida people, and the speakers may have used the English terms to make that distinction. They also have borrowed the English word "acre," Oneidacizing its pronunciation to "ekel," even though they developed descriptions using native words for many other English measurements, such as inch, yard, and quart. Apparently the dominant land measure for farming was a concept outside native ways.

These examples raise the question of what happens when a native term is stretched to cover a new and foreign meaning instead of borrowing an English term. Oneida has a root term ("-kal-") that is often translated as "cost," "price," or "debt." Coincidentally, "-kal-" happens to be the same as the root for "story." Much of the Oneida vocabulary for finances, mortgages, and the like is based on this root. One wonders what these terms really meant to Oneidas when they started dealing with mortgages, tax levies, collateral, and other terms from whites but continued to use their native vocabulary.

There are also a few items about which the speakers of that time had not quite made up their minds. Dennison Hill at one point uses the English word "stable" and at another time Oneidacizes it with a native suffix to "ste·blne." Oscar Archiquette uses both "ba·n," the Oneida pronunciation of "barn," and "yehwaʔektá·ke," an Oneida description meaning "the threshing place." And Guy Elm uses both the English "log house" and its Oneida variant "tekalu·tátu." Other buildings apparently fit more comfortably in native vocabulary and descriptions.

The generation of speakers who participated in the WPA project lived at a key time in the balance between the use of English and Oneida languages, and their choices and codeswitching can give us some clues about how they viewed their world.

Notes

1. Jack Campisi and Laurence M. Hauptman, "Talking Back: The Oneida Language and Folklore Project, 1938–1941," Proceedings of the American Philosophical Society 125 (December 1981): 441–448; Herbert S. Lewis, ed., *Oneida Lives: Long-Lost Voices of the Wisconsin Oneidas* (Lincoln: University of Nebraska Press, 2005).

2. Floyd G. Lounsbury, *Oneida Verb Morphology*, Publications in Anthropology 48 (New Haven, CT: Yale University Press, 1953); Clifford Abbott, *Oneida*, Languages of the World Series 301 (München, Germany: LINCOM EUROPA, 2000); Clifford Abbott, Amos Christjohn, and Maria Hinton, *An Oneida Dictionary* (Oneida, WI: ONIW, 1996); Karin Michelson and Mercy Doxtator, *Oneida-English English-Oneida Dictionary* (Toronto: University of Toronto Press, 2002).

3. A Web site of Oneida language tools is developing at www.uwgb.edu/oneida.

Table I. English Words Used in the Oneida WPA Texts

Collected by Dennison Hill
1. high school
2. insurance
3. merry-go-round
4. picnic ground
5. wagon

Collected by Guy Elm:
1. airplane
2. celery
3. chief
4. citizen
5. cornet
6. day school
7. deed
8. magneto unit
9. mechanical arts
10. mission
11. olives
12. relief
13. schoolroom lesson
14. station
15. swimming hole

Collected by Oscar Archiquette:
1. biscuit
2. blueprint
3. bump bump pull away
4. button button
5. croquet
6. Episcopalian
7. Farmer in the Dell
8. grade foreman
9. hide-and-go-seek
10. jackass
11. lightning rods
12. mile
13. one week
14. picnic
15. saw logs
16. steel forms
17. tenor saxophone

Table 2. English Words Incorporated into Oneida Words

From the WPA Texts		Incorporated English Word	
Oneida word	*Translation*	*English*	*Oneida*
wahakwatkyantítslanute	he gave us some candy	candy	kyanti
kyentiho·kú	lots of various candies	candy	kyenti
waʔtyakwatpiknik	we had a picnic	picnic	piknik
tetyukwatkli·náb	we cleaned up	clean up	kli·náb
katmʌ́nhne	in the government	govern (ment)	katmʌ́n
yukwabás	our boss	boss	bás
yukwatkámp	our camp	camp	kámp
latifá·mas	they are farmers	farmers	fá·mas
tehotitsyabslakwʌ́hne	they had taken jobs	job	tsyab
tehotitsyá·bsloteʔ	they hold jobs	job	tsyá·b
nusakattsyabslo·lʌ́neʔ	I found another job there	job	tsyab
tuktsyabsliyóneʔ	I got a good job	job	tsyab
sakattsyabslisákhaʔ	I went looking for another job	job	jobtsyab
wa ʔtektsyabslakwa·nʌ́	I got a big job	job	tsyab
tsiʔ nikatsyabsló·tʌ	the kind of job I had	job	tsyab
wakatyoʔtʌhslo·lʌ́neʔ	I found work		yoʔt
— *from Dennison Hill's texts*			
mitshinho·kú	various machines	machine	mitshin
uskah kwátah	one quarter (in school)	quarter	kwátah
ukwakémslayʌ	we had games	game	kém
lokwʌná·ta Lá·sʌn	old man Larsen	Larsen	Lá·sʌn
— *from Guy Elm's texts*			
nya ʔtekamisinslake	various kinds of machines	machine	misin
tehutfá·m	they have farms	farm	fá·m
ukwatfaʔmkʌ́	the farm we used to have	farm	faʔm
nyaʔtekakyemslake	various kinds of games	game	kyem
uktsyobslo·táneʔ	I held a job	job	tsyob
uktsyobslu·tí	I lost a job	job	tsyob
tsifkʌ́	a former chief	chief	tsif
kuttsyá·mʌns	German women	Germans	tsyá·mʌns
tetyutdream	she had a dream	dream	dream
porchne	on the porch	porch	porch
kitsyʌ́nhne	in the kitchen	kitchen	kitsyʌ́n
— *from Oscar Archiquette's texts*			

Cherry Picking: A WPA Story in Oneida and English

by Lewis Webster

Cherry Picking

Kwah tsiꞋ náheꞋ tsiꞋ ké·yaleꞋ kwah tsiꞋ ni·kú tsyóhslat okhaleꞋ wahuhtʌ·tí·kaꞋi·kʌ́ lanukwehu·wé eliꞋkó wahú·yak<u>ha</u>. Státsyʌn Bey nu kaꞋi·kʌ́ yehuhyák<u>ta</u>. TsiꞋ niháti lonatatsuná·lu kaꞋi·kʌ́ ahu·yak<u>ha</u>. O·nʌ́ ótyahkeꞋ lonahtʌ́ti. O·nʌ́ kiꞋ uni ne tsiꞋ nikú neꞋn áhsu teꞋyakohtʌ·tí· úwaꞋ ok luhtʌtyú·ne. Ne kaꞋi·kʌ́ tsiꞋ niwʌhnisles akwe·kú kʌs ne lonatataskénhꞋ lotiyo·<u>te</u>. Nok tsiꞋ lonatuhweskwá·tu kʌs kiꞋ ne anyoh áti tsiꞋ só·tsiꞋ lotiluhya·<u>kʌ</u>. Ne kʌs kaꞋi·kʌ́ o·nʌ́ sahatikhwtá·ne neꞋn yoꞋkalásha kaꞋi·kʌ́ tsiꞋ ka·yʌ́ kʌꞋ nithotiyʌ́·saꞋ tehutsiꞋkwá·eks ahtá·nawʌ kaꞋi·kʌ́ lotikstʌhokú<u>ha</u>. Latikalatʌnyúne kʌs nʌ ne aleꞋ kʌs oni uwkehuwehnéha tehotilihwáhkwʌ. Swatye·lʌ́ kʌs o·nʌ́ tho yahá·laweꞋ latsihʌ́statsi tho yahatlAnyahyʌ. OtyahkeꞋ shohwistakatáti o·nʌ́ sá·laweꞋ okhaleꞋ ótyahkeꞋ kwh ne yah úskah kwénis tʌsahota·túh<u>le</u>. TsiꞋ ka·yʌ́ neꞋn áhsu tehonahtʌ́ti o·nʌ́ kiꞋ uniꞋ ne ta·t yowʌtutáu ne ok neꞋn tekníhatut luhtʌtyʌ́h<u>ne</u>.

— *Told by Lewis Webster*

Cherry Picking

As far back as I can recall every summer some of our people would leave Oneida and go to Sturgeon Bay to pick cherries. People took names of those people that wanted to go cherry picking. Some had already left. The ones that were still here would be leaving soon also and during the day everyone worked hard. But they also had fun even if they worked hard. When they had had supper and the younger people would play baseball, the older people sat around and told stories and some would be singing Oneida hymns. Sometimes their pastor came and then they had prayer service. Some would come back with a bit of money and some would not have even a penny left. The ones that had not left yet would be leaving about Monday or maybe Tuesday.

A Tribute to "She Remembers" [Maria Christjohn Hinton]

With Reflections on Oneida Language Classes in the 1970s

by Ernest Stevens Jr.

Introduction

THIS IS A STORY ABOUT PART OF THE LIFE of my father's mother, Maria Christjohn Hinton, now ninety-nine, whose Oneida name means "She Remembers." Two things stood out to me as she recalled her life experiences. The first is how tough life was for Indians then, and the other was how they found ways to survive these terrible circumstances. Hers is a lifetime marked by historic world events: two world wars, the Great Depression, and — quieter but just as deadly — government policy intended to wipe out the last vestiges of Indian identity and legal rights. Her experience is an example of what Indian children and their families endured in this terrible period, during which families were separated and their so-called trustees systematically marginalized their governments and communities. That she survived is an inspiration to me and a symbol of the fortitude of our ancestors. What follows is a compacted version of some of the important events in her life and her feelings about them, as well as the differences she made to her family, her community, and other Indians with whom she worked in a lifetime of service.

Personal History

An Oneida midwife brought Maria Hinton into this world on June 5, 1910, in Oneida, Wisconsin. Maria was raised by David and Louisia Christjohn, grandparents on the side of her father, Moses Christjohn. Louisia, or Lucy, was born in Oneida Castle, New York, and came to Wisconsin when she was a child with her father and sister. As a child bride at the age of fifteen, Louisia married David, a sixty-year-old Civil War veteran. David, only a young teenager when he went to war for the Union with other Oneidas, survived, but many others did not. As a result of his Civil War experience,

David could speak some English, but Lucy had no opportunity to acquire it. Oneida was their first language, as well as that of the children. At this time, most Oneidas were first language speakers of Oneida, though some, such as David, were fluent or partially fluent in English. This language shift to English is still happening.

Education

As did other Oneida and Indian children, Maria attended government boarding schools, separated from her family for extended periods of time. She was fortunate enough to be accompanied by an older brother and sister, and that was something she clung to. Grinding poverty, resulting from government oppression of Indians on the reservations, was one motivating factor for families who allowed their children to be sent to these boarding schools — some of which were hundreds of miles from their homes. Because of forced relocations and dispossession of their land, the Oneidas' traditional food sources had been replaced by unhealthy government substitutes: refined and often weevily flour, lard, and sugar. Food was always scarce. Trusting that children would have enough to eat was as strong a motive as education to induce Indian families to allow the separation.

As was common for many young Indian children, Maria was shuttled from school to school at ages as young as four or five. She attended four boarding schools, one Catholic school, and a public high school in Kansas City. Her first school was the Oneida Government School. Though she was too young to attend classes, at age three, she followed her older sister, Anna, and brother, Amos, to the boarding school. The thought of my grandmother as little more than a toddler, existing in boarding school shadows while her older sister and brother were in class, is a heart-wrenching example of how tough life really was then.

She then went to Bethany Indian Mission School in Wittenberg, Wisconsin. She does not remember how long she stayed there but recalls that she attended the Oneida Catholic School, probably in fifth and sixth grades, after returning to Oneida with her grandparents.

She was then sent to Mount Pleasant Indian Boarding School, in Michigan, for the seventh, eighth, and ninth grades. She doesn't recall her age at the time. Following this, she attended high school at Haskell Indian School in Lawrence, Kansas. She left in the twelfth grade to work for a family for whom she had previously worked during summer outings in Kansas City.

Despite what is generally said about the Indian boarding school era, it was at least a means for Indian children to survive. Make no mistake, though. These boarding schools were intended to destroy the most critical parts of the Indian way of life: the extended family and cultural continuity.

Oneida Government School Experiences

Maria often shared memories of the Oneida Government School with me. Because she was too young for classes, she would sometimes stand in front of the Oneida Government School when her grandpa, David, would pass the school with his team of horses. He never looked at her as he rode by, because the school's policy forbade family contact. Instead he told her in Oneida to wait there until he came back. When he returned, he would throw candy to her. So, my grandma and her grandpa found a way to follow the rule and still make the forbidden contact. The family connection, forbidden by government policy, was ingeniously and tacitly maintained by an elderly grandpa and his granddaughter, even under the most terrible conditions. That simple, bittersweet silent exchange meant a great deal to both of them, and it still does to the rest of our family. Its memory lingers as a reflection of the power of the love that has helped us endure.

Not even in first grade, Maria roamed around the school unsupervised. One woman who worked in the laundry would feed her and talk to her in Oneida, which at the time was the only language Maria spoke. But there came a time when there was an epidemic in the community and the school was converted to a community hospital. Grandma never saw the woman again. She heard that the Oneida laundry woman had been a victim of the epidemic and was left unable to care for herself.

Under a cloud of controversy and over the objections of the Oneidas, the school was sold to the Catholic Diocese in Green Bay. This school was located on the only unallotted land on the Oneida reservation and was finally returned to the tribe in the 1980s. Today it houses the Oneida tribal headquarters, the Oneida tribal high school, and Oneida day care and Head Start, among many other tribal offices.

Grandma often explained that, after she returned to the school from a visit home, the school's workers would scrub her whole body with a brush. But sometimes the older girls would take care of her, so that she would not be scrubbed so hard.

Her older brother, Amos, did not like school and often ran away, even when he was very sick. Grandma said Amos was frequently sick at night with earaches. Her grandmother would blow pipe smoke in his ear to help his pain.

Bethany Indian Mission School

Maria's strongest memory about the mission school was of being over-crowded with other Indians who also resented being treated this way. This was another aspect of culture shock. The other Indians were Ho-Chunk, then called Winnebagoes. Many years later, Grandma worked with some of her classmates as language and culture teachers.

The period just before she attended Bethany is one of the few times Maria recalled living with her parents. They lived in Tigerton, where they had seven younger children, and Maria guesses they were probably having another baby when they sent her and Amos to the boarding school. Deeply unhappy, Amos wrote to their grandpa David. When their grandpa came to get Amos, Maria was not about to be left alone. She and her older brother returned to their grandparents' home.

Throughout her life, Grandma maintained a close relationship with her older brother and sister. Each became a respected tribal elder in a different area, based upon their voluntary involvement in the community, in tribal government, and in the education of young people. Most importantly, they had an unshakable sense of family loyalty. Tough as they were, they were unfailingly courteous and respectful, a trait that has descended to their fam-ilies. Maria's sister Anna, in particular, was known for her public outspo-kenness; she didn't hesitate to bring the Tribal Council, or anyone else, to account for their behavior. During World War II, Amos served in the U.S. Navy in the South Pacific, but the family never lost contact. Later their sons would serve in Korea and Vietnam, and their grandsons in Iraq.

Saint Joseph's Catholic School

My grandmother did not recall much from the time she started at the Oneida Government School to when she attended junior high in the Mount Pleasant Boarding School in Mount Pleasant, Michigan. She lived with her grandparents, her two older siblings, and her younger cousin Emily, with whom she attended Saint Joseph's Catholic School in Oneida.

This was a hard time in her life, as it was for most Indians. It was clear that memories of her time at St. Joseph's agitated her, and though she was reluctant to talk about it, she did when I pressed her. Her first response was that she was happy when she left to attend Mount Pleasant with her brother Amos, because she did not enjoy walking to school and taking cold lunch. She recalled how the nuns tried to convert her from using her left hand through various abusive acts, never once accepting that left-handedness was a natural phenomenon. In spite of their efforts, she always would go back to using her left hand. Finally, she told her grandfather, and it was when he visited the school to talk to the head nun that this abuse stopped.

Indian students were forbidden to speak their first languages or have regular contact with their families. Theirs was the worst kind of oppression. The ignorance and the intentional abuse young Indians faced is appalling to us now, but it was part of their world. At the same time, tribal governments were also being subjected to political duress that would be felt for many years. To say this period was a particularly hard time for Indians is a gross understatement.

Mount Pleasant Boarding School

Their aunt Marie was responsible for taking Maria and Amos to the Mount Pleasant Boarding School in Michigan. Maria's aunt and uncle worked at the boarding school, and during a visit one summer break, her aunt Marie told Maria's grandmother that she was going to take Amos with her because he was a good worker. Here Maria imitated her grandmother's reaction: a dismissive shake of the head and the words, "Take her with you, too."

Grandma, Amos, and many other Oneidas did a lot of beadwork

during this time to sell, yet they were never properly paid. The Saginaw Chippewa tribe in Mount Pleasant has since made a humble memorial of the site of the old government boarding school. As one of the most progressive of Michigan tribes, this community has used its economic success to educate both its membership and the general public about their contributions to the local non-Indian community. They have internally invested gaming revenues to create a wonderful museum as well as an entire education system, which in no small part was inspired by the old boarding school.

Haskell Boarding School

Though Maria is a mild woman, she was not afraid to stand up for herself or others when the situation required it, and she is still quietly forceful and readily confronts misbehavior or bullying. At Haskell Boarding School in the middle 1920s, there was one matron who continually abused and arbitrarily punished her. This abuse continued until Maria's last year at Haskell, when the superintendent, Mr. Hart, talked to the matron. Although some Oneidas were suspicious of his reputation for trustworthiness, Grandma felt close to the superintendent, who had also worked at the Oneida Government School and who treated her kindly. After this incident, she told the superintendent that she wanted to go back to Kansas City to work for a family with whom she had lived in three previous summer work placements. Hart notified the family, and they arrived right away. Maria ended up finishing school at the Southwest High School in Kansas City, Missouri. She graduated but did not attend the ceremony. The Missouri family wanted her to stay on with them, but she got homesick and returned to Oneida.

After WWII

Although Maria began her quest for education with her older brother and sister, only Maria and Amos finished high school. Amos then joined the navy, after which he returned to Oneida. Anna worked in Green Bay and married when she was quite young. Both Anna and Amos remained in Oneida most of their adult lives to raise their families.

After completing high school, my grandmother returned to the Oneida reservation, where she had one son: my father, Ernest Stevens Sr. This was during the Depression Era, and while my grandmother went to Milwaukee seeking employment, her own grandmother Louisia raised my father in the Oneida language until he was two. At that time Oneida language and culture were still very prominent. In fact, my father did not acquire English until he began school at age five. My grandmother brought my father to Milwaukee once she was able to establish herself, but because she worked long hours, my father was taken care of by English-speaking people and did not maintain the Oneida language. He lived in Milwaukee until the seventh grade, when he went to live with Louisia in the small farm town of Tigerton, Wisconsin, where he finished high school. (He is still remembered for his academic and athletic achievements at Tigerton High School.) My father then joined the Marine Corps and served two combat tours in the Korean War.

After his service, my father returned to Oneida, where he met my mother, Marge Powless. They married and relocated to California, where they had four children. Upon the birth of their first child, Maria moved to California to help take care of the grandchildren. My parents' marriage lasted only seven years, and my grandmother stayed with us the majority of the time. She always said my father told her to stay with us. For about six years after the divorce, both of my parents stayed in California, where they were involved in Native American politics. California was a favorite destination for Indians being relocated in the 1950s, but, as my parents had, many more arrived on their own. My father eventually went to work for the Department of the Interior in Washington, D.C., under the Nixon administration. My siblings and I moved back to Wisconsin with my mother. My grandma followed us to Milwaukee.

In Wisconsin, my mother became very active with the American Indian Movement, which resulted in one of her most significant accomplishments, the creation of the Indian Community School in Milwaukee. In the fall of 1970, tired of their children being bullied in the public schools, my mother and two of her friends started the Indian Community School in our living room. These mothers, all single parents, were inspired by the Minnesota AIM chapter, which had started a Native American survival school called the Red School House.

During this time, a traveling college group known as the White Roots of Peace came to the local university to provide a presentation about the Haudenosaunee people. One of the main speakers was Tom Porter, a young Bear Clan chief of the Mohawk Nation from New York. Tom was fluent in his Mohawk language, and I had never encountered such a young person who spoke a Native language. He encouraged us to learn our own and asked to visit my grandma because he was told that she could speak Oneida. Because the Mohawk language is so closely related to the Oneida language, Tom and my grandmother had a long visit in their respective languages. He encouraged my grandmother to teach Oneida to the young people.

At the same time, my uncle Percy Powless, then chairman of the tribe, told my grandmother's cousin Emily Swamp about a new program at the University of Milwaukee. The program was looking for Native speakers to hire. So, at sixty-three, my grandmother began a new career. At an age when most people are retiring, she returned to school to become an Oneida language teacher, which she remains to this day. Hardly a day goes by when she is not visited by teachers, former students, and others seeking her assistance with some aspect of the Oneida language or culture.

While she was participating in this program, Gordon McLester visited my grandmother. He told her that he was working on the WPA stories and would like her to work with him. My grandmother told him that first she wanted to finish her program to become a teacher and then she would return to Oneida.

While Grandma was still in school, my mother got a job in Green Bay. My grandmother and I stayed in Milwaukee to continue her schooling. When she finished the semester, we moved back to Green Bay with my mother. Grandma completed her B.A. in education and received the degree from University of Wisconsin at Green Bay, where she graduated magna cum laude. At last she was ready to work for Oneida, but it was not easy for her.

Having been gone for so many years, she was in for some culture shock. After years of urban life, Grandma had to reacclimate to the reservation. For this transition Grandma relied on her large, extended Christjohn family. Once again the family came together: Amos and Anna helped her readjust to the community. Because of her hard work she was not only accepted but appreciated, particularly for her accomplishments in furthering her formal education at such an advanced age. She had earned the respect of everyone she met, both in and out of the tribe. She taught as a volunteer at the Soaring Eagle School in Green Bay, another Indian school started by concerned Indian parents, as she had at the Milwaukee Indian School. She also worked for the Oneida language programs but was then recruited to work for the Oneida Tribal School. It was from this position that she touched the lives of so many Oneida people and was able to share her extensive knowledge of the Oneida language and culture.

In the 1970s, Maria was named a Faith Keeper of the Turtle Clan in the traditional Oneida longhouse and has worked there as well as at the Oneida Tribal School. At present, she is still working to complete an online dictionary with Professor Cliff Abbott, a distinguished linguist at University of Wisconsin at Green Bay. She is also the author of several books of Oneida stories and an Oneida dictionary she completed with her brother, Amos, in the 1990s.

I am proud of my grandmother, Maria Hinton, and of all that she has accomplished, and I work hard to live up to her legacy. I am happy that our family has shared her with hundreds of Oneida youth and their families, here in Wisconsin; in Ontario, Canada; and in New York. In this sense, she is a symbol of all Oneida grandparents, leading by her example of hard work, kindness, and devotion to the Oneida people.

Afterword

Maria Hinton's story reflects an old-time Indian woman whose life of poverty, oppression, isolation, and little opportunity is interwoven with courage, family loyalty, cultural awareness, and personal achievement. Today she is one of the few remaining first-language speakers of Oneida. When she was born, virtually the entire Oneida community spoke the Oneida language exclusively. Ninety-nine years later, there remain only a small handful of Oneida first-language speakers.

In her life, terrible displacement evolved into purpose and determination to improve herself through education, experience, and sticking by the cultural values of family loyalty with which she was raised. Maria has devoted her time and energy to her belief that family matters more than anything else. This is the centerpiece of her ethic, which is that the Oneida language and culture are gifts to the Oneida people and that all Oneida children should know and practice our old ways. She is often called upon to share her knowledge of the Oneida language in many different venues both on and off the Oneida reservation. At an age when others were settling in to retirement, she began a career as a teacher, writer, and storyteller, and, though she formally retired in 2004, she maintains this work. Maria has left the need for recognition to others while she made herself useful. Her doctor persuaded her to quit driving four years ago, but otherwise she shows no signs of slowing and continues to be an inspiration to all who know her, especially her family.

Oneida Education

Past, Present, and Future

by Thelma Cornelius McLester

IN ITS BROADEST CONTEXT, the term "education" has wide implications covering many aspects of our lives. We begin learning early in life from our immediate families. We learn how we fit into the society in which we live, which includes learning about our past, present, and future. As we grow older, we discover the expectations placed on us by the community and beyond.

This essay will look at how we as Oneidas have prioritized education and have made it an important part of our lives, for education defines our future and our continued survival. Some of us use the phrase "seven generations," while others simply say, "the generations coming after us," but this concern for the future is relevant for American Indians across the country.

Oneida education must include concern for the natural world, the protection of our wildlife, and the preservation of our lands, as we believe we are all connected.

A great deal of growth has taken place in Oneida, especially in the field of education. The Oneida tribe offers funding for every enrolled Oneida to attend institutions of higher learning anywhere in the United States, provided they maintain certain grade point averages and attend accredited educational institutions. Many Oneidas are now attaining degrees they wouldn't have been able to in earlier times. In a recent issue of the *Chronicle of Higher Education*, an article entitled "America Falls Behind in Degree Attainment" noted that, nationally, fewer people are earning associate and bachelor's degrees, due to schools' inaccessibility and lack of capacity and cost-effectiveness.[1] This national decline is in direct opposition to what is happening in Oneida, where increasing numbers are receiving associate, bachelor's, master's, and doctoral degrees. We hope this continues, as we have a lot of catching up to do.

Another recent article in *Indian Country Today* addressed Indian students specifically.[2] This article reiterated the need to prepare the younger generation to gain the knowledge necessary to lead Indian communities and defend their cultures and tribal interests. In order to succeed, Native students need two things: strong identities and strong employability skills, not only for the benefit of Indian communities, but to survive in mainstream society.[3]

To a certain extent, we Native peoples now have more control over the education of our students than we did in the past. Today there are at least thirty-four tribally controlled community colleges in the United States and Canada. Enrollments in American Indian community colleges have more than doubled, from 76,000 in 1976 to more than 165,900 in 2002.[4] And there are more than 124 college-level Indian studies programs and departments. The most recent university to offer a major in American Indian studies is the University of Wisconsin at Green Bay (UW–Milwaukee and UW–Eau Claire also offer majors in American Indian studies).

This essay discussion will focus on two studies of the Oneidas published in 1956 and 1958. These may be the only in-depth studies to compare educational skills and employment in Oneida, Wisconsin. More important, they show how the Oneidas have viewed education throughout the past fifty years.

The first study, which began in 1950 but was not published until 1956, was by the League of Women Voters from Appleton, Wisconsin.[5] The second study, known as the Thorson Study, was performed by a professor at the University of Wisconsin–Madison and was published in 1958.

The first, "Study of the Oneida Indians of Wisconsin," began by examining elementary and secondary levels of education at Oneida. In 1950, there were approximately 3,527 on the Oneida tribal roll, with 40 percent residing on the Oneida reservation. Then, as now, the Oneida students attended several different public school districts surrounding the reservation. Bus service was provided for attendance at West De Pere, Seymour, and Green Bay, all in Brown County, and Freedom in Outagamie County.[6] The Pulaski school district was not mentioned at that time, though some of today's Oneida students do attend Pulaski.

During the 1955–1956 school year, according to the study, Seymour High School had a total enrollment of forty-nine high school students, with three students graduating that year. The superintendent of schools in Outagamie County reported that attendance of Oneida students was increased due to bus service, the availability of extracurricular activities, and the hot lunch program.[7]

The study showed that 21 percent of Oneidas had completed the eighth grade, 14 percent had received a high school diploma, and 9 percent had attended Green Bay Vocational School. Two Oneida women had attended nurses' training in Neenah, Wisconsin.[8] There were no records showing the use of any federal scholarships for attendance at institutions of higher learning at this time. Many young men volunteered for military service during this time period.[9]

On the economic side, at least 13 percent of married or heads of household in Oneida earned less than one thousand dollars per year. Thirty-two percent of single men and women in Oneida earned less than one thousand dollars per year.[10]

The median income for married and heads of household was approximately thirty-five hundred dollars per year. No sufficient data could be given for single men and women.

The occupations were entry level and unskilled, temporary or seasonal, and some permanent employment. Temporary and seasonal positions included stevedores, golf caddies, landscapers, factory workers, wood cutters, orchard workers, some construction workers, and farmworkers. Permanent positions included paper mill workers, truck drivers, railroad workers, construction workers, and farmworkers.[11]

The results of the survey showed that approximately 12 percent were unemployed at this time, with approximately 8 percent retired, 7 percent in school, 4 percent disabled, a little more than 2 percent in the military, and just .02 percent not seeking employment. A very few were incarcerated.[12]

The second survey, "A Report on the Labor Force and the Employment Conditions of the Oneida Indians," or the Thorson Study, was conducted by research assistant Douglas Thorson from the University of Wisconsin–Madison and published in 1958.[13] This study aimed to help with the development of an industrial program for the Oneida community. Thorson interviewed approximately six hundred Oneida people and thirty employers, with the main objective of identifying the labor force in Oneida. The results showed that 23 percent of the men were engaged in permanent work. The major temporary and seasonal occupations were stevedoring and canning factory work, while construction, paper mills, and farms were the main sources of permanent employment.[14]

At least 10 percent of the Oneida women were employed in seasonal work, while 20 percent of Oneida women were engaged in permanent work. Seasonal occupations included working in orchards and in canning factories, while permanent work consisted of domestic and factory work. The median wage was $1.00 per hour for women and $1.95 an hour for men. The median income was $2,800.00 per year.[15]

Again, as in the first survey, education tended to end at the elementary and secondary levels, with the median education being the completion of eighth grade. However, this was shown to be true of a younger age group; those nearer the ages of fifty and sixty were more likely to have stated completing only up to the sixth grade. In all age groups, women held the highest median educational attainment.[16]

At least 2 percent of those who completed the survey attended some college. Less than .02 percent actually received a bachelor's degree, while 9 percent attained vocational training during this period.

These studies were the first to be done of the Oneidas at this time, and the Oneida leaders took advantage of the chance to use the data in their grant applications. After President Johnson's Great Society in the mid 1960s, the Oneidas applied for and received grant monies to begin offering the federal Head Start program on the reservation. They also applied for and received other grant funding that had become available not only to American Indian governments but to other governments with low-income, disadvantaged people in their populations.

In 1972, Congress passed the Indian Education Act. In 1975, the Indian Self-Determination and Education Assistance Act was passed, which set new directions for all American Indian tribes, nations, and bands. And finally, in 1978, the Tribally Controlled Community College Act was approved, and this has become a stronghold in all of Indian country.

The Oneida tribe now has a continuous offering of preschool, elementary, and secondary schools right on the reservation. In their curricula, the schools offer a major focus on the Oneida language and culture, which is not offered in the public schools. The reservation is situated near several fine universities, and so the tendency is to attend these rather than to build the Oneida nation's own community college.

Today, the Oneidas are a scattered nation, with most of our population residing off the reservation. Yet our communication efforts with all students tell us that they are successful. We have more students attending post high school than ever before. With the educations they receive, these graduates are attaining employment both on and off the reservation, and they are being promoted. That is success in every way.

Notes

1. Peter Schmidt, "America Falls Behind in Degree Attainment, Report Warns," *Chronicle of Higher Education*, March 16, 2007.

2. "Education Must Prepare Students for Leadership, Citizenship," *Indian Country Today*, April 4, 2007.

3. Ibid.

4. From "The Path of Many Journeys, The Benefits of Higher Education for Native Communities," a report by the Institute for Higher Policy in collaboration with the American Indian Higher Education Consortium and the American Indian College Fund, February 2007.

5. "Study of the Oneida Indians of Wisconsin," League of Women Voters of Appleton, made possible with the approval of Oneida Leaders of Wisconsin, published in 1956.

6. Ibid.

7. Ibid.

8. Ibid.

9. Ibid.

10. Ibid.

11. Ibid.

12. Ibid.

13. "A Report on the Labor Force and the Employment Conditions of the Oneida Indians," special study with approval from Oneida leaders of Wisconsin by research assistant Douglas Thorson, University of Wisconsin–Madison, October 1958.

14. Ibid.

15. Ibid.

16. Ibid.

The Origins of the
Oneida Nation Library

by Judy Cornelius

THE ORIGINS OF THE ONEIDA NATION LIBRARY date back to at least 1906, the same year the *Green Bay Advocate* published an article headlined, "[Bishop] Grafton Has Returned Home; Dedicated the New [Episcopal] Parish House and Library Building at Oneida."[1] Yet the modern history of the library begins in the 1960s.[2]

Helen Henderson was the first VISTA (Volunteers in Service to America) worker to enter our community around 1965–1966, and it was through her efforts — along with those of community members such as Alberta Baird, Lucille Cook, and Barbara Denny — that the library was brought back to life in the very same building in which it had been housed in 1906.

Brown County Library donated the initial collection of five hundred used books. In 1968, even though the roof of the building leaked and the winter was cold, the library opened to a supportive community. The late 1960s and early 1970s saw a major renewal of community voluntarism, with individuals and churches working together to establish service programs. A number of VISTA workers, some of them Oneidas, began to assist community volunteers in seeking funding that would establish programs and services that included the development of the library as well as delivery of day care and health care, educational programs such as Head Start, summer school and tutoring, and the founding of an Oneida newspaper. Once funding became available from the federal, state, and tribal governments, the Oneida Community Library blossomed. The Oneida Nation supported what the grants could not cover, including space requirements, utilities, and wages for employees. Library director Barbara Denny was a major force in the development of a magnificent Native American collection, focusing on the Iroquois (Haudenosaunee).

In 1987, Barbara Denny retired and I became the library's director. By this time, the library (now located in the Oscar Archiquette building along with the post office and Enrollment Trust Department) had been relocated and expanded three times on the reservation. Elder Ernest Stevens Sr., a strong supporter of the library, deserves special recognition for his work to help the library expand into this facility.

We again sought an expansion before I resigned in 1995, and the library added footage to the western portion of the building. Chris Doxtator, the free-thinking director of the Wisconsin Oneida Office of Land Management, helped us develop the "satellite" library on the other end of the reservation in De Pere. Eleanor Danforth was the first director of this satellite branch, which was named the Green Earth Library. This growth has continued: we repurposed an old mobile home used for Head Start to expand our services to the children and elders, and the Oneida Housing Department now has a small space devoted to library services in the Three Sisters Housing area on the far eastern side of the reservation.

During my tenure as librarian and director, we sought and obtained funds that allowed for terrific growth. The library joined the Nicolet Federated Library and later the Outagamie Waupaca Library systems, which have been extremely supportive financially and with training for library staff. The Iroquois collection and other Native American materials have grown into what I believe is one of the best Native American resource libraries in Wisconsin. Barbara Denny and I were also motivated and assisted by the Nicolet Library System to provide computers for the public — no small task.

Around 1993, an Oneida community trainer named Terry Hetzel and I wrote a resolution to the tribal council (Oneida Nation Business Committee) requesting the establishment of a community arts program, which has evolved into the program it is today, offering programs in basket making, beadwork, pottery, lacemaking, reading, and storytelling. Originally, the program was housed in the library under my supervision. The supervision has since changed, but the arts program continues to grow, offering instruction in basketry, beadwork, calligraphy, corn-husk doll making, and pottery. Other library initiatives include oral history, storytelling, latchkey, literary, and summer reading programs, as well as outreach programs to schools and civic groups.

In 1993, the library received the international Clarion Award for our participation with other libraries in hosting a poetry contest, a book-signing event with Michael Burke (author of *Dances with Wolves*), and a Native American social gathering at Heritage Hills.

My successor, Brian Doxtator, spent a good number of years working in library services and became well known for his storytelling abilities, particularly his specialty of Native American stories. Doxtator was followed by Lew Williams, the current director. Our staff, then and now, believes that the library should be a safe place, where people young and old can come to learn. We also believe it is crucial to remember that all of us learn in different ways. The various materials that trip our mental triggers are critical to how and what we learn. Our library staff is committed to providing those learning materials, to networking with others to promote the written word, and to ensuring our future as Oneidas. This is one way of fulfilling the traditional task of preparing for the next seven generations to come.

Notes

1. News clipping file, Oneida Nation Library, ONIW.

2. Much of the material presented is based on files at the Oneida Nation Library, which I directed for eight years.

Sybil Carter and Her Legacy

by Patricia Matteson

IN THE LAST DECADE OF THE NINETEENTH CENTURY, Sybil Carter began a lacemaking tradition on the Oneida reservation in Wisconsin that has been a source of community pride to the Oneidas ever since. What became the Sybil Carter Lace Association involved a dozen Indian nations and formally lasted more than thirty years.

Born the privileged daughter of a Louisiana plantation owner in 1842, Carter taught in Chicago and traveled broadly in the United States, Palestine, China, and Japan before starting her lacemaking enterprise, observing in her travels the condition of women's work and lives.[1] Why did this non-Indian woman and her New York association of women sponsors come to the Wisconsin Oneida community and establish this lacemaking tradition? Carter was influenced by four distinct movements: (1) women's rights, (2) late-nineteenth-century missionary activities, (3) the flourishing arts and crafts movement of the time, and, most importantly, (4) Indian policy reform.

Carter's work and travels started when the Civil War took her father's life and led to the destruction of his family plantation house: the newly impoverished young woman traveled to Chicago to make her own way. "[A] kind friend," she noted, "found me school work." She began to teach, among others, impoverished women and girls, later recalling that only then did she understand her father's early wisdom:

> I remember, when I was a little girl, he used frequently to say that he wanted his girls to have a good education, that they might be helpful women in the world. Shortly after I became a woman that good father was taken home, and the war broke over us and closed, leaving me penniless. Then I was so glad to have received the idea in my young days that it was honorable to work. I am glad that I did not sit down at home to be dependent on some of my male relatives in the South, to add one more to their burdens.[2]

Carter added: "When I was in Chicago, I had a great deal to do in getting work for poor women." For instance, she met and taught an "intelligent" English woman whose husband had run away. "The one thing [Carter] knew how to do was to make lace," and so she set up a lacemaking class for the woman to teach other women.[3] By 1884, as a special agent for the Domestic and Foreign Missionary Society of the Protestant Episcopal Church, she was "responsible for visiting branches of the Women's Auxiliary" and observed many Indian women in their tribes in the Southwest as well as the Ojibwa's White Earth reservation in northern Minnesota.[4]

These experiences, both at home and around the United States and abroad, inspired Carter's early feminism, her desire to be a "helpful [woman] in the world," and the sure knowledge that she would be able to help other women support themselves through teaching and lacemaking. This time period also saw the rise of women's benevolent associations in both England and America dedicated to helping women who, through no fault of their own, found themselves impoverished.[5] Of her work, an increasingly financially independent, emancipated, and empathetic Carter later observed: "When I was among my Indian sisters, I used to wish that I could do something to add to their power of earning money. I had earned all my own for twenty years; and I was sometimes glad that I could spend every dollar I had, if I wanted...and [some] 'John' could not say a word."[6] In this statement Carter seems clearly conscious of the potential fate she had avoided: the disempowerment of any woman cast in the role of a "burden," dependent on some male.

Then came the moment when she put all these elements together. She explained this awakening at the Lake Mohonk Conference of Friends of the Indian in 1890:

> [Within the first ten days], [w]hen I was in Japan I was invited to go and see a lace school, and I went and saw a hundred women, girls and women, make lace, pillow lace. I sat and looked at them, and I said to myself, Sybil Carter, why didn't you remember that? I could scarcely stay in Japan until my time was up. I wanted to get on to the Indian reservation, and see if I could not help my friends to do that.[7]

In Japan her non-Indian friends had tried to discourage her, for at the time for her white friends, it was beyond belief that the genteel white

Carter could want to go live among Indians — beyond belief in the narrow thinking of the time that Indian women could learn to make "dainty" or clean work.[8] But Carter ignored them, telling her friends that she wanted to spend the summer "twenty-two miles from anyone who can speak English." With encouragement and authorization from Episcopal bishop Henry Benjamin Whipple, she started teaching twelve Ojibwa women at the White Earth reservation in Minnesota. Whipple was delighted with the initial results. The bishop later quoted Carter's description of her accomplishment: "I was amply repaid by taking back to the East twelve bits of pretty lace, thus proving two things; first, they [Ojibwas] could learn; second, they wanted to work for their living."[9]

Thus Carter feistily countered her friends' prejudices about Indian women and herself. Those prejudices stemmed in part from a mainstream nineteenth-century ideology called the "woman's sphere" by American historian Nancy Cott. Just before Carter's birth in the early nineteenth century, Cott states, women's roles began to evolve through three stages within the period's "ideology of domesticity": that is, they changed from being a prisoner/victim to using their position to claim special agency within the domestic sphere and, finally, began to promote that sphere as an identity supporting a resource-rich "sub-culture" that "enhanced their status" in society at large.[10] Certainly this three-part evolution was what Carter herself had embodied: she had changed from a young woman dependent on a breadwinner to a young dependent woman victim to an independent woman teaching other women skills with which to empower themselves in the "society at large." It seems clear that she hoped to pass on that progression of empowerment to other women, including the Oneidas.

Carter's efforts must also be viewed in the context of nineteenth-century Christian religious thought and missionary activity. Laywomen's public involvements outside of church attendance arose from an increasingly volatile millennial contention that American society had strayed from the path of grace and needed religious reform. In the early 1870s, Frances Willard founded the Women's Christian Temperance Union,[11] the largest association of women up to that time in America. In the decades that followed this organization's founding, a growing number of middle-class white women were able to write and speak at the meetings — to aid in the reform of society's ills, such as poverty, alcoholism, homelessness, and child abuse. The fear was that such sins and abuses would leave America unredeemed and unsaved at the day of God's judgment. This belief sanctioned the women's participation in reform work and allowed those who had heretofore been kept privately and chastely within their domestic sphere to go outside their private homes and do missionary work and to attend evangelical reformers' public events.

The success of Sybil Carter's lace enterprise relied as much on her genuine identification within the women's and the religious reform movements as it did on two other national reform movements in the second half of the nineteenth century: the arts and crafts movement and the Indian reform movement. Her work required her to engage in ever-larger circles of networking, public speaking, competition, and persuasive skills.

The arts and crafts phenomenon was a major force in the last decades of the nineteenth century and the first decade of the twentieth century. English art critic John Ruskin and his disciple William Morris began the movement as a reformist faction that influenced English and American architecture, decorative arts, and gardening. This reform came about as a reaction to the Industrial Revolution's massive changes in culture, politics, and the American and English economies during the span of the nineteenth century. Over all, arts and crafts promoters viewed the Industrial Revolution as diminishing the quality of life for the middle and lower economic classes.[12] Ruskin and Morris wanted to revalue the creation of fine art by a creative individual versus industrial, factory-made goods. Whereas before the movement a handmade textile might have been seen as pretty or useful for the family, in the movement's view such an item expressed a higher distinction — a finer, more natural, and simpler virtuous art; a more spiritual piece by its maker. Moreover, among the intelligentsia and fashion mavens, a handmade item not only represented the spiritualized ideals of a preindustrial economy but also signified an economy of individuals who *rejected* the mainstream industrialized culture.[13] American arts and crafts reformers meant to reinterpret European arts and crafts ideals via the "craftsman" style of architecture, furniture, and other decorative arts, such as the designs Gustav Stickley promoted in his magazine *The Craftsman*. The movement also influenced studio potters, textile makers, weavers, designers, metal workers, and all sorts of artists.[14]

More than a decade before Carter started teaching at White Earth, the Philadelphia International Centennial Exhibition of 1876 highlighted — for the first time in America — that everyday, handmade, useful, and traditional objects for home use and decor were of special worth compared to manufactured goods. Among these objects were pottery, silver, furniture, glass, metal, paintings, sculpture, and a collection of textiles including wall hangings, embroidery, needlework, and lace. Nor was Carter alone in devoting her time to organizing training for unemployed women. One booth at the 1876 Philadelphia Exhibition displayed textiles from England's Royal School of Art Needlework, founded by wealthy English women in 1872 to provide "suitable employment for Gentlewomen" in need, of all economic classes, and to bring renewed attention to ornamental needlework as a valued decorative art. Another socially-minded entrepreneur, the influential American interior designer Candace Wheeler, noted that when she saw this exhibit she put two and two together, and she "jumped at the possibility of work for the army of helpless women of NY who were ashamed to beg and untrained to work."[15] The overall goal of the Royal School was for women to run businesses that economically benefited other women by providing training and a market for their products and also revived traditional hand skills of the pre-Industrial time in more modern forms.

In the late 1870s, Candace Wheeler initiated women's organizations comprising aspiring artists and needy gentlewomen "by professionalizing home decoration for women and developing an American style in textile arts."[16] During the next decade, the popularity of art needlework expanded rapidly. Wheeler directed the Bureau of Applied Arts in the Women's Building for the 1893 Chicago World's Columbian Exposition, where lace made by Indian women under the direction of Sybil Carter won prizes.[17] Indian lace also won medals at the 1900 Paris Exposition, the Pan-American Exposition in Buffalo in 1901, Liege in 1905, Milan in 1906, and the Australia Exposition in 1908, and Oneida lace won a gold medal at the St. Louis World's Fair of 1904. Such accomplishments garnered more public attention and enhanced the value of Oneida lace on an international scale.[18] A particular point for the Oneidas was the Episcopal church's request to create some twenty-five pieces of altar cloths for the 1911 inauguration of the Cathedral of St. John the Divine in New York City (several of the cloths survive in the cathedral today).[19]

In her excellent work on the history of the arts and crafts movement in America, Eileen Boris points out that changes in the thread industry "brought design patterns within reach of working class women."[20] Textile-related projects of the arts and crafts movement spread rapidly to poor whites in Appalachia, and the work was centered at Berea College in Kentucky. In order to "save" immigrant women from the factory system, urban reformers established handicraft workshops at settlement houses, including at Jane Addams's Hull House in Chicago.[21] To Ruskin and others in the movement, cottage industries not only exercised the fingers, limbs, and brain but also had "great moral value" by binding families together,[22] and Sybil Carter fit precisely within these philosophies and ideals. Boris puts it best:

> Women leaders of the arts and crafts movement reinforced what Victorians understood as women's culture: the knowledge and skills transmitted from one generation of women to the next, no matter their class or ethnic origins. They discovered this culture in the work of their foremothers, but they also identified its presence in artifacts from other cultures, particularly those of the Appalachian highlander, Russian serf, Italian peasant, and the Amerindian. In the eyes of crafts promoters, the baskets, pottery, and — most of all — textiles produced by women from "folk" or "primitive" societies became symbols of the self-expression possible within the family economy. As such, they suggested an alternative to the factory system for women forced to enter wage labor. Philanthropic art industries would tap the potential of women's culture to provide wholesome, creative labor for the needy.[23]

The ethical and economic reform basis of the arts and crafts movement was clearly evident in Carter's thinking. For her, it meant that needy Indian women would gain sustainable economic skills, be recognized as creative artists, and maintain their families by working at home in a rural setting, far away from the evils, corruption, and temptation of the modern industrial world. One brilliant aspect of Carter's scheme was that, once trained, the lacemakers could do their work at home and part-time; between their domestic obligations of raising children and caring for their families, Indian women could produce valuable lace that Carter's networks sold virtually at once.

The fourth — and perhaps greatest — influence on Carter was the 1880s movement to reform Indian policies. Inspired by a popular wave of revulsion toward the massacres of Indians during and after the Civil War and by the writings of novelist Helen Hunt Jackson, this reform movement was led by relatively liberal social and religious leaders from the Northeast.[24] After 1883, many of these reformers crossed paths once a year at the Lake Mohonk Mountain House, a Quaker resort hotel in New Paltz, New York, founded by Albert K. and Daniel Smiley. The brothers were to each serve consecutively on the Board of Indian Commissioners from 1873 to 1930. Each autumn at Mohonk between 1883 and 1916, and again in 1929, the Smiley brothers hosted annual conferences of Friends of the Indians and the Federal Board of Indian Commissioners' meetings.[25]

By the late nineteenth century, the lay reformist "Friends of the Indians" belonged to such regional and national groups as the Indian Rights Association, the Boston Indian Citizenship Commission, the Federal Commissioners of Indian Affairs, and various Protestant and Catholic church subgroups as well. It is important to note here that women's work and religious reform came together with Indian reform. Mary Bonney and Amelia Stone Quinton (both white women) founded the Women's National Indian Association (WNIA) in 1879, uniting against the encroachment of white settlers and railroads on land supposedly set aside for Indians. Another motivation was telling: according to Bonney, it was that such encroachments would "greatly hinder the work of Christianizing Indians...." Carter was an active member of the WNIA and, just prior to her death in 1908, was the national president of the association.[26]

Historian Patricia Limerick has perceptively observed: "Like the humanitarian advocates of removal, the reformers [of Indian policy] of the 1880s saw the situation as urgent, even apocalyptic."[27] They saw that even earlier advocates of "removal" such as Presidents Madison and Jackson had not succeeded in ending conflict with the Indians. They still feared that the Indians would be annihilated. So they focused on these problems from a government policy standpoint: Congress should address Indian security rather than continue to either promote or ignore the wars and massacres. Both strategies — the removals and the later reform efforts — were at the least crude efforts to prevent additional bloodshed. At the same time, they were both one-sided, disastrous instruments of massive land-grabs and trauma. With the Plains Indian and Southwestern Indian wars still fresh in people's minds, many of these reformers saw their task as vital to "save" the Indians by encouraging private property, industrial education, Christianity, and the "reward" of United States citizenship that would lead, they believed, to protection under American law.[28] In 1890, the first year that Carter attended the Mohonk Conference, Amherst College president Merrill Gates opened the proceedings with a welcome to "intelligent patriots." "We meet," he stated, "in the earnest desire to secure justice, education, citizenship, and Christianity for that weaker race whose destinies Providence has entrusted to this nation in its strength. It is for this reason that the Mohonk Conference has come to have a name and an influence throughout our land."[29]

Despite their optimistic expectations that the General Allotment Act of 1887 would lead American Indians to become self-sufficient and independent individuals within the framework of American capitalism, the policies that followed — namely the Burke Act (1906) and the Federal Competency Commissions (1915–1921) — proved devastating to reservation communities, including the Wisconsin Oneidas.[30] Yet many of these same reformers, including Carter herself, believed that the Indians were on a perilous slope to extinction and that transformation was their only hope to survive as a people. Ironically, while reformers were pushing for allotment to end the reservation system, they were also encouraging Carter to instill pride and give Indian women the necessary skills to maintain a semblance of life on those very same reservations. In the case of the Oneidas, what reformers did not foresee was that within the scheme of lacemaking their efforts to end the reservation system and individualize the Oneidas were subverted by the women's collective pride engendered from the perceived value of the lace and their strengthened abilities to keep their families — and thus, the tribe — together. Indeed, Carter's introduction of European lacemaking at Oneida, Wisconsin, actually helped in some ways to counter the very same assimilationist agenda promoted by federal officials of the era!

Because women were generally not made a part of the formal proceedings at the annual Mohonk conferences, Carter was invited to speak in 1890 under the auspices of Bishop Whipple's authority among the reformers. She described her intentions and how she had come to see the teaching of lacemaking as a way of showing Indian women how to become more independent. She showed the group several pieces of lace made by Indian women and concluded her presentation by emphasizing the benefits of Indian self-determination:

> There is nothing better than giving people a chance to make their own way of life. It is one of the best things that we can do for Indian women, and girls and Negro women and all poor people. If we can only give them the chance in life that you and I have had, I am quite sure that that would solve many questions which have been problems to us heretofore.[31]

At Mohonk, Carter made many connections among wealthy Northeastern men and, more especially, their wives, who later would help promote and sell the lace in New York, Boston, Philadelphia, and Pittsburgh. With the help she received following her speech at Mohonk, Carter was to expand teaching to several other reservations in Minnesota and Wisconsin, and in 1892 she hired a second and a third teacher.

Carter spoke again at the 1892 Mohonk Conference, this time on "Work and Wages for Indian Women." She emphasized to the assembled conferees that on the reservations she had visited, the Indian women would repeatedly ask her for teachers to instruct them in work that paid. While she had once wondered if these people were lazy, Carter went on to say that she had come to know that they were very hard workers: "They are more industrious than I had any idea of till I lived among them." Finally, she called for assistance from among the audience: "O my friends, I am trying to work out this problem. I need your sympathy and your help. The best work of all in our mission field is that which helps to make men and women self-supporting and self-respecting."[32] The sympathy and help she called for was given.

Carter was named an Episcopal deaconess in 1893 and subsequently founded more lacemaking projects. Her frequent attendance at Mohonk meetings of reformers cemented ties to policy makers, prominent businessmen and their wives, missionaries, and educators who helped her immensely in her efforts to institute and spread lacemaking projects. Another quality that aided the circulation of Carter's work was persistence. As a frequent correspondent with the Office of Indian Affairs, she beseeched officials to allow her to take lacemakers from White Earth to the Columbian Exposition, she wrote letters asking for government quarters to house her lace teachers, she questioned the dismissal of one of the teachers at a government-run school, she recommended women for government positions in the Indian Service, and she promoted the establishment of a new government school.[33] Relentless in her push to promote Indian lacemaking, Carter even enticed the commissioner of Indian affairs with promises of free samples of the lace.[34]

Mrs. Charles Bronson was the first lacemaking teacher to work at Oneida, arriving in 1898. At first she taught a dozen women, but the numbers soon grew, according to the report of *The Church's Mission to the Oneidas*, published in 1899:

> At the close of that year *i.e.* September 1899 the class numbered seventy-five women who had made over 500 pieces of lace.... This brought them in a cash return of about $425...it is always a pleasure to see the women's delight in this fascinating art. The coming year should bring greater returns...and we have a hope of even sending some good specimens to the Paris Exposition.[35]

By 1904 Carter had founded the Sybil Carter Indian Mission and Lace Industry Association and was able to set up a store at 289 Fourth Avenue in New York City. Oneida lace would also be sold at private gatherings at homes of well-to-do New Yorkers. In the year of Sybil Carter's death, the wives of prominent Americans, including the Cuttings, the Vanderbilts, and the Sages, were on the association's board, as was Eleanor Roosevelt. Four years later, the association was still going strong, sponsoring 196 lacemakers on six reservations.[36] At Oneida, Josephine Hill Webster administered the lacemaking enterprise that at its height included 150 women.[37] While the New York City Sybil Carter Lace Association ended in 1926, the Wisconsin Oneidas continued to make and market lace for several decades after that. In her goal of helping Indian women achieve economic independence, Carter shrewdly chose skills and items that were not only immediately marketable but also increasingly valued in society. Bishop Whipple would note in May 1898: "There have been many instances where the Indians would have suffered from hunger by the loss of their crops had it not been for this industry."[38] Lacemaking helped mitigate the destruction of morale, community ties, and family groups. Yet the financial remuneration from the project could be overemphasized. Of course, the association paid for teachers, supplies, mailing, transportation, and so forth; however, the payment to individual lacemakers was only about fifty dollars per year in 1912. Nevertheless, the wage scale for this time-intensive skill was sometimes greater than for Indian beadworkers during the same period.[39]

For the Oneida women, the opportunity to work together in a guild replicated their ancient tradition of women's societies and created a bond that renewed their position of importance in the community. The project helped promote pride and self-confidence that were perhaps greater than the financial reward. Not all women in the project made lace — some were in charge of packing, mailing, transporting, and marketing the lace at fairs.[40] Thus, this cooperative labor reinforced community cohesiveness. Although Sybil Carter's name is largely forgotten by the Oneidas today, her legacy lives on with the Oneida's modern efforts to revive lacemaking as part of their own tradition in the community. Modern critics may rightly view Carter's lacemaking enterprise as just as paternalistic, colonialist, and racist as contemporaneous efforts to "kill the Indian in him and save the man" as Captain Richard H. Pratt, founder and first superintendent of the Carlisle Indian Industrial School, so infamously stated in 1892. Perhaps a more realistic way of interpreting this little-known chapter in Indian-white relations is to understand, from our twenty-first-century viewpoint, that in complex ways, Carter's creative enterprise saved many people's lives, families, and dignity. Carter's effort, regardless of her intentions, accomplished several valuable ends — not only Indian women's emancipation and self-determination and self-esteem, but also financial blocks against the disintegration of tribal, community, and family ties in the aftermath of the Dawes Act.

Notes

1. Bob Neslund, "Native American Lace: An Experiment in Mission and Self-Help," *The Historiographer* [National Episcopal Historians and Archivists, Historical Society of the Episcopal Church] 41 (Pentecost 2003): 18–21; Kate C. Duncan, "American Indian Lace Making," *American Indian Art Magazine* 5 (Summer 1980): 28–35; Laurence M. Hauptman and L. Gordon McLester III, eds., *The Oneida Indians in the Age of Allotment, 1860–1920* (Norman: University of Oklahoma Press), 92–95, 109–111.

2. Isabel C. Barrows, ed., Proceedings of the Eighth Annual Meeting of Lake Mohonk Conference of Friends of the Indian [hereafter cited as *LMC*], 1890 (New Paltz, NY: Lake Mohonk Conference of Friends of the Indian, 1890): 46–47. For other upper-class women of the South seriously affected by the Civil War, see Drew Gilpin Faust, *Mothers of Invention: Women of the Slaveholding South in the American Civil War* (Chapel Hill: University of North Carolina Press, 1996; New York: Vintage paperback edition, 2004).

3. *LMC* (1890): 47.

4. Neslund, "Native American Lace," 18. For Carter's lacemaking project at White Earth, see Melissa L. Meyer, *The White Earth Tragedy: Ethnicity and Dispossession at a Minnesota Anishinaabe Reservation, 1889–1920* (Lincoln: University of Nebraska Press, 1994), 83–86.

5. Candace Wheeler called this fallen position "untoward circumstances." Amelia Peck and Carol Irish, *Candace Wheeler: Art and Enterprise of American Design, 1875–1900* (New Haven, CT: Yale University Press and the Metropolitan Museum of Art, 2001), 24.

6. *LMC* (1890): 47.

7. Ibid., 47–48.

8. Ibid.

9. Henry Benjamin Whipple, *Lights and Shadows of a Long Episcopate: Being the Reminiscences and Recollections of the Right Reverend Henry Benjamin Whipple, D.D., LL.D., Bishop of Minnesota* (New York: Macmillan Co., 1899), 173–175.

10. Nancy F. Cott, *The Bonds of Womanhood: "Woman's Sphere" in New England, 1780–1835* (New Haven, CT: Yale University Press, 1977), especially 197–206.

11. For Frances Willard and her organization, see Ruth Bordin, *Frances Willard: A Biography* (Chapel Hill: University of North Carolina Press, 2001). Many temperance reformers attended the Lake Mohonk conferences, including Clinton Fisk, Prohibition Party candidate for president of the United States and founder of Fisk University.

12. Eileen Boris, *Art and Labor: Ruskin, Morris and the Craftsman Ideal in America* (Philadelphia: Temple University Press, 1986), xi–xvi.

13. Ibid., 10–12.

14. Ibid., especially 3–11, 99–138, for an excellent analysis of the movement.

15. Quoted in Peck and Irish, *Candace Wheeler*, 24.

16. Boris, *Art and Labor*, 115.

17. Peck and Irish, *Candace Wheeler*, 23–24.

18. Duncan, "American Indian Lace Making," 34.

19. "News and Notes," *The Indian's Friend* [National Indian Association, formerly Women's National Indian Association] (June 1911): 4. This brief article identifies the Cathedral lace as being made by the Wisconsin Oneida women. For the opening displaying the lace, see "Set of Altar Linen Made by Indian Women for Cathedral of St. John the Divine," *New York Herald,* April 9, 1911, 6.

20. Boris, *Art and Labor,* 116.

21. Ibid., 126–134.

22. Ruskin quoted in Ibid., 129.

23. Ibid., 122.

24. For Helen Hunt Jackson, see her *A Century of Dishonor* (1881; repr. New York: Dover Books, 2003); Valerie Sherer Mathes, ed., *The Indian Reform Letters of Helen Hunt Jackson* (Norman: University of Oklahoma Press, 1997); see Patricia Matteson, "'A Stain on the Blood': Indian-Loving and Nineteenth-Century Women's Literary Strategies" (unpublished PhD dissertation, University of Colorado, 1996): 172–255.

25. Francis Paul Prucha, *American Indian Policy in Crisis: Christian Reformers and the American Indian, 1865–1900* (Norman: University of Oklahoma Press, 1976). For a selection of the reformers' writings, see Prucha, ed., *"Americanizing" the American Indian: Writings by the "Friends of the American Indian," 1880–1900* (Cambridge, MA: Harvard University Press, 1973). For a harsh critique of these reformers, see Wilbert H. Ahearn, "Assimilationist Racism: The Case of the 'Friends of the Indian,'" *Journal of Ethnic Studies* 4 (Summer 1976): 23–32. For the work of the Indian Rights Association, see William T. Hagan, *The Indian Rights Association* (Tucson: University of Arizona Press, 1985). The proceedings of the Lake Mohonk conferences of 1883–1916 and 1929 are on microfilm. *The Indian Truth* (Indian Rights Association) and *The Indians' Friend* (Women's National Indian Association, later changed to National Indian Association) are the two major publications of these longstanding, but now defunct, organizations.

26. For the Women's National Indian Association, see Helen M. Wanken, "'Women's Sphere' and Indian Reform: The Women's National Indian Association, 1879–1901" (unpublished PhD dissertation, Marquette University, 1981). See the masthead of any edition of *The Indians' Friend* in the first months of 1908.

27. Patricia Nelson Limerick, *The Legacy of Conquest: The Unbroken Past of the American West* (New York: W. W. Norton and Co., 1988), 197.

28. See the succinct treatment in William T. Hagan, "Private Property: The Indians' Door to Civilization," *Ethnohistory* 3 (Spring 1956): 126–137; and Hagan's "Reformers' Images of the American Indians," in *"They Made Us Many Promises": The American Indian Experience, 1524 to the Present,* 2nd ed., ed. Philip Weeks (Wheeling, IL: Harlan Davidson, 2002).

29. *LMC* (1890): 8.

30. See Hauptman and McLester, eds., *The Oneida Indians in the Age of Allotment.*

31. *LMC* (1890): 47–48.

32. *LMC* (1892): 117–119. Carter attended the Mohonk conferences in 1889, 1890, 1892–1894, 1896–1899, 1901, 1903, and 1906.

33. Sybil Carter to R. V. Belt, April 24, 1893, #15027-1893 [to quarter teachers]; Carter to commissioner of Indian affairs, July 12, 1894, with attached letter of dismissed teacher Nettie Knickerbocker, July 6, 1894, #26806-1894; Carter to Belt, November 30, 1891, #42775-1891 [to start industrial school]; John M. Ewing [chief special agent] to Belt, April 15,1893, #13500-1893 [relative to Carter's request to send lace and lacemakers to Columbian Exposition]; Carter to Commissioner William Jones, January 12, 1899, #1912-1899 [employment of field matron], all found in Records of the BIA, Letters Received, 1881–1907, RG75, NA.

34. "I will prepare the lace for you freely." Sybil Carter to commissioner of Indian affairs, January 12, 1899, #1912-1899, Records of the BIA, Letters Received, 1881–1907, RG75, NA.

35. *Oneida: The People of the Stone* (Oneida, WI: Episcopal Church of the Holy Apostles, 1899), 47–49. The material on Oneida lacemaking appeared again in Julia Bloomfield's *The Oneidas*, 2nd ed. (New York: Alden Bros., 1907), 343–349.

35. Sybil Carter Lace Association, Annual Reports, 1908–1912, Records of the Sybil Carter Lace Association, (Smithsonian) Cooper-Hewitt Museum, New York City.

36. For Josephine Webster, see Thelma McLester, "Josephine Hill Webster, 1883–1978," in *The Oneida Indian Experience: Two Perspectives*, ed. Jack Campisi and Laurence M. Hauptman, 116–118 (Syracuse, NY: Syracuse University Press, 1988). For Josephine Webster's own writings about the Oneida lacemakers, see the brochure she wrote in Hauptman and McLester, *The Oneida Indians in the Age of Allotment*, 109–111.

37. Neslund, "Native American Lace," 19.

38. Ibid., 19; Duncan, "American Indian Lace Making," 28–35.

39. See note 38.

40. Woodrow Webster, interview, June 4, 2004, Oneida, WI.

Reviving Oneida Lacemaking

by Betty McLester and Debra Jenny

BETTY MCLESTER: Fifteen years ago, I read a booklet on the history of the Holy Apostles Episcopal Church at Oneida [*Oneida: The People of the Stone: The Church's Mission to the Oneidas*], which mentioned the Oneida women lacemakers. The ladies had learned this art to supplement their family incomes, but no one in Oneida makes lace anymore. I thought perhaps we could learn it again. I talked with Beth Bashara of the Oneida Arts Board, who found a teacher, Debra Jenny. The Oneida Nation Arts Board then instituted a class on lacemaking at Oneida, which I immediately joined. We now have hopes of reviving the art.

DEBRA JENNY: The one word to characterize the work of the Oneida lacemakers of the past was "efficient." They did it all. They did exacting work determining yardage — namely, how many inches of lace you could make in an hour — making Indian motifs, finishing off the lace, and submitting the final product to international competitions. They won many prizes, including a medal at the Paris Exposition in 1900 and first place at the St. Louis World's Fair in 1904. These ladies were good!

. . .

BY WORLD WAR I, more than one hundred women were involved in the project. Every two weeks, they delivered lace to the association [Sybil Carter Lace Association] in New York City. The Oneida women were very busy. They did one-hundred- to three-hundred-dollar commissioned pieces for the ladies in New York City. The association ended its work in 1926; however, [Oneida postmaster] Josephine Webster [and other women] kept up lacemaking until her retirement in 1953. A lady named Sister Augusta tried to revive lacemaking in the region after that time.

Today we are again attempting to revive the interest in Oneida lacemaking. The effort needs to be encouraged from an early age, and there is a definite learning curve in becoming a skilled lacemaker, a highly labor-intensive endeavor. Woody Webster [Josephine Webster's son] donated a bushel basket full of bobbins to the Oneida Nation Museum, and from them we can see that the women used whatever wood was available to make the bobbins. Some look like wooden dolls chopped off at the legs. Others look like Belgian, Bohemian, and German bobbins.

We have studied the lace made by the Oneida women of the earlier times. They made every type of lace known, though we have not yet found any surviving examples of pillow lace, which is made by attaching thread to a wooden bobbin and twisting it in a certain way and then pinning it onto a pillow as work continues. The Oneida women employed four-strand braiding, used simple geometric designs, or mastered complicated lace patterns [that resulted in their masterpiece at the Cathedral of St. John the Divine]. It is nearly impossible to differentiate lacemaking styles used by the Oneidas from other expert lacemakers of the time, though one way is to note that some of the Oneida lace had Indian motifs. But because any lacemaker could get ideas about patterns out of a book, styles were borrowed, and this was fair game. The Indian women who worked on the eight projects supported by the association [two others were short-lived among the Senecas and Onondagas in New York] also copied patterns to guide their work. These patterns were often on architectural blue paper or linen or from select diagrams on tissue paper.

By studying the work of these past lacemakers, we can see how precise they were. Looking at two original photographs of the St. John the Divine lace, at the exactness of the pinhole, we can appreciate how incredibly great this piece is. The women's talent of working from a simple outline and expertly crossing and twisting the pattern is amazing. The grapevine ivy design in the lace is actually the theme of the cathedral. The lace also depicts an eagle — regarded by Oneidas as a protector, rising above everyone and everything, watching for danger — an image that clearly had spiritual meaning to the Indian women.

Reminiscences of Oneida Life
in Milwaukee, 1920–1975

by Opal Skenandore

AFTER THE FIRST WORLD WAR AND MAINLY INTO THE 1920S, many of our Oneida people began to move to Milwaukee seeking jobs and better living conditions.[1] Families such as the Archiquettes, Bairds, Coopers, Coulons, Danforths, Doxtators, Johns, Metoxens, Parkers, Powless, Schuyler, Skenandores, Summers, Websters, and Wheelocks were just a few. During World War II, others moved to Milwaukee to work in war-related industries. And in the 1950s through the 1960s, the government introduced a program of urban relocation as the means of ending reservation poverty and accelerating assimilation. They promoted the advantages of city life to reservation communities. As many more Oneida people moved to Milwaukee, they encountered and interacted with other Wisconsin tribes, mainly Chippewas, Menominees, Potawatomis, Stockbridge, and Winnebagos.

The folks who raised me, Julius Summers and his wife, Susan Metoxen Summers, were typical of those who had come to find work and live in Milwaukee. Both were born and raised in Oneida, Susan in October 1897 and Julius in May 1900, and both attended an off-reservation Indian boarding school at Flandreau, South Dakota. Many other Oneida children attended this school or others, for boarding school was mandatory for Indian children. These schools were designed to immerse Indian children in white culture as well as to educate them. In 1917, the army recruited many male students from the boarding schools. Julius and others enlisted to serve during World War I.

After the war, Julius moved to Milwaukee. Susan also moved there to find work. They would marry about 1928 and spend the rest of their lives in this city. Along with their own daughter, Ethel Summers, they raised several Oneida foster children, including three Steffes sisters — Ruth, Esther, and Mildred — in the 1930s. After the Steffes girls left, I came to live with them, around 1943; around 1945 they took in four more Oneida

girls, again all Steffes sisters: Dolores, Celia, Shirley, and Doris. In the late
1920s, the Summerses' closest neighbors and friends from Oneida were
Alpheus Smith and his wife Delia, who lived right across the street.
Another friend and Oneida family neighbor was Ami Skenandore, his wife
Jane (Powless), and their family. The Summerses always kept active within
the Indian community, and we girls also participated, for instance, learning Indian dancing through the Consolidated Tribes of American Indians.
My folks were both active members of that organization, and they made
sure we stayed connected with our Indian community and Oneida people.

Many regularly traveled back and forth to Oneida on weekends to visit
family members and attend weddings, funerals, or social events. Others
stayed away and returned only when necessary, and others lost touch and
never returned. People traveled by train or bus but mainly by car. Back
then, it took about four hours of travel time, so most Oneida families
packed a lunch. A large ring of bologna and sweet rolls was said to be very
popular to snack on.

From the 1920s onward, many intertribal centers sprung up in major
cities, including Milwaukee, in response to the need to be with fellow Indians. Oneida life centered around activities sponsored by the Consolidated Tribes of American Indians. In 1937, Alpheus Smith founded the
organization and served as its first chairman for many years. (His great-
grandfather, Henry Cooper, had been the interpreter as Oneidas moved
from their homelands in New York to Wisconsin starting in the 1820s.)
Alpheus's Oneida name was Hanging Corn. He attended two Indian
boarding schools, the first at Tomah, Wisconsin, and the second at Carlisle
School in Pennsylvania, from 1916 to 1918. He came to Milwaukee in
1927 and worked at the International Harvester Company from 1929 until
his retirement in 1963. In March 1969, he died of leukemia at the age of
seventy-one.

In the early years, the Consolidated Tribes met in schools or at homes
and occasionally rented halls for their meetings or activities. In 1960, they
were able to secure their own center at 1872 North Twelfth Street. This
organization was open to all Indians of different tribes to keep alive and
interpret to others Indian history, dances, songs, and Oneida singing as
well as to promote fellowship among the Indian people of Milwaukee,

and they sponsored social events for all ages. For example, they began an Indian dance group in 1938. Because our Oneida people had little knowledge of powwows, songs, or dances, we had help from the Chippewas, Potawatomi, and Winnebagos. These tribes and some Indian dancers from Chicago, as well as other dancers from tribes from around our state, came to help out at our dance gatherings. Some of our first Oneida dancers that I can recall included Eli and Kenneth Powless, Frances Coleman, Florrean Skenandore, Rupert Smith, Esther Steffes, and Ethel Summers. The Consolidated Tribes held many fund-raising events to buy dancers regalia; when they raised one thousand dollars, the Chippewas made the outfits for them. An outfit was given to an individual to use while he or she was in the group, but it was to be returned when one stopped dancing. Dance outfits were very expensive; most could not have afforded to buy their own.

In the mid-1940s, other young Oneidas began to learn and started dancing with this group. They included many family members or brothers and sisters such as Jim and Ellen Danforth; Hoyan Doxtator; Dewey (we called him Babe), Marlene, and Eugene Silas; Donna, Kenneth, Myron (Chub), and Joyce Skenandore; the three Steffes sisters, Dolores, Shirley, and Doris; Stan Webster; and myself. Some of the dances our group did included the friendship dance, pipe dance, shield dance, and eagle dance, performed by Babe Silas, an Oneida, and Joe Webster, a Chippewa. Marlene Silas, Joyce Skenandore, and I all learned to do the hoop dance. Doris Steffes did what was called a feather dance, which taught the dancer to keep time with the drum by dancing around the feather; then the dancer would bend over, keeping time, and pick up the feather with her mouth. She also did so while doing a back bend. Some of the dances were done by the whole group, and others were done just by the boys or by the women; some of these dances were fast and others were slow, depending on the song that went with the dance.

Over the years, our group danced for hundreds of places and events in and around Milwaukee. We did some television appearances and were featured many times in the newspaper. We participated beginning in 1943 in the Holiday Folk Fair, and we danced at the one hundredth anniversary celebration of the founding of Milwaukee as well as the celebration parade for the arrival of a major-league baseball team in 1953. When the Milwaukee Braves won the World Series in 1957, the Braves organization presented my foster dad, Julius Summers, and other Consolidated officials with rings commemorating the event. I still have Julius's ring. In the mid-1940s through most of the 1950s, the Consolidated sponsored an annual dance on the third Saturday of September at the Bohemian Hall, for which our dancers put on an hour-long program. Donald Cornelius would sing a few modern songs, which the people enjoyed, for he was a fine singer.

In June of 1957, the Consolidated began holding their powwows outdoors at Heidelberg Park. Jay Silverheels, a Mohawk actor who played Tonto on radio, on television, and in movies, was the featured celebrity, and he helped draw large crowds. Silverheels knew his Mohawk language, and our people who could speak Oneida could converse with him, because Oneida and Mohawk are so similar. This was really enjoyable for our people. In 1969, the powwow moved to Croatian Park in Franklin, and that year the celebrity guest was Iron Eyes Cody, an actor best known for his television commercial to clean up our environment. In 1970, I was the featured dancer for having been selected as Miss Holiday Folk Fair 1968 and for my ability to do the hoop dance.

The Consolidated also sponsored other activities, which they publicized through a monthly newsletter, flyers, telephone calls, and the "moccasin telegram," namely, word of mouth. According to Ronald Skenandore, in the late 1940s and 1950s, the organization sponsored a lacrosse (an Indian game) team that competed against the Menominee and Chippewa teams down at the Milwaukee lakefront. Some of the players were Ronald Skenandore, Kenneth Powless, Dewey and Eugene Silas, Rupert Smith, and Myron Skenandore. Oneida teachings say that the game of lacrosse was given to us by our creator, and the game was played well before the coming of Europeans. It is played with sticks a little longer than three feet that have pockets on one end about the size of a baseball. Players can toss a ball up to fifty yards. The object is to catch the ball and carry it in the stick while running toward the goal. Two poles are stuck in the ground about four feet apart, and the ball has to go through the posts to earn a point. Because of all the running up and down the field, the players wore no protective equipment or much clothing. The game is very rough, and injuries frequently occurred.

According to Edith Schuyler Wolf, from the late 1920s into the 1940s the Milwaukee Oneidas also had a baseball team known as the Iroquois. (Oneidas are members of the Iroquois Confederacy.) Some of these players included Alpheus Smith, Julius Summers, and the three Schuyler brothers, Arthur (whose nickname was Jonas), Melvin, and Harold.

The Oneida women achieved success in sports as well. The All Saints Indian Women's Guild sponsored a girls' softball team in the 1950s. We called ourselves the Bravettes and wore red and gray uniforms, and the guild paid for equipment and uniforms. Floyd Skenandore and Frank Baird were the coaches. The Bravettes played in the city league and also at Oneida and Wisconsin Dells against other Indian teams. Members included Ellen Danforth, Alberta House, Lydia Parkhurst, Marlene Silas, and Erma Wheelock, as well as some Menominee girls. Both Lydia Parkhurst and I were named to the All-City team. We also organized a girls' basketball team that was composed of two Menominees, three Winnebagos, and me. We played in a tournament in Chicago against Chicago's Indian girls' team.

The Consolidated also sponsored the Miss Indian Milwaukee contest, which three Oneida girls won: Victoria Patterson, 1966; Patricia Powless, 1967; and Patricia Cornelius, 1977. All three went to Bismarck, North Dakota, to compete in the Miss Indian USA contest. I was selected Miss Holiday Folk Fair at the event's twenty-fifth anniversary in 1968. More than fifty-four thousand people attended the fair that year, and the honored ethnic group was the American Indian. Robert Bennett, an Oneida who was the commissioner of Indian affairs, was the honorary guest. I made many public appearances on behalf of the fair and was on television and in the newspaper a number of times. A highlight was a trip to Washington, D.C., to attend a Wisconsin congressional dinner, where I met Mr. Bennett. I also attended the Wisconsin Governors Conference Dinner and met and dined with Governor Warren Knowles. That year was a very exciting experience.

Many Milwaukee Oneidas were involved in the operations of the Consolidated Tribes. Both my folks held offices at one time or another. Lois

Powless served as treasurer. Morris Wheelock, who in 1937 was the first elected Oneida tribal chairman under the IRA, served as chairman of the Consolidated Tribes in the late 1950s. Agnes Powless and Elizabeth Pierce were both charter members. Bill and Elizabeth Cornelius, Eli Powless, Ruth Baird (who served as secretary) and her husband LaBoy, Frank Baird and his wife Grace, and Nathan Smith (who served as chairman) all helped to keep the organization active.

The Oneidas of Milwaukee also helped shape Oneida reservation life. For example, Oscar Archiquette was vice chair of the tribe from 1939 to 1942, 1950 to 1951, and 1967 to 1968, and Purcell Powless was Wisconsin Oneida tribal chairman from 1967 into the 1970s. Raymond Parkhurst was chairman from 1940 to 1942, Morris Wheelock from 1937 to 1938, and Andrew Beechtree from 1946 to 1947. Dewey Silas became an Episcopal deacon and later an ordained priest in Milwaukee, and he also served in Oneida at the Holy Apostle Episcopal church. Lois Powless now serves on the Wisconsin Oneida Appeals Commission in Oneida and is a member of the Oneida hymn singers.

In addition to the inspiration and encouragement of the Consolidated Tribes, other factors influenced the lives of Oneidas in Milwaukee through the mid-1970s. The Episcopal Church of All Saints cathedral, located at East Juneau Avenue near the lakefront, played a central role for many Oneida families. There, Ruth Baird founded the Indian Women's Guild, which was quite active within the church. They held meetings and fund-raisers, and they served breakfast once a month after mass and fish fries during Lent. Membership was about fifteen ladies, and some were Susan Summers, Helema Skenandore, Reka Smith, and Emily Swamp. The Women's Guild held a harvest dance in 1955, where they served traditional corn soup and featured an Indian dance program, square dancing called by Oscar Archiquette, and an arts and crafts sale. When we were children, we girls, meaning the Steffes girls and myself, attended Sunday school class and helped with kitchen duties. Other Oneidas attended St. John's Episcopal Church on Milwaukee's south side, located at Mineral Street. This church became a meeting place for various Indian groups and for social activities and meals for the elderly.

Oneida prayer singers go back to the days when our people still lived in New York. As the Oneidas accepted Christian teachings, they also learned Christian songs, and hymn singing became an important part of our communities. This tradition has been passed down from one generation to the next since the 1700s and maybe even earlier. Many fine Oneida hymn singers moved to Milwaukee, particularly Oscar Archiquette, Eli Powless, Ruth Baird, Lucy Cornelius, Ruth Coleman, Curtis Denny, Evelyn and Sheldon Hill, George Ninham, and Edith Wyland. The group made a few records so the songs would be preserved, and Oscar, Ruth, and Edith taught the Oneida hymns to those who wanted to learn. New singers such as Shirley Lafleur, Russell Metoxen and his son Kirby, and Lois Powless began to sing with this group at the wakes of Oneida people, at church, or wherever they were asked to perform.

Two outreach health clinics providing social services opened in 1972. These clinics on the north and south sides of the city became known as the Milwaukee Indian Community Health Centers. The American Indian Council for Alcohol and Drug Abuse has served the Milwaukee Indian community for many years. Herb Powless was its first director.

Numerous Oneidas have worked in health-care occupations. In 1949, Ramona Skenandore was the first Oneida girl to win a nursing scholarship, given by the National Society of the Daughters of the American Revolution. Dorothy Danforth, Sandra Schuyler, and Sharon Skenandore all worked in the nursing profession. Marilyn Skenandore, known as Mindy Minidmoye, also worked in the drug-abuse-prevention programs. Marlene Silas focused her attention on serving the needs of the elderly and was given recognition and an award for her services.

A new organization was started in the 1970s: the United Indians of Milwaukee. They met first at St. John's Episcopal Church, and years later they acquired the use of an unused firehouse station located at Fifteenth Street and Bruce Street. It is an active center, teaching arts and crafts and Indian dancing. There, the group holds fund-raisers, special commemorative dinners, Christmas parties, wakes, and their business meetings.

The Milwaukee Oneidas have had many accomplishments: athletic, professional, and artistic. On August 1, 1950, John Danforth Sr. was the first Indian to hold the position of commander of the General William Mitchell American Legion Post. I was a featured hoop dancer at many powwows throughout the country and Canada. In 1964, I was on the *Original Amateur Hour* television program. Spider Denny and brothers Dale and Mark Powless made a name for themselves in amateur boxing, with matches held at the Eagles Club in downtown Milwaukee. They learned their skills at a club called Ace Boxing under a Chippewa Indian instructor by the name of Dell Porter. Jonas Schuyler won several awards from the Milwaukee Recreation Department for his batting average, which was never under .300 in all the years he played baseball. Melvin Schuyler's son Arthur was also honored for his skills in baseball in the 1950s and 1960s. Maxine Elm Smallish, now retired, was a student adviser at Marquette University.

Oneidas in Milwaukee have made their mark in other fields of endeavor. At least eight Oneida families ran taverns in Milwaukee from the 1940s to the 1970s. Max and Lucy Skenandore's bar was known as Aragon Bar, located on Sixth Street and Bruce. This was the first Indian-run licensed establishment in the city. It was followed by Guy and Nomie John's Wigwam on Sixth and Walker, John and Nancy Danforth's Indian John's at Fifth Street and Bruce, Edith Doxtator's The Comet on South Fifth Street, Tony and Dorothy Danforth's Tony's Bar on Seventeenth Street and Highland Avenue, Emily and Coleman Swamp's Thunderbird on Muskego Avenue, Marlene Silas's Arrow Inn at South Twentieth Street, and Eugene Baird's Geno's Tavern on South Pearl Street. These taverns were gathering places where Oneidas and other Indians held fund-raisers, dances, and birthday parties; maintained social ties; and organized events and sports teams — bowling, basketball, softball, and darts. Today, however, none of these taverns still exist in Milwaukee.

The American Indian Movement (AIM) came on the scene in the late 1960s, founding chapters throughout the country, including in Milwaukee. In 1971, a group including Herb Powless Sr. and other Oneidas took over the abandoned coast guard station at the Milwaukee lakefront. Eventually, city officials turned the building over to the Indians, and the site became the first Indian community school.

The school was eventually relocated from the lakefront site to an unused campus near downtown Milwaukee, where it served American Indian children for many years. Besides teaching the ABCs, the school has had guest speakers from different tribes; dancing, drumming, culture, and history classes; and performances by Native actors. The school has really grown over the years. In September 2007, a new ten million dollar Indian school opened in the Franklin district of Milwaukee to meet the needs of the growing Milwaukee Indian community.

Notes

1. For more on the early history of the Oneidas in Milwaukee, see Nancy O. Lurie, "Reflections on an Urban Indian Community: The Oneidas of Milwaukee," in *The Oneida Indian Experience: Two Perspectives*, ed. Jack Campisi and Laurence M. Hauptman (Syracuse, NY: Syracuse University Press, 1988), 101–107. For an earlier portrait, see Robert Ritzenthaler and Mary Sellers, "Indian in an Urban Setting," *Wisconsin Archaeologist* 36 (1955): 147–161.

Part 2

Wisconsin Oneidas Polish the Chain of Alliance, 1917–1975

Introduction

A NY CASUAL VISITOR TO ONEIDA, WISCONSIN, quickly realizes the importance of American military service to the community. Indeed, family military service is ingrained, and children and grandchildren follow in the footsteps of their elders, much as with the military tradition in parts of the United States' South; however, there is more to it than that. The frequently used metaphor of the chain of friendship — formed in colonial times and reinforced by the American-Oneida alliance during the Revolutionary War — still helps define Oneida identity. From Oriskany in 1777 to Baghdad in 2010, Oneidas have served. In their minds, serving in the armed forces is a way to remind Americans that they, Americans, have an obligation to fulfill their part of their alliance with the Oneidas, an alliance made in 1777 and confirmed by two treaties in 1794.[1]

This is especially noticeable at the Wisconsin Oneidas' annual July 4 powwow. After the grand entrance dance that initiates the doings, the flag ceremony begins. The announcer then invites both Indians and non-Indians who served in the United States armed forces to enter the circle and join the honor dance. The sentiment expressed at the powwow is no mere ploy for tourist dollars; it is a deeply felt respect for this sacrifice. This feeling is also evident in the recent dedication of an impressive monument and park on the Wisconsin Oneida reservation to honor all tribal veterans who served in the United States armed forces, from the American Revolution to the present time.

Indeed, Oneidas periodically remind outsiders of their impressive military service throughout American history, particularly stressing their role in the War of Independence on the side of George Washington. Although Oneidas still want to remain culturally distinct, they also have a desire to be recognized and included in the larger sweep of American history. They are saying to the United States, "We were there with you at the darkest days of your history — at the Saratoga campaign of 1777, at the British blockade of Lake Ontario in the War of 1812, at the siege of Atlanta in the Civil War, in the trenches on the western front in World War I, at the Battle of the Bulge in World War II, at Pork Chop Hill in the Korean War,

at Khe Sanh in the Vietnam War, and at Fallujah in today's war in Iraq."
This is a reminder that they too remain important and have had distinguished leaders. But military service holds an even more significant place
in Oneida life than this. Oneidas once used ancient condolence council
ceremonies (one of the most revered ceremonies of the Iroquois peoples)
to reinforce their feelings about the greatness of the past and to remind
both Oneidas and their guests of their mutual obligations.[2] Now Oneidas
use their extraordinary military record as a cultural touchstone, to reinforce their heritage, their collective memory, and their national identity —
an identity that is not entirely exclusive from the American national
identity.

While some Oneidas splintered off and joined the sizable contingent
of the Six Nations on the British side during the American Revolution, the
vast majority of Oneidas (and their allies the Tuscaroras), encouraged by
their pro-American missionary Samuel Kirkland, faithfully served George
Washington's rebel army. Eleven Oneidas served as officers in the American army, and, to this day, Oneida oral history is filled with references to
their service in the patriots' quest for independence. Among the Oneida
heroes of the Revolution are Peter Bread, Blatcop, Henry Cornelius (later
the founder of the Handsome Lake religion among the Oneidas), Hanyost,
Paul Powless, and Thawengarakwen (Honyery Doxtator). At Oriskany, a
major battle of the Saratoga campaign, Blatcop heroically charged the
enemy three times while under intense British fire, while Honyery Doxtator's wife, Dolly Cobus, took her husband's place in the battle after he was
wounded in the right wrist. Hanyost distinguished himself at the siege of
Fort Stanwix as a lieutenant under General Peter Gansevoort. Moreover,
Oneida chiefs Skenandoah and Good Peter, despite their advanced ages at
the time, faithfully served the Americans as messengers from General
Philip Schuyler, only to be arrested by the British and harshly confined as
prisoners of war in 1780.[3]

During the War of 1812, in May of 1814, a military detachment of more
than 120 irregulars, mostly Oneidas but including a sprinkling of Brother-
town, Onondaga, and Stockbridge Indians, made their way through rough
terrain north of Oneida Lake, unaware that their forced march would lead
to a dramatic American victory at Sandy Creek. The Oneidas, who in-

cluded some of the most prominent tribesmen of the era — Peter Elm, Daniel Bread, Henry Cornelius, and Adam Skenandoah — were also a vital part of the overall defense of Sackets Harbor, the only American-held ship-launching center on Lake Ontario during most of the war. The British navy was ambushed by Indians coming from the south, as well as by other American marines, dragoons, and riflemen on the north shore of the creek, coming from Sackets Harbor. The British forces were cut to pieces in the ensuing firefight, now known as the Battle of Big Sandy or Sandy Creek. Fourteen British sailors were killed, and twenty-eight were wounded. American forces captured the three British gunboats containing Congreve rockets, thus weakening British control of Lake Ontario.[4]

During the Civil War, the Wisconsin Oneidas served as volunteers in Company F of the Fourteenth Wisconsin, part of General William Tecumseh Sherman's Grand Army of the West. Their service was most noteworthy in the Atlanta and Carolina campaigns from May 1864 to the end of the war. At least 111 Wisconsin Oneidas served in the Union army and navy out of a total reservation population of 1,100. Although estimates vary, at least 46 of these volunteers were killed, went missing in action, or died of disease while at war.[5]

Oneida servicepeople in all of the American military conflicts were remembered again and again. In their festivities throughout the nineteenth century, in the manner of the traditional condolence council ritual, chiefs would address gatherings of tribal members and non-Indian guests to their Wisconsin reservation, telling of the great Oneida leaders of the past and their heroic exploits at Oriskany and Valley Forge. A conscious effort to generate goodwill in their new Wisconsin location, this gesture showed their non-Indian guests that they were loyal Americans worthy of respect.[6] Later, as Oneidas attempted to fight off the conversion of trust lands to fee simple patents subject to taxation and foreclosure after the Burke Act of 1906, Oneidas once again brought up the stories of the American Revolution and made reference to Oneida military service and loyalty to the United States. In a letter of July 23, 1918, addressed to President Woodrow Wilson, Paul Doxtator pointed out that his family members had fought on the American side from Bunker Hill onward; that they had been killed in action fighting the British in the War of 1812; that he and his brother

George and his father, Cornelius, had served in the Civil War; and that his son John was now part of the American Expeditionary Force fighting Germans in Europe.[7]

. . .

IN THE FIRST ARTICLE IN PART 3, tribal chairman Jerry Danforth, himself a thirty-year veteran of the United States Navy, describes his visit to a military cemetery in France in search of the grave of a Wisconsin Oneida killed in action during World War I. His poignant essay clearly shows the links between the past and present and that contemporary Wisconsin Oneidas hold military service in high regard. Danforth's article is followed by that of Loretta Metoxen, who herself served two decades in military service. Metoxen, the Wisconsin Oneida tribal historian, outlines the experiences of Wisconsin Oneidas in World War I and then focuses on the life of Dr. Josiah Powless, an Oneida physician who was killed on the western front just one month before the armistice.

In an excellent recent work on the twelve thousand American Indians who served in World War I, Susan Applegate Krouse adds to Metoxen's essay, expanding our knowledge of Oneida service in World War I. She focuses on the military service of Chauncey Powless, who was in Company D, 165th Infantry, 42nd Division. According to his white commanding officer, the twenty-seven-year-old Oneida from West De Pere was a hero, surviving the heaviest fighting of the war: "Powless came to us over a year ago. He was in all battles, Champagne, Chateau Thierry, St. Mihiel, Argonne, Sedan. He was a great runner, carrying messages through heavy shell fire. Magnificent at liason [sic] work."[8] In addition, several Wisconsin Oneida nurses, including Cora Elm Sinnard, also served in France.

During World War II, several hundred Wisconsin Oneidas were among the twenty-five thousand Native Americans in military service. Even before the attack on Pearl Harbor, the United States Army attempted to recruit Oneidas and other Indians into the Signal Corps of the Thirty-second Infantry, "for the express purpose of radio communications."[9] Later, as has been well documented, the Marine Corps used Navajo and Comanche languages to foil the Axis powers. Wisconsin Oneidas were with the Fourth Infantry Division that liberated Paris in 1944 and drove the Germans back across France and Belgium.[10] In the third essay in Part 2, a group of three first-person accounts of Oneida military service, Edmund Powless describes his wartime experiences as a paratrooper. He fought at the Battle of the Bulge in the winter of 1944 and parachuted behind enemy lines in order to secure a key bridge over the Rhine to allow American entry into Germany.

The second of the first-person accounts is from Franklin L. Cornelius. At barely eighteen years of age, Cornelius enlisted in the Marine Corps during the height of the Korean War. He received a commission and became a marine drill instructor and platoon leader in Korea. In his twenty-two years of service, he also served two tours of duty in Vietnam. On the other hand, Kenneth William Webster was a draftee sent to fight in Vietnam. In his account, he describes the horror of jungle warfare, the bonds among fellow soldiers in his company, and his impressions about Vietnam and its people.[11]

Notes

1. *Treaty with the Six Nations, Stat.* 7 (1794): 44; *Treaty with the Oneida, etc., Stat.* 7 (1794): 47.

2. For the best treatment of the Iroquois condolence council, see William N. Fenton, *The Great Law and the Longhouse: A Political History of the Iroquois Confederacy* (Norman: University of Oklahoma Press, 1998), 3–18, 135–142. For its importance in Iroquoian diplomacy, see Fenton, "Structure, Continuity and Change in the Process of Iroquois Treaty-Making," in *The History and Culture of Iroquois Diplomacy: An Interdisciplinary Guide to the Treaties of the Six Nations and Their League*, ed. Francis Jennings et al., 3–36 (Syracuse, NY: Syracuse University Press, 1985). For its legacy among the Oneidas, see Laurence M. Hauptman and L. Gordon McLester III, *Chief Daniel Bread and the Oneida Nation of Indians of Wisconsin* (Norman: University of Oklahoma Press, 2002).

3. See, for example, the stories recounted by Gloria Halbritter and Loretta Metoxen, "Oneida Traditions," in *The Oneida Indian Experience*, ed. Jack Campisi and Laurence M. Hauptman (Syracuse, NY: Syracuse University Press, 1988), 144–145. For Oneida history during the American Revolution, see Barbara Graymont, "The Oneidas in the American Revolution," in Campisi and Hauptman, *The Oneida Indian Experience*, 31–42; Graymont's *The Iroquois in the American Revolution* (Syracuse, NY: Syracuse University Press, 1972), 132–141; Karim M. Tiro, "The People of the Standing Stone: The Oneida Indian Nation from Revolution Through Removal, 1765–1840" (unpublished PhD dissertation, University of Pennsylvania, 1999): 99–146; and, most recently, Joseph T. Glatthaar and James Kirby Martin, *Forgotten Allies: The Oneida Indians and the American Revolution* (New York: Hill and Wang, 2006).

4. U.S. Congress, Senate, Committee of Claims, *Report Regarding Compensation for the Capture of Three Gun Boats* [in the War of 1812 — petition of Oneida Indians], 32nd Cong., 1st

sess., 1852, Senate Report 286, Serial Set 631. See also A. D. Bonesteel to A. B. Greenwood [commissioner of Indian affairs], July 8, 1859, OIA, M234, Records of the Green Bay Agency, Microfilm Reel 323, RG75, NA; J. Mackay Hitsman, *The Incredible War of 1812: A Military History* (Toronto: University of Toronto Press, 1998), 155; Douglas R. Hickey, *The War of 1812: A Forgotten Conflict* (Urbana: University of Illinois Press, 1989), 185; Greg Chester, *The Battle of Big Sandy* (Adams, NY: Historical Association of South Jefferson County, 1981). For the war, see also Carl Benn, *The Iroquois in the War of 1812* (Toronto: University of Toronto Press, 1998).

5. For accounts of Oneidas in the Civil War, see Byron R. Abernethy, ed., *Private Elisha Stockwell, Jr., Sees the Civil War* (Norman: University of Oklahoma Press, 1958), 32–33, 79–80, 88; Stephen Ambrose, ed., *A Wisconsin Boy in Dixie: The Selected Letters of James K. Newton* (Madison: University of Wisconsin Press, 1961), 138–139; Robert Smith and Loretta Metoxen, "Oneida Traditions," in Campisi and Hauptman, *The Oneida Indian Experience*, 150–151; Laurence M. Hauptman, *The Iroquois in the Civil War: From Battlefield to Reservation* (Syracuse, NY: Syracuse University Press, 1993), 67–83.

6. See, for example, *Green Bay Advocate*, July 4, 1854. See also Hauptman and McLester, *Chief Daniel Bread*, 117–126.

7. Paul C. Doxtator to President Woodrow Wilson, July 23, 1918, #64300-18-312 (Oneida), BIA, CCF, 1907–1939, RG75, NA.

8. Quoted in Susan Applegate Krouse, *North American Indians in the Great War* (Lincoln: University of Nebraska Press, 2007), 79. For more on American Indian involvement in World War I, see Thomas A. Britten, *American Indians in World War I: At War and at Home* (Albuquerque: University of New Mexico Press, 1999).

9. Kenneth William Townsend, *World War II and the American Indian* (Albuquerque: University of New Mexico Press, 2000), 144.

10. Alison R. Bernstein, *American Indians and World War II: Toward a New Era in Indian Affairs* (Norman: University of Oklahoma Press, 1991), 55.

11. For a moving portrait of Native American veterans of Vietnam, see Tom Holm, *Strong Hearts, Wounded Souls: Native American Veterans and the Vietnam War* (Austin: University of Texas Press, 1996).

Remembering Oneida Veterans and Their Sacrifices

A Personal Journey

by Jerry Danforth

I SERVED IN THE UNITED STATES NAVY from July 1964 to July 1994. In November 1988, I was stationed aboard the USS *Leyte Gulf*, a guided missile cruiser assigned to the Roosevelt Battle Group. We were preparing for a six-month deployment to the Mediterranean and scheduled to depart in December. During the predeployment briefings, I learned that my ship would be making several port visits to France.

I knew from past family conversations that I had a relative who had been killed in World War I: my great uncle, Private First Class Antone Danforth, Thirtieth Infantry, Third Division, died in a battle at Aisne-Marne on July 15, 1918. My aunt Agnes had said that all she knew was that Antone was killed in the war and buried in France. With that limited information, I wrote to the Battle Monuments Commission in Washington, D.C. In very short order, an agent of that organization contacted me with information on Antone's branch of service and rate as well as the name of the cemetery where he was buried. The agent also provided me with a point of contact at the American embassy in Paris.

During the last week in May 1989, my ship pulled into Toulon, France, for our middeployment maintenance upkeep. Because this in-port period was going to be longer than normal, I decided this would be the best opportunity for me to visit the cemetery. I received four days' leave and set out to Paris on the TGV, a high-speed train.

I spent the first night in Paris and got directions to Château-Thierry, a town near Belleau Wood. Château-Thierry was fifty miles east of Paris, and the train for that leg of my trip was quite the opposite of the TGV. This train was something straight out of the 1930s, a coal-fired locomotive with passenger cars that had side aisles and sliding doors to enter the seating area. En route to Château-Thierry, we made seemingly countless stops, often halting for a simple junction at a dirt road. Finally, after several hours, I saw in the distance a monument-type structure standing off in a wooded area, and I wondered if that was the monument that marked the battlefield and cemetery I was looking for.

The train came to a stop at Château-Thierry. With the wooden train platform, a stack of mailbags, and the people coming and going, it was like a scene from an old movie. Unlike Paris, where many people understood and could speak English, here a man dressed in a uniform interrupted my first question to tell me that he could not "speak American." We communicated through gesturing, however, and he advised me to go across the street to a café, where there would be a man who could speak English.

I entered the café, where there were three men standing at the bar, drinking their espresso and talking. I asked the man behind the bar if he could speak English. He told me he couldn't, but, pointing to his watch, he indicated that there would soon be someone coming who could. I ordered a coffee and waited, and within fifteen minutes a man walked in. Immediately the bartender started explaining to him that I was an American and had some questions. The gentleman and I introduced ourselves, and I soon learned that he did not know too much more of English than I did of French. Nonetheless, with the help of the brochures I had, he understood what my goal was and called a taxi for me.

The taxi arrived, and the gentleman explained to the lady taxi driver where I wanted to go. Away we went. We drove out into the country and continued for what seemed to me to be quite a long way. I was trying to calculate what I thought the distance was in relation to the monument I had seen from the train. Soon we arrived at the gated entrance to the cemetery. By this time, I had a growing concern that I might not have enough francs to pay the taxi fare, but I figured I could sort that out later.

Just inside the cemetery grounds there was a building for visitors, and a man emerged from the entrance. He spoke first to the taxi driver and then greeted me in English. He asked me how long I would like to stay at the cemetery; I told him about three hours. He spoke to the taxi driver and she left.

A map of the cemetery was available in the reception building, and the caretaker helped me locate my great-uncle's grave marker. As I proceeded to walk through the cemetery, I noticed several individuals going grave to grave, placing a French flag and an American flag on each marker. The caretaker had explained to me that the cemetery held a special service each Memorial Day, and with the holiday just a few days away, they were making preparations.

I found Antone's grave marker and spent some time there, trying to envision what he and his comrades buried with him must have experienced on this battlefield. To walk on the ground where the actual battle took place was a somewhat eerie and calming feeling all at once.

After a while, I joined the people who were placing the flags on the graves. Even though we couldn't communicate very well, I could see they appreciated my offer to help. Even more so, I could see their appreciation for those who were buried there. When I got ready to leave, the caretaker removed the two flags from Antone's grave and presented them to me.

The taxi driver returned after about three hours, and I headed back to Château-Thierry. We stopped at the café where my local trip had begun. When I got out of the taxi and asked how much the fare was, the driver just smiled and said, "Merci," thanking me for my relative's sacrifice on behalf of the French people.

Later, as the train pulled away, again I saw the Château-Thierry monument. An excerpt of the inscription on the monument reads: "The last German offensive of the war, on 15 July, included an attack in the Eastern part of this Salient and there the 3rd American Division and elements of the 28th were important factors in the successful defense of the Allied positions." The train ride back to Paris gave me time to reflect on the day's experience. While it was somewhat sad, it also gave me a sense of satisfaction for having fulfilled a family responsibility by visiting Antone's grave.

When I returned to the States, and ultimately to Oneida, I told my aunt Agnes the story of my trip and presented her with the flags from her brother's grave. She was very touched by this and has kept those flags on display in her living room ever since.

Oneidas in World War I

by Loretta Metoxen

IN APRIL 1917, THE UNITED STATES CONGRESS declared war on the Central powers. The United States quickly mobilized, sending Major General John J. Pershing with his American Expeditionary Force (AEF) to France. In mid-June 1917, the AEF arrived in Paris. On July 4, 1917, after Pershing laid a wreath of flowers on the grave of General Marquis de Lafayette at Picpus Cemetery in Paris, Colonel Charles E. Stanton uttered the famous words: "Lafayette, we are here."[1] For the Oneidas in the AEF, those words had a very special meaning, for their great-grandfathers had served with General Lafayette in the American Revolution.[2]

Lafayette was the boy general of the Revolutionary War and at times the taskmaster of General George Washington. Later, he was adopted by the Oneidas, and there seems to be reason to believe that he may have Oneida descendants. Now the AEF was returning the great favor of Lafayette and France.

World War I introduced chemical warfare to the world when the German army utilized asphyxiating gases against the French on April 22, 1915, leaving many men comatose or dying in the trenches. Five chemicals were manufactured, but the most common and most feared was mustard gas, which some Oneida soldiers experienced in the field. Though mustard gas rarely caused immediate death, it did cause immediate blindness, which was overcome only with lengthy treatment. The gas also caused severe blistering of the skin and was very effective in completely immobilizing its targets. The United States responded with its own research, development, and supply of chemical gases, but the process was relatively slow and inefficient. Large-scale production materialized in England in the summer of 1918, by which time the French were ready to use their product on the front. Calaway Doxtator was one of the Oneidas who suffered the immediate effects of mustard gas and probably had residual effects for the rest of his life. Not much was known about battle fatigue (now known as post-traumatic stress disorder) among the Oneidas who returned to their families and homes in Wisconsin.

At least 115 Wisconsin Oneidas served in World War I. This number is not definitive, because it was calculated by researching all the cemetery records on the Oneida reservation; we know, however, that there are others buried at King Veterans Hospital and Cemetery at Waupaca, Wisconsin, and undoubtedly still others interred in all parts of the United States and cemeteries in France.[3]

The Oneidas from Wisconsin served in diverse capacities during the war. About ten of the Oneidas we tracked served in the navy. Most Oneidas were enlisted men and served as privates, privates first class, and corporals in the United States Army. A significant number served in the Quartermaster Corps and at supply depots. John R. Doxtator was a cook. Alfred Powless was in the 120th Field Artillery Band. Herman Willie Kelly served in the 429th Battalion, Signal Corps, while Reuben King served as corporal with Company C, 9th Field Signal Battalion. Brothers George and Wallace Cooper, George and William Cornelius, Chauncey and Levi Baird, Milton and Philip Summers, and Hyson and Julius Hill also served in the AEF, as did the three sons of Daniel and Cassie (Webster) Denny. Emanuel Powless, a veteran of the Spanish-American War, also fought in France during World War I. A few Wisconsin Oneidas, including Roderick Cornelius, served in both World War I and World War II.[4]

Several Oneidas served at higher ranks: Parker Websters was a staff sergeant in the 54th Pioneer Infantry, Joel Howard Cornelius was a pharmacist mate first class in the navy, and Cora Elm Sinnard, a Carlisle graduate and a highly trained nurse, also served in the war zone in France.[5] But without a doubt the most famous Wisconsin Oneida to serve in the war effort was Dr. Josiah Powless, first lieutenant in the Medical Detachment of the 308th Infantry, 2nd Division, who gave his life in the fighting on the western front in 1918.[6] Powless's sacrifice was not forgotten: on November 6 and 7, 2003, the United States Army honored his extraordinary courage as a physician and soldier in a ceremony at Fort Sam Houston, San Antonio, Texas, by dedicating a building in his honor. Powless's grandchildren, Roy Huff (World War II veteran) and Elizabeth (Betty) Bins, and four of his great-grandchildren attended the honoring ceremony.

Josiah Alvin Powless was born on the Oneida reservation on August 1,

1871, the son of Peter A. and Rebecca Powless. He attended grade school on the reservation, probably at the Holy Apostle's Mission School, where he graduated at age fourteen. Afterward, he entered the United States Indian Industrial School at Carlisle, Pennsylvania, where he continued studies for another six years and graduated in 1891 at the age of twenty. (Powless was one of 492 Oneida students at Carlisle; at least 27 of these Carlisle-educated Oneidas eventually served in the military during World War I.[7]) He then availed himself of a short course at Dickinson Preparatory School at Carlisle before returning home to Wisconsin to teach at the Oneida Indian Boarding School (the Government School) that opened in 1893.[8]

Powless yearned to become a physician, but he had no means to attain his goals. It was at this time that the Reverend Mr. Merrill, Holy Apostle's pastor, made a trip east to seek funds for the Oneida Hospital, for a badly needed water plant, and for the establishment of a small industry. During his presentation to a group in the Chapel of Old St. Paul's Church, Merrill mentioned the great need for a resident physician to care for more than two thousand Oneida people at the mission. Merrill said of this meeting:

> God indeed blessed that small meeting to us and to the Oneidas. One of the number there assembled, Miss Ethel M. Cheney, President of the Junior Auxiliary of St. Paul's Church, came forward to gladden the heart of the Missionary and all his people with a promise that she would undertake to provide means for the education of a physician for Oneida.[9]

As a result of this support, Josiah Powless was able to enter Milwaukee Medical College in 1900. According to one source: ". . . this young Oneida Indian, in his twenty-eighth year, had finished with great credit a four years' course of study at the College and graduated, not only with honors but with the same splendid record for moral character and attractive personality as he won while at Carlisle."[10]

At home on the Oneida reservation, Powless was a principal participant in church events. Additionally, he was among seven Oneida men who made up the very first election board, allowing Oneidas to vote in public elections. On November 1, 1897, he married Electa Skenandoah. After graduation from medical school in 1904, he returned to Oneida as the director and physician of the Oneida Hospital. His wife served as assistant director and nurse. The hospital had been established in 1898 by Solomon S. Burleson, an Episcopal missionary. For twelve years, Dr. Powless carried out his duties at the hospital while also caring for the Oneida children at the Oneida Boarding School, which also had a small hospital on site.

Dr. Powless enlisted on April 1, 1918, and on June 11 was sent overseas to France, where he served with the Medical Detachment of the 308th Infantry, 77th Division. He was also in the "Lost Battalion" in the Argonne Forest: a battalion of six hundred men who went on patrol in the forest and returned with only two hundred. On October 14, 1918, near Chevieres, France, Lieutenant Powless crossed an area of intense machine gun and artillery fire to go to the aid of a wounded comrade, Captain James M. McKibben. Powless dressed McKibben's wounds and carried him to the rear. McKibben did not survive, and Powless was seriously wounded.

Five days before the end of the war, Powless died from his wounds at the age of forty-seven. He was posthumously awarded the Distinguished Service Cross by the commanding general of the American Expeditionary Forces, General John J. (Blackjack) Pershing, according to direction of President Woodrow Wilson and under provision of an act of Congress.[11] He is buried in the Holy Apostles Church cemetery in Oneida, Wisconsin.

· · · ·

WORLD WAR I ENDED when the German delegates signed the armistice on the eleventh hour of the eleventh day of the eleventh month (November 11, 1918). Millions of innocent people, military and civilians, perished in the Great War — Oneidas among them. As was true for many who enlisted, they may not have completely understood the war or the rationale of heads of state who caused the whole world such damage, but they answered the call and enlisted at unusually high rates to protect the land and the liberty of a free people.

Notes

1. Charles E. Stanton was the nephew of Edwin M. Stanton, Lincoln's secretary of war. At least one source claims that Pershing stated the same phrase three weeks earlier. John

Bartlett, comp. and ed., *Familiar Quotations*, 13th Centennial Edition Revised (Boston: Little, Brown and Co., 1955), 789.

2. Barbara Graymont, "The Oneidas and the American Revolution," in *The Oneida Indian Experience: Two Perspectives*, ed. Jack Campisi and Laurence M. Hauptman (Syracuse, NY: Syracuse University Press, 1988), 31–44.

3. Records of the following cemeteries were consulted: Assembly of God; Church of Christ; Greenwood Cemetery; Holy Apostle; Immaculate Conception; Oneida Methodist; Wisconsin Veterans, King; Zion Lutheran.

4. Oneida Military Records, Oneida Nation of Indians of Wisconsin (ONIW), Oneida Cultural Heritage Department (OCHD), Oneida, WI.

5. Ibid.

6. Ibid.

7. Oneida Boarding School Records, ONIW, OCHD, Oneida, WI. For the names, see Laurence M. Hauptman and L. Gordon McLester III, eds., *The Oneida Indians in the Age of Allotment 1860–1920*, appendix (Norman: University of Oklahoma Press, 2006).

8. For the Oneidas at Carlisle, see Barbara Landis, "The Oneidas at Carlisle," in Hauptman and McLester, *The Oneida Indians in the Age of Allotment*, 48–55. See also Linda Witmer, *The Indian Industrial School: Carlisle, Pennsylvania, 1879–1918* (Carlisle, PA: Cumberland County Historical Society, 1993).

9. Julia Bloomfield, *The Oneidas*, 2nd ed. (New York: Alden, 1907).

10. Ibid.

11. Josiah Powless Military Service Records, ONIW, OCHD, Oneida, WI.

Three Memoirs of Veterans

by Edmund Powless, Franklin L. Cornelius, and Kenneth William Webster

World War II

EDMUND POWLESS: Directly after Pearl Harbor, I enlisted in the United States Army, as did my brothers. I eventually landed in France while my brothers went off to the Pacific. I had been working in the fields for the Larson Company and had just finished Civilian Conservation Corps work. I was only seventeen years of age, and so I needed my parents' approval. Other Oneidas, Ervin Doxtator, LeRoy Lemerond, and Kenneth Hill, joined when I did. I was then shipped off to Camp Cook in California, where I spent about a year in quartermaster training.

I volunteered for parachute training, and at the end of my stay at Fort Cook, I was sent to Georgia for three months of "jump school." I enjoyed the training. Even though I had a hernia on the right side, it never bothered me. The doctors told me that the army would not be held responsible if I aggravated it while parachuting; nevertheless, after many simulated jumps and three real ones, I was deemed qualified and given my "jump wings." I accomplished this while stationed at Fort Bragg, North Carolina, where I undertook combat training after jump school. A man named Karnatchio, a twenty-year-old from New York, was my best buddy. He was an expert with the bazooka and my right-hand man.

From North Carolina, we were shipped off to England and received two more weeks of training there. Then, after D-Day in 1944, we were sent to France, where we became foot soldiers and marched off to the town of Bastogne in Belgium and soon became combatants in the Battle of the Bulge. Marching to Belgium proved to be difficult, because supplies often did not catch up to our forward advance. We did not have the appropriate footgear for a winter campaign, and many of our soldiers suffered frostbite. My buddy Karnatchio was next to me when he was blown to pieces. Initially, the Germans who surrounded the town appeared to be well prepared, but their resistance soon fell apart. We took Bastogne. On

Christmas Day in 1944, I remember our dinner was made up of boiled beans without salt or any flavoring whatsoever. Our platoon was trapped in the town by the Germans; however, American soldiers retook the town for keeps when General Patton came in. During this period I was promoted from buck private to buck sergeant and then to staff sergeant.

We then parachuted across the Rhine, attempting to secure German-held territory for Allied forces, but we landed about ten miles short of our planned destination. I was the last man out of the airplane. As I came down, I remember maneuvering around a hill, a farmhouse, and another soldier; however, my parachute was caught up in the limbs of a tree. I cut myself down, but then an older man came out of the house and started shooting at me. I was equipped with an M-1 rifle and a pistol, and I returned fire.

I then quickly left and marched to the Rhine, since our mission was to secure the [Remagen] bridge across the river before the Germans would blow it up to stop the Allied forces from advancing. We saved the bridge, but at a high price: I was the only paratrooper of my company of twenty-two to survive. After helping to secure the bridge, I received medical attention, because my feet had been frostbitten. From this rest area, I was shipped to Camp McCoy in Wisconsin in April 1945. I was discharged with medals that included the Purple Heart and the Bronze Medal of Honor. I came back home soon after and married Blanche Hill.

Korea and Vietnam

FRANKLIN L. CORNELIUS: My father, Anderson W. Cornelius, had been in military service in World War II. In 1952, during the Korean War, I enlisted in the United States Marine Corps. On September 17, my Wisconsin platoon was shipped out of Green Bay. When I reached Milwaukee, I learned that I needed my birth certificate. I had been born at home in 1934 and had to prove my date of birth. I jumped on a train back to Green Bay and then hitchhiked back to the reservation to secure a copy of my baptismal record. At 4:00 a.m. the next day, I hitched back to Green Bay and took the train to Milwaukee, only to find out that my entire troop had already left.

This did not stop me. I was transported by the marines to San Diego, where I attended basic training. After graduation, I was selected for

Officers Candidate School. On completion, I became a marine drill instructor as second lieutenant SBC (Special Basic Course). Despite a twenty-one-year age requirement, I became a commissioned officer at the age of twenty! After serving as a drill instructor in San Diego, I was sent to Quantico to serve in that capacity. After five months of training at Quantico, I was sent to Bridgeport, California, to get ready for Korea. The training included cold weather training, being sent out with nothing much on in twenty-degrees-below-zero conditions.

In 1953, the Korean War was beginning to wind down, and I would spend thirteen months in Korea along the DMZ [demilitarized zone]. I was platoon leader over about sixty men for Dog Company, Second Battalion, First Marines. Our mission was to hold the line for those battalions that were falling back, and also to take specific areas. I was also involved in prisoner exchanges in the DMZ. By the time I was set to return home, I had been promoted to first lieutenant. After my service in Korea, I left military service and returned home, deciding to go to the Chicago Technical Institute. I later decided that I could go to school while continuing my military service, and consequently I re-enlisted. I did not have to go through basic training again. I was made a sergeant and served as a drill instructor at Camp Pendleton.

While serving as a staff sergeant in Tennessee, I received a new commission, one I had not requested. I was again commissioned as second lieutenant, just as the war in Vietnam was heating up. I was then sent to Vietnam, where I served two tours of duty. Because of severe allergies to inoculations for typhoid, plague, and cholera, I was transferred to Hawaii, where I finished up my twenty-two-year military service.

I have some vivid memories of certain aspects of my military service. I met other Oneidas in the service, including Don Cornelius and Huston Doxtator, and shared "liberty" with them. I remember crossing the Equator on an aircraft carrier. The onboard ceremony was filled with good humor. I was also engaged in mine-sweeping operations in the Suez Canal in 1962 or 1963. At another time, our ship was caught in a hurricane, and we were almost forced to abandon ship.

When I retired from military service, I went to work for the 3M Corporation. After a year, I realized that I did not like "civilian life"; I was so used to regimentation and wanted a more structured environment. I applied for a position with the BIA and worked at Oneida for three or four years. I then worked for the United States Postal Service, serving as a maintenance electrician. In total, I have spent fifty years of my life in governmental service, in the military or as a civilian employee.

Vietnam

KENNETH WILLIAM WEBSTER: I was born on the Oneida reservation in 1943. In 1966, I was drafted. I attended basic training at Fort Knox, Kentucky, for nine weeks and at Fort Polk, Louisiana, for another nine weeks. I was a member of the First Cavalry Division, Company B. After Fort Polk, we were sent to Oakland, California, then on to Wake Island, then to the Philippines, and finally to Saigon.

In September 1966, I found out what a guerrilla war was all about. The weather was mostly hot and humid; when the rainy season, or monsoons, came, about three months straight would be mostly wet. The rest of the year was wet but not as bad, and we could occasionally dry off in the afternoon. The terrain in the area where I was stationed was hilly, with lots of jungle and rice paddies.

My company consisted of approximately seventy men, who would be paired up and sent out into the field (combat) together. Fighting in Vietnam was a strange experience in that one did not always know who the enemy was. United States infantry soldiers were sent out into the field to draw fire, and at that point the soldiers would know where to search for the enemy, or Viet Cong, but the Viet Cong did not always wear uniforms, so it was hard to detect who the enemy was. It was also strange because once a spot of land was cleared or burned out, the enemy could and would often move back into the area just covered. I can describe for you what "going on patrol" meant: constant moving from one place to another, searching out the enemy, often moving into an open area to draw fire. If it rained, we would set up a makeshift tent out of our ponchos and often had to sleep in these "tents." Usually, but not always, each group of GIs at nightfall would return to a rudimentary camp where they would regroup. Going to Ahn Khe, a base where supplies were housed and better food provided, gave GIs a break from combat for a while. Unfortunately, I visited the camp at Ahn Khe only a few times, since I was locked into a combat zone for nine months straight. I had only one R&R, for five days in Hong Kong, during my twelve-month tour of duty.

As were most Native Americans in the service, I was referred to as "Chief" and was thought to possess all those stereotypical attributes we read about in books. As an "Indian," I was appointed "lead man" and would be the first GI sent out to lead a patrol. This occurred at least nine out of ten times when a "lead man" was needed. On one occasion, I was relieved of being the lead, and the man who replaced me was killed.

Most of the men I served with in the field were just out of high school, and the war really affected some of them in a negative way. I figured there was no sense getting upset about anything and just did what I had to. Land mines were a problem, and although I did not run into any, I did witness some men being blown up, maimed, or killed. Nothing ever prepares you for war.

The Vietnamese people were friendly but very poor. One big surprise was finding a Catholic church way out in the middle of nowhere. I understood that the church or any religious place was not to be bothered. I was also fascinated with a set of hand-carved wooden gears used to draw water in one of the villages.

After spending twelve months in the combat zone, I was given the option to serve three more months in Vietnam or be shipped home and serve six more months there. I chose to come home and landed in Washington, D.C. I arrived at a time when protest marches were happening in the capital, but the "returnees" were not called on to assist in monitoring these events. I remember being harassed because of my military service in Vietnam, but not all that much.

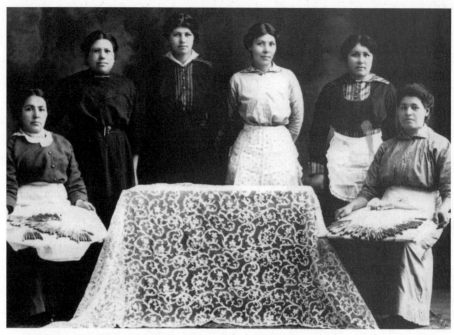

Oneida lacemakers in the early 1900s, showcasing a tablecloth and lacemaking tools. From left to right: Mrs. Jonas Skenandore, Mary James, Josephine Webster, Tillie Baird, Angeline Hill, and Mrs. Levinia John.
Image courtesy of the Oneida Nation Museum

A group of women doing lacework
Image courtesy of the Oneida Nation Museum

The school at Oneida, Wisconsin, circa 1905
Image courtesy of the Oneida Tribe of Wisconsin

Oneida activist Laura Minnie Cornelius Kellogg, seen here in 1911, advocated the pursuit of land claims
Image courtesy of the Oneida Tribe of Wisconsin

Oscar Archiquette and Esther House Archiquette standing in front of their log home
Image courtesy of the Milwaukee Public Museum Collection

A house built by the Works Progress Administration, shown in 1966
Image courtesy of the Oneida Tribe of Wisconsin

Ida Baird and Hanna Cornelius making baskets
Image courtesy of the Milwaukee Public Museum Collection

People congregated around Holy Apostles Episcopal Church in Oneida.
Image courtesy of the Oneida Nation Museum

Dr. Josiah Powless,
an Oneida physician
who was killed on
the western front
in WWI, upon
graduating from
school at Carlisle,
PA, in 1891
Image courtesy of the
Oneida Tribe of Wisconsin

Edmund Powless, seen
here in 1945, fought in
the Battle of the Bulge
in World War II.
Image courtesy of Edmund Powless

Oneida veteran Loretta Metoxen, seen here in 1951 at Kelly Air Force Base, Texas, is a former member of the Oneida Business Committee.
Image courtesy of Loretta Metoxen

Oneida veteran Franklin Cornelius, seen here in 1953, served tours in Korea and Vietnam.
Image courtesy of Franklin Cornelius

Kenneth Webster,
shown here in 1966,
is an Oneida veteran
of the Vietnam War.
*Image courtesy of Kenneth
Webster*

Jerry Danforth is an
Oneida veteran and
former tribal chairman
of the Oneida Nation
of Indians of
Wisconsin.
*Image courtesy of Jerry Dan-
forth*

Morris Wheelock, shown here in the 1930s, was a central leader in establishing the IRA government for the Oneida tribe.
Image courtesy of the Oneida Tribe of Wisconsin

Irene Moore is sworn in as the first Indian woman in Oneida tribal history to serve as chair of the executive committee, Aug. 6, 1963. From left: Irene Moore, Lee McLester Jr. (vice chairman), Althea Schuyler (treasurer), Eva Danforth (secretary). Far right is Melda A. Radtke, of federal government's Great Lakes Indian Agency.
Image courtesy of the Press-Gazette *Collection of the Neville Public Museum of Brown County, Green Bay, Wisconsin*

Robert L. Bennett shakes hands with President Lyndon B. Johnson circa 1966, the year Bennett was named commissioner of Indian Affairs.
Image courtesy of the Oneida Tribe of Wisconsin

Althea Schuyler served as Oneida Nation of Indians of Wisconsin tribal treasurer from 1956 to 1965.
Image courtesy of the Oneida Tribe of Wisconsin

The Oneida Business Committee, August 9, 1967. Back row from left: Oscar
Archiquette (vice chair), Purcell Powless (chair). Front row from left: Loretta
Metoxen (Secretary), Joycelyn Ninham (treasurer).
Image courtesy of Press-Gazette *Collection of the Neville Public Museum of Brown County, Green
Bay, Wisconsin*

Norbert Seabrook Hill, Sr., circa 1975, served on the Oneida Business Committee for many years.
Image courtesy of the Oneida Tribe of Wisconsin

Oneida elder Maria Hinton, seen circa 1990, worked with Clifford Abbott and her brother Amos Christjohn to compile *An Oneida Dictionary*, published in 1996.
Image courtesy of the Oneida Tribe of Wisconsin

Amos Christjohn, seen here September 23, 2008, compiled *An Oneida Dictionary* with Maria Hinton and Clifford Abbott.
Image courtesy of the Oneida Tribe of Wisconsin

Purcell Powless, seen here in 1990, served 24 years as Oneida tribal chair.
Image courtesy of the Oneida Tribe of Wisconsin

Part 3

Wisconsin Oneida Responses to Federal Policies, 1900–1975

Introduction

*U*NTIL THE PAST DECADE, historians have divided the period from 1887 to 1970 into three parts when discussing American Indian history and federal policies: (1) the age of allotment, 1887 to 1933; (2) the liberal era of the so-called Indian New Deal; and (3) the conservative era of termination.[1] Yet, in many ways, this paradigm ignores the fact that the Indian New Deal was hardly a true effort at real self-determination for Native Americans.[2] New Deal programs did bring noticeable temporary improvements, but within a paternalistic framework, adding a new level of bureaucracy to an existing — and already oppressive — colonial order. As historian Kenneth Philp rightly points out, the limitations of New Deal reform led both liberals and conservatives, do-gooders and outright racists, as well as some Native Americans themselves, to once again consider throwing out the baby with the bath water, or termination.[3]

Termination policies, which were formulated from World War II through 1954, called for an end to the federal-Indian treaty relationship and a shift to state jurisdiction over Indian nations. This federal withdrawal from Indian affairs was devastating to certain Wisconsin Indians, especially the Menominees, in that it ended Washington's support for Indian economic, educational, and medical programs and development. For the Wisconsin Oneidas, who managed to escape termination, it would have meant an end to all their litigation in federal courts. Yet, the policy of termination that resulted from problems with the Indian New Deal was well rooted in American Indian policies of the past. As we have already seen, federal efforts to buy out treaty obligations to the Wisconsin Oneidas had been going on since the end of the first decade of the twentieth century. Hence, the period prior to the brief interlude of the Indian New Deal had much in common with the policies that emerged during World War II. Instead of breaking up the reservation system by converting trust patents to fee simple title, now the policy centered in transferring jurisdiction to the states and encouraging the Indians to relocate to the cities.

As was true of the earlier Dawes Act and the Indian difficulties that followed it, the federal withdrawal policy after World War II was presented as "emancipating" the Indians from the oppression of BIA wardship.

In the first essay in Part 3, L. Gordon McLester III surveys the federal allotment policies and how the Wisconsin Oneidas dealt with the resulting crisis. Former tribal attorney Loretta Webster follows, explaining how the Wisconsin Oneidas were affected by the provisions of the Indian Reorganization Act and how they restructured their existing world. They quickly took advantage of the opportunities provided, however limited they were, knowing full well from history that federal policies were fickle. For instance, the Wisconsin Oneidas jumped at efforts to obtain a small portion of their treaty lands by largely reclaiming what had been designated "submarginal." By 1945, the Wisconsin Oneida tribal lands had grown to 2,168 acres.[4] As Oscar Archiquette clearly showed in Part I, the astute Oneidas took advantage of work-relief projects ranging from road and house construction to the establishment of the Oneida Language and Folklore Project under the auspices of the WPA and the University of Wisconsin.

Then, Ada Deer describes how federal termination policies in the 1950s were applied to the Oneidas' Menominee Indian neighbors. The Wisconsin Oneidas selected two strategies of resistance: (1) to file a series of cases before the Indian Claims Commission, which Karim Tiro analyzes here; and (2) to refuse to accept a lump-sum payout of federal treaty obligations to them. Next, Laurence Hauptman discusses how, although the Wisconsin Oneidas were split politically in the 1950s, after a meeting with BIA officials in Des Moines, they coalesced in opposing other federal efforts at termination.

In the concluding essay in Part 3, Loretta Webster explores how, by the 1960s, the Wisconsin Oneidas wisely made use of new federal programs, including those initiated by the Office of Economic Opportunity and Housing and Urban Development. Although these programs — such as HUD, Head Start, and VISTA — were designed for inner-city African Americans, a new and more determined Wisconsin Oneida tribal leadership, led by Irene Moore, Norbert Hill Sr., and later Purcell Powless, quickly took advantage of the availability of these programs for reservation residents. In 1963, the Wisconsin Oneidas established the Oneida Housing Authority and applied for sixty-six units of HUD housing and loans to build houses. This was followed by a second application for forty units the next year. Although there were complaints about the low quality of the first HUD Indian housing units, the program brought desperately needed housing to the reservation.[5]

Other major changes were in the air by the mid- and late 1960s. By 1965, the Oneida Nation had begun to strengthen its ties to its kin in central New York and Canada, holding meetings with delegates from all three Oneida communities. They contracted with George Shattuck of the Syracuse law firm of Bond, Shoeneck, and King in a collaborative effort to pursue their New York Indian land claims.[6] In 1968, the Oneidas began formulating plans to develop an industrial park along West Mason Street in the city of Green Bay, mostly on lands that the Nation had discovered still belonged to them. These lands, which today feature a casino and a Wal-Mart, are now a major source of revenue for the Wisconsin Oneidas and clearly show the vision of tribal leadership four decades ago.[7] In the mid- and late 1960s, the Wisconsin Oneidas also had a more friendly ear in Washington, D.C. President Johnson's appointment of Robert L. Bennett, who had been born on the reservation and whose relatives still live there, gave the Wisconsin Oneidas hope that the termination era was coming to an end.[8]

Notes

1. For example, see Peter Iverson, *"We Are Still Here": American Indians in the Twentieth Century* (Wheeling, IL: Harlan Davidson, 1998), 77–138.

2. The Indian New Deal was "liberal imperialism," or enlightened "indirect rule," modeled on British colonial policies in Africa. See Laurence M. Hauptman, "Africa View: John Collier, the British Colonial Service and American Indian Policy," *Historian* 48 (May 1986): 369–374.

3. Kenneth R. Philp, *Termination Revisited: American Indians on the Trail to Self-Determination, 1933–1953* (Lincoln: University of Nebraska Press, 1999), xi–xiv.

4. Oneida Nation of Indians of Wisconsin (ONIW), Oneida Tribal Business Committee (OTBC), Minutes, 1945.

5. ONIW, OTBC, Minutes, 1963–1965.

6. George C. Shattuck, *The Oneida Land Claims: A Legal History* (Syracuse, NY: Syracuse University Press, 1965), 9–12.

7. ONIW, OTBC, Minutes, 1968.

8. For the best treatment of Bennett, see Thomas Clarkin, *Federal Indian Policy in the Kennedy and Johnson Administrations* (Albuquerque: University of New Mexico Press, 2001), 227–269.

The Wisconsin Oneidas, 1887–1933

by L. Gordon McLester III

THE ONEIDAS HAD NOT YET HAD TIME to empty their backpacks after arriving from New York when attempts were already under way to either allot their Wisconsin reservation or move them farther west. In 1868, Senator Timothy Howe of Green Bay introduced a bill to allot the Oneida Indian reservation. His first attempt failed, but he continued the effort.[1] Finally, in 1887, the United States Congress passed the General Allotment Act, better known as the Dawes Act, which went into effect at Oneida in 1892 and had a different impact on each of the Indian nations in Wisconsin. It had a devastating effect on Oneida natural resources, both land and timber.[2] The act and its subsequent modifications led to the sizable alienation of land and loss of timber resources at Oneida.

A review of the Dawes Act shows that sections 2, 3, 5, 6, 9, and 10 applied to the Oneida Indian reservation. According to section 2, individual Oneidas could select their own allotment parcels, but this did not happen. Section 3 required that special agents look after allotments of orphans and resolve disputes. Section 5 created a twenty-five-year trust period during which time the United States would hold those trust patents and Oneidas could not sell, lease, or use the land to secure credit for twenty-five years. The trust period would end in 1917 but could be extended by the president if he felt it was necessary. Section 5 also stated that when all the Indians received their allotments and there were excess reservation lands, the balance of the lands would be declared "surplus land" and opened to non-Indians to purchase. In Oneida, all the land was allotted, so there was no surplus land, but on other reservations, millions of acres of Indian land were declared surplus. Section 6 specified that state criminal and civil law would apply to the allotments at the end of the twenty-five-year trust period, and Indians who accepted fee simple title would become United States citizens after conversion of their trust patents. In section 9, the U.S. government appropriated $100,000 to survey the reservations. Section 10 reconfirmed Congress's right to grant railroad right-of-way across Indian reservations.[3]

In 1906, Congress passed the Burke Act, which gave the secretary of the interior the discretion to issue fee simple patents before the end of the twenty-five-year trust period. Thus, the passage of the 1906 Burke Act shortened the length of the trust period that would have given the Indian people time to adjust to the changes set forth in the Dawes Act. Once the Indian person received a trust patent, the Indian agent had the authority to declare the Indian competent, and those trust patents were then converted to fee simple ownership status. When the Indian land was converted into fee simple status, the land became subject to state laws and taxation and the Indian became a United States citizen, subject to state criminal and civil law. Because of the Oneidas' poverty and their inability to pay taxes, they were now also susceptible to outside land sharks, aided by local and state politicians as well as some Oneida tribal members.[4]

In 1903, three years before the federal Burke Act, the state legislature of Wisconsin had passed a bill to create the town of Hobart and the town of Oneida within the Oneida reservation.[5] The two townships would be the keys to gaining control of Oneida lands. When the two town boards were formed, Oneidas initially served on them. Within two decades, Oneidas had lost political control of these positions, because many outside non-Indians were buying up Oneida lands that had been converted to fee simple title and subsequently lost because of tax foreclosures or sold off by impoverished Indians.[6] By 1930, non-Indian residents of the Town of Hobart outnumbered the Indians by a three-to-two advantage, thus outvoting the Oneidas.[7]

From 1903 to the early 1930s, many Oneidas resisted converting trust patents to fee simple title, because fee simple brought with it the new imposition of town, county, and state taxation. This protest movement was first led by the Indian Party, headed by Paul and Henry Doxtator, and later, in the mid- and late 1920s and early 1930s, by Willie "Fat" Skenandore. Both the Doxtators and Skenandore refused to pay taxes and defended their refusal in court actions (e.g., *Town of Hobart v. Doxtator*).[8] Although the courts ruled against the Doxtators and required the Oneidas to pay taxes, Skenandore continued to file briefs, which he sent to federal officials well into the 1930s, to no avail.[9]

In 1917, the Federal Competency Commission came to Oneida. By the time its work was complete in 1920, Oneidas had lost more than fifty thousand acres of the original sixty-five-thousand-acre reservation. The commission, headed by James McLaughlin, pushed for the remaining trust lands to be converted to fee simple title. Once again both land specula- tors and local and state political forces were pushing this agenda, and once again the federal government gave impetus to this movement. In so many ways, this effort was a harbinger of later federal initiatives, namely the termination policies after World War II. In both instances, the United States government was pushing for an end of its trust responsibilities to the Oneidas, as set forth in two treaties in 1794. Yet from 1909 to 1918 and again in the 1950s (described in Part 3 of this book), the Wisconsin Oneidas rejected a lump-sum buyout of federal obligations under the pro- visions of the Treaty of Canandaigua of 1794.[10] If the federal officials suc- ceeded in buying out the 1794 treaty provisions, then Washington could end all of its economic, educational, health, and land-claims obligations to the Oneidas.

The WPA projects contain many poignant stories told by Oneida elders who remembered these sad events. As children, they would come home to find their things set outside their houses, the sheriff's men telling their parents that because they did not pay their taxes, they had to leave right then.[11] To most of the Oneida people, the Dawes Act and Burke Act arrived like tornadoes in the night. With the creation of the two townships as well as the misuse of the Burke Act and the Federal Competency Com- mission, many Oneidas lost their lands. An Oneida tribal protest sent to the commissioner of Indian affairs in 1922 summarized this loss of land after 1906. The petitioners described what befell their tribal members after the passage of the Burke Act, when Oneidas were recommended by the Indian agent as "competent" and subsequently applied for fee patents:

> . . . It appears that the Act allowing the issuance of fee patents prior to the twenty-five year period contained a provision to the effect that the Indian may procure payment for his land before he received his fee patent if he worked it through the representative of the Secretary of the Interior, or, the Indian Agent. We wish to say that this provision also was in- discriminately abused so far as the spirit of your honorable Office is

concerned in making that provision. It was used to promote the interests of the land speculators who would and did seduce the ignorant Indians to go with them to the Indian Agent so that there would be an appearance of complying with the law regarding getting the permission of the Secretary of the Interior, and the speculator would pay a certain sum so that the Indian may sign his fee patent over to the speculator as soon as the Agent procures it for him. When the fee patent comes the speculator goes and tells the Indian that his fee patent is at the Agent's Office and takes him over there and has him sign over to the speculator. Much of this signing over to a speculator has been done even without having been done through the Agent. The perpetration of these frauds is evidenced by the fact that probably as much as 95% of the lands, sold immediately upon receipt of a fee patent, has been sold to speculators who have made it a business to wrest the lands from the Indians through fraudulent means and apparently aided by the Indian Agent as shown by the apparent disregard as to the competency of the Indian.[12]

The Wisconsin Oneida petitioners then added:

The Competency Commission [that] visited the reservation reported the Indians as being quite competent to receive fee patents as the Commission traveled through the reservation and saw good houses, barns and stock but they saw the property of white people who live on lands owned by speculators or are paying for such lands on the installment plan....Fee patents were issued through the recommendations of the Competency Commission and excessive taxes are levied so that we are not able to pay them and apparently we will lose our holdings entirely through our inability to pay taxes. [Oneidas] are assessed for taxes although it appears that Indians who receive annuities are not citizens.[13]

They concluded with a desperate appeal:

We respectfully petition your honor to cause a relief from our lands being taxed as we do not feel capable at the present time of meeting the responsibilities of full citizenship and we feel that we have been dragged into our present deplorable condition through mismanagement of our affairs at a critical period. We [Oneidas] believe that the spirit of your

Office has always been to care and protect our interests but that those in the field who are or have been entrusted with our affairs either betrayed the trust or were incompetent....[14]

. . .

IN THE FACE OF THESE FEDERAL, STATE, AND LOCAL ACTIONS at times aimed at tribal dissolution, the Wisconsin Oneidas continued to maintain their presence in Brown and Outagamie counties. Their overall tribal population increased yearly (with the exception of 1914). As late as 1930, 442 Indians still resided in the town of Hobart out of a total of 1,105 residents.[15] Despite the extreme pressures of poverty, racial discrimination, tax foreclosures, and the machinations of land sharks, the Wisconsin Oneidas were able to hold things together and maintain a culturally rich Indian community life in these two counties. Having been in Wisconsin for a century, they were rooted in the Midwestern soil, with cultural attributes — language, custom, kinship, rituals — brought from their homeland in central New York.

Notes

1. James W. Oberly, "The Dawes Act and the Oneida Indian Reservation," in *The Oneida Indians in the Age of Allotment, 1860–1920*, ed. Laurence M. Hauptman and L. Gordon McLester III, 181–182 (Norman: University of Oklahoma Press, 2006). See *Green Bay Gazette*, December 11, 1869, January 29, 1870.

2. *General Allotment Act (Dawes Act)*, Stat. 24, (1887): 388–391.

3. Ibid.

4. *Burke Act*, Stat. 34 (1906): 182–183.

5. Oberly, "The Dawes Act," 184–199.

6. Ibid., 201; Ida Blackhawk, "Hard Times at Oneida," WPA, Oneida Language and Folklore Project (OLFP), Oneida Cultural Heritage Department (OCHD), Oneida, WI.

7. U.S. Census for 1930, Town of Hobart, Brown County, WI.

8. For the Doxtator protests, see Paul C. and Henry Doxtator to Senator Robert M. La Follette Sr., June 7, 1917, May 13, 1918, File: "Indian Affairs: Oneida, 1912–1913," La Follette Family Papers, Series B-29, LC. See also Paul C. and Henry Doxtator to Senator Irvine Lenroot, June 22, 1912, #52706-18-312 (Oneida) and Paul's letter to President Wilson, July 23, 1918, #64300-18-312 (Oneida), both in BIA CCF, 1907–1939, RG75, NA. The case fills nearly three boxes of correspondence and legal briefs housed at the National Archives.

9. For Skenandore, see Francis Skenandore, "William Skenandore," in *The Oneida Indian Experience: Two Perspectives*, ed. Jack Campisi and Laurence M. Hauptman, 126–130 (Syracuse, NY: Syracuse University Press, 1988). See also Hauptman, *The Iroquois and the New Deal* (Syracuse, NY: Syracuse University Press, 1981), 77, 205 nn. 24, 25, 26, 27.

10. Federal Competency Commission (Oneida) Report, August 31, 1917, James McLaughlin MSS, Box 1, Wisconsin Historical Society, Madison, WI. See also Laurence M. Hauptman, "The Wisconsin Oneidas and the Federal Competency Commission," in Hauptman and McLester, *The Oneida Indians in the Age of Allotment*, 200–225.

11. Jack Campisi, "Oneida," in *[Smithsonian] Handbook of North American Indians*, vol. 15, *The Northeast*, ed. Bruce Trigger, 481–490 (Washington, D.C.: Smithsonian Institution, 1978). For Oneida opinion, see Filmore Cooper, "[Dawes] General Allotment Act"; Levi Baird, "In Deceit"; Rachel Swamp, "Before They Started to Pay Taxes"; Guy Elm, "Property and Loss of Land," all found in WPA, OLFP, OCHD, Oneida, WI.

12. Wisconsin Oneida Petition to the Secretary of the Interior, March 27, 1922, #30709-08-313 (Oneida), BIA CCF, 1907–1939, BIA, RG75, NA.

13. Ibid.

14. Ibid.

15. U.S. Censuses for 1900, 1910, 1920, and 1930, Town of Hobart, Brown County, WI.

The Wisconsin Oneida Tribal Government under the Indian Reorganization Act

The New Deal Years, 1933–1941

by Loretta Webster

THE ONEIDAS IN WISCONSIN SETTLED HERE IN THE 1820s, with their 64,500-acre reservation eventually defined by the United States federal government in 1838. By this time, the Oneidas had suffered over one hundred years of disruption to their social and political structure by encroaching foreign governments. Still, they continued to govern themselves according to the ancient principles of the Great Law of Peace, as did all of the Iroquois Nations (Oneida, Mohawk, Onondaga, Cayuga, Seneca, and Tuscarora). Many Oneidas and other Iroquois believe that the Great Law evolved over two thousand years ago[1]. But this approach to governance was nearing its end. The last attempt to govern according to the Great Law of Peace occurred in 1925, when Oneida chiefs from Canada went through a condolence ceremony on the Oneida reservation in Wisconsin to raise up nine new Wisconsin Oneida chiefs. These new chiefs, and their assistants, were brought to these positions by centuries-old standards. This attempt would fail, however, because of new forces that led leadership to leave the reservation to make a living, not to mention poor health, death at an early age, and generally poor living conditions on the Oneida reservation.

A picture of this condolence ceremony came to my attention this past year, and I was stunned and excited to see my father in the crowd of people watching the ceremony. He was twenty-five years old and a fluent speaker of the Oneida language. Everyone in the picture probably spoke fluent Oneida, and so they understood the words of a ceremony that had changed very little since first performed hundreds of years earlier thanks to the efforts of the Peacemaker and Hiawatha.[2] I wonder whether my father was certain, or possibly just hopeful, that these new chiefs would lead the Oneidas into a level of self-sufficiency and governance equal to what they held two hundred years before. Leadership and governance were sorely needed in Oneida, Wisconsin, where many leaders had formed many groups, all moving in different directions with the goal of benefiting the Oneida people.[3] Churches had split the minds and hearts of Oneida people along doctrinal lines and condemned the traditional leadership who would attempt to govern. The reservation land was almost gone, so what was the territory to be governed? The leaders who were condoled on October 10, 1925, would have to be as effective as the Peacemaker himself to reconcile the diversity of minds they had agreed to serve.

The picture of the 1925 Oneida condolence ceremony captured a glimpse of peace, power, and righteousness as idealized in the words of the Great Law of Peace. At the time, the Wisconsin Oneidas were well settled in their new reservation along Duck Creek, although land had already been lost at a rapid pace since the Allotment Act individualized all land holdings. Some Oneidas in 1925 would have been considered quite prosperous, but most were stuck in the quagmire of discrimination, poor health, inadequate housing and education, insufficient full-time work, and the generally substandard living conditions chronicled in the Meriam Report of 1928. Oneidas as a whole were considered well on their way to full acculturation, as many took advantage of free non-Indian education and training, dropped their "Indian ways," and left the reservation to seek their profits and adventure. As was true for traditional tribal leaders throughout America at this time, the leaders condoled in 1925 never gained recognition by the state and federal governments. For reasons that are perhaps lost in time, the nine new Oneida leaders condoled for life in 1925 were gone by 1933, some having left the reservation and others having died. So by 1933, reservation groups were again attempting to organize a condolence ceremony to name some more new chiefs.[4] Only the chiefs' assistants were left, and they were considered to have no authority. The Oneidas were still desperate for strong, stable leadership.

By 1934, another Indian group was organizing on the Oneida reservation. They were called the New Deal group, with a new goal of passing the Indian Reorganization Act (IRA) and using it to organize a totally different type of government that would be "recognized" by the federal government. Most tribal governments up to this time did their work and went unrecognized by either the state or federal governments — in fact, there was a time when many traditional Indian governments were essentially banned by the federal government. With a New Deal government, the federal government could assist and protect the Oneida tribe from the advancements or encroachment of the state of Wisconsin. This was crucial to the Oneida people, even though it meant adopting a boilerplate constitution written by the Bureau of Indian Affairs. The Oneida tribe did receive governmental "recognition" — but at the price of relying on the BIA for direction on everything. This established a paternalistic relationship with the BIA, which is still present to this day.

．．．

LED BY MORRIS WHEELOCK, the New Deal group also had other well-known advocates, such as Oscar Archiquette, as active members. First, the group formed a state corporation [headed by Archiquette] so they could act as an organized voice for the Oneida tribe. The New Deal group successfully drafted and received approval from Oneida people for a new constitution and bylaws, but this took several years. At least three other groups within the Oneida community opposed the New Deal group and its constitution, preferring to continue with traditional leadership.

Everything about the New Deal constitution differed from the principles of the Great Law of Peace: the land was held in individual fee simple title rather than communally; business was conducted in English instead of Oneida; government was elected every few years rather than "condoled" for life. In addition, in the New Deal group's constitution, the decisions were by majority rather than consensus, and written laws, rather than oral principles and teachings that were believed to be thousands of years old, were the rule. The spiritual basis for governing had permeated the Great Law of Peace, and this foundation was completely gone from the New Deal constitution.

Traditionalists who opposed the newly drafted constitution did not participate in the New Deal meetings, nor did they vote. In spite of this, at a meeting held on November 14, 1936, the New Deal group won approval of the Oneida constitution by a vote of 790 for and 16 against. After many meetings and a great deal of effort by the New Deal group, the constitution and bylaws of the Oneida Nation of Indians of Wisconsin was accepted by the U.S. Department of the Interior on December 21, 1936. The Oneidas now had a federally recognized government.[5]

The IRA included principles that Indian people had supported in a series of Indian Congress meetings held throughout the country (the Oneidas attended the last Indian Congress on April 23 and 24, 1934, in Hayward, Wisconsin). The act came on the heels of centuries of failed Indian policies by the federal government. Many saw it as a salvation for tribal governments, but at the same time, other tribal members viewed it as the death knell for the spiritual and cultural values traditionally expected to be part of everyday life as well as government. The IRA was, pure and simple, a recipe for full acculturation of Indians by imposition of a foreign governance structure, one completely unknown to the tribes and easily controlled by the Bureau of Indian Affairs through its agents.

On the positive side, however, besides providing basic self-governing powers to tribes within their reservations (which traditionalists argued they already had), the IRA released some burdensome federal policies regarding the land and provided a viable vision of people and territory for self-governance: (1) stopped allotment and made restoration of lands possible, (2) extended land trust period indefinitely, (3) provided funds for purchase of land and self-governance, (4) established a revolving loan fund for tribal economic development, (5) established a revolving loan fund for tribal education, and (6) established preference for Indians to fill vacant positions in the Bureau of Indian Affairs.[6]

The New Deal group in Oneida organized the first tribal election under the new IRA constitution, and it took place on January 14, 1937. Morris Wheelock was elected chairman; Anderson Skenandore, vice chairman; Harrison Smith, treasurer; and Katie Cornelius, secretary. This was a temporary committee until the regular election in July 1937, when the same officers were elected except for Katie Cornelius, who was replaced as secretary by Lydia W. Powless. The Oneida constitution set one-year terms between regular elections, so each year the officers expended some effort just getting a quorum for elections, which was seventy-five of the eligible voters within the Oneida reservation. Obtaining a quorum for the first election was not a problem: 169 Oneidas attended this first General

Tribal Council meeting (the General Tribal Council, rather than the Executive Committee, was designated as the governing body in the constitution). The Executive Committee was composed of these four elected officers, but they could act only when directed by the General Tribal Council. Difficulty in getting a quorum for council meetings became a chronic problem with the new Oneida government, which had no funds to send out notices.[7] In addition, very few of the tribal members had phones, and membership lived all over the country. In addition, the new committee did not fully understand its role in getting the tribal government to move forward, and it had little or no help from the federal government or other mentors. The new government relied on the Bureau of Indian Affairs and reservation church leaders to prepare written documents (even letters), type up materials, and mail correspondence well into the 1950s. Few Oneida people had verbal skills or writing skills in English.

If you can imagine being elected to lead a brand-new government, I am sure you would want a clear understanding of your duties as soon as possible. Not surprisingly, the first Executive Committee members spent several months meeting with the BIA and discussing the meaning of the constitution and how they should implement it. At the same time, they worked with their BIA agent to draft a federal charter for an Economic Development Corporation. This charter was easily approved at a meeting on May 10, 1937, by a vote of 349–0, the Oneidas being exceedingly accommodating to the federal advisers who recommended it. The usefulness of the charter, however, had yet to be determined by the Oneida tribal government. At the General Tribal Council meeting where the vote was taken, there was more discussion of a recommended tribal seal than of the federal charter. For the seal, the Executive Committee had recommended a shock of corn, but after some discussion, the group at hand decided to go with the cheaper wheat design.[8] Later in the same meeting they accepted a motion to have monthly socials to raise funds for committee expenses. The socials must have been successful, because at their next meeting they voted to have a social every two weeks. At the same time the Executive Committee sent a proposal to Washington, D.C., requesting funds for their expenses.[9]

This first year, the Executive Committee dealt with both Oneida

Indian and non-Indian groups who provided a variety of dissents to the new government. The Oneida Indian groups felt the new government was not legal because it had not obtained the required number of votes to support the constitution before it was sent in for federal approval. A non-Indian group gathered 538 signatures on a petition protesting the new government and questioning their inclusion as "Indians" as defined in the IRA, section 19. Even today, a petition with more than 500 signatures of protest would indicate a pretty hostile environment. To their credit, the Executive Committee met with the town of Oneida and Outagamie County officials and explained the benefits of the IRA to the white people as well as to the Indians. No further reference is made about these protests in future minutes, but we know these same antigovernment sentiments still exist today.[10]

Land issues were a part of every agenda of the Executive Committee from the start. The IRA directed the BIA to buy certain lands for the Oneida tribe to assign to tribal members who had none. There were also options to purchase placed on other pieces of land, which the BIA presented to the Executive Committee for their recommendation, but initially the committee — uncertain it had any authority in this area — rendered few decisions.[11]

Tribal enrollment was another responsibility for the new Executive Committee. They verified eligibility for enrollment by accepting birth certificates at their meetings. Birth certificates were then sent on to the BIA for further processing.[12]

Planning started so the Executive Committee could request IRA funds for its own revolving loan fund. By the end of the first year of tribal government, they had begun to formulate the rules for giving out loans.[13]

The Works Progress Administration and Civilian Conservation Corps provided jobs on the reservation, and it appears that the new Executive Committee was used to screen and recommend Oneida people for open positions. Due to the scarcity of work and its desire to spread this economic boon as far as possible, the Executive Committee moved that no two people from one family would work on a project.[14]

By 1938, problems of getting a quorum for the General Tribal Council meetings were obvious. The Executive Committee elected in 1937 continued on through the year because an election could not be organized. But without a General Tribal Council meeting, the Executive Committee members could not get clear direction on what their duties were. Nonetheless, the Executive Committee was able to further strengthen the government in the areas of finances, organization, and decision making.

Throughout these early years, one can see the dependence on the BIA in all the Executive Committee's minutes, which were always sent to the BIA. They scheduled meetings so that the BIA agent could attend. The BIA agent provided frequent advice, offered written forms and applications for adoption by the Executive Committee, and even wrote letters on the tribe's behalf. Funds received for IRA initiatives such as loans to Oneida people were held in an Oneida-designated BIA account and disbursed by the BIA after the Executive Committee had approved the loan request. The BIA agency in Tomah assisted the Executive Committee, and the committee held several meetings at the Tomah office.[15]

Decisions were made by motion of the Executive Committee, which met at least monthly. Major decisions in 1938 included approval of certain WPA projects, fifty dollars for a women's sewing project, approval to submit a request for a fifteen thousand dollar loan to the BIA, approval of a membership ordinance, and approval of a land purchase plan for 1939.[16]

The Executive Committee remained hesitant to make day-to-day decisions about land use without the General Tribal Council's approval or direction. For example, the BIA had purchased five hundred acres of land for the Oneida tribe, and in one meeting the agent warned the Executive Committee that if it did not make a decision on how to use the present acreage, the BIA would not purchase more for the tribe. Despite the critical need for housing, farming acreage, and woodlands for the many landless Oneidas, the Executive Committee refused to make any new decisions on land use that year without clear direction from the General Tribal Council. They accepted applications and tried to conceive of a method for processing them through the BIA, but there was no actual transfer of land use to an individual.[17]

The BIA's initial five hundred–acre purchase was called "redeemed" land, and this term has continued to the present time. The BIA "redeemed" land from foreclosure, tax liability, or bankruptcy proceedings, and if it happened to be land held by an Oneida Indian, the tribe would usually assign that land to the same Indian after it was purchased. If the purchased land had been held by a non-Indian person, it was added to a growing backlog of applications until the Executive Committee could make a decision on how to disburse it. The acreage purchased through IRA funds was all titled to "the USA in trust for the Oneida Tribe of Indians of Wisconsin."[18] The land in trust is tax exempt, but the trust process forever linked Oneida decisions on land use to the maintenance of a "title report" with the U.S. government, and to the use of federal forms for transfer of land use. In other words, the individual assigned the land would never own it or be able to sell it. This was probably never clearly understood by the Oneida people, most of whom spoke only the Oneida language and did not understand the ancient white laws associated with land title.

In January 1939, the first set of amendments to the IRA constitution were presented to the General Tribal Council and approved. The most notable action was to lower the quorum of a General Tribal Council meeting to "50 qualified voters of the Tribe."[19]

The initial elected leadership had diligently worked for almost three years before a major change occurred on the Executive Committee. An election in August 1939 gave the Executive Committee two new members: Mark Powless was now chairman, Chauncy Adams was vice chairman, Ray Parkhurst was treasurer, and Lydia Powless was secretary. By the end of 1939, Chauncy Adams, who had been on the Executive Committee since November 1937, resigned. He was replaced by Andrew Beechtree, giving the Executive Committee three new members to forge on with.[20]

. Upon his retirement as chairman, Morris Wheelock, who had been a leader in the formation of the tribal government for almost ten years, eloquently summarized the committee's accomplishments:

> You no doubt recall that we had to start from scratch. The sum total of the Oneida tribal assets at the time we took office amounted to 85 acres of tribal land valued at approximately $4250.00. There was no cash capital to carry on the work. Your tribal officials have spent many hours, week after week, on tribal matters, on their own time and at their own

expense. I do not raise this point with any thought of complaining and I am sure it is not in the mind of any member of the Committee[,] as each one has unselfishly given the best he had to the work. However, I feel that it is worthy of mention and may help the few who sometimes want to criticize to understand that your tribal officials are working under a decided handicap.

Our tribal assets at the present time have reached a value of approximately $77,366.00 and are listed as follows:

Land purchased by the Federal Government and turned over to the Tribe: 1,289.943 acres

At a cost of: $49,591.00

Grants of Rehabilitation Funds to the tribe by the Federal Government, amounting to: $27,775.00

Of this amount there has been an expenditure of, the most of which is out on loans to members of the tribe for houses, house repair and wells: $22,755.00

The balance on hand in this fund amounts to: $5,020.00

Repayments on loans to date amount to: $260.00

The entire balance of Trust Funds, to the credit of the tribe on deposit with the Tomah Indian Agency is: $5,280.00

I should like to mention at this time that WA has furnished labor and materials in the amount of $21,261.50 in the construction of new houses for which no charge has been made to members of the Tribe.

Out of rehabilitation funds there [have] been constructed the following:

20 new houses

57 houses repaired

23 wells drilled

Of the Government land purchased for the Tribe, there [have] been 30 assignments made and there still remain 310 acres which have not been assigned.

Medical services [have] been provided for the people and a clinic is held each week where individuals may go for medical care.[21]

Although this seemed to be a peaceful transition from one set of leadership to another, the end of 1939 saw a need for an audit in the monthly

Executive Committee minutes. Even though, as the BIA pointed out, the committee had made all expenditures for the tribe through the Tomah agency office, a three-person audit committee was selected from the tribal membership. By this time, the tribal government had collected more than two carloads of material, which were transported from the former chairman's house to the new chairman's house for auditing.[22]

One notable decision by the General Tribal Council on September 18, 1939, was to give power to the Executive Committee to select the members for the Land Committee and Credit/Loan Committee. Slowly, the General Tribal Council was empowering the Executive Committee to handle day-to-day responsibilities of the Oneida tribe.[23]

The number of meetings in 1940 was sparse, but each one had the same types of items on the agenda. The committee approved or rejected loan applications and then sent the applications on to the BIA for payment out of the rehabilitation fund. They assigned land, and for the first time in the minutes, a dispute over land between two assignees was discussed and settled.[24]

Elections were held in August 1940, and the new officers were Ray Parkhurst, chairman; Oscar Archiquette, vice chairman; Anderson Cornelius, treasurer; and Lydia Powless, secretary. This particular group would be the officers of the Executive Committee for almost three years.[25]

Because the General Tribal Council is the legislative body in the constitution and the Executive Committee follows its directives, the committee prepared these directives in resolution form for General Tribal Council approval. The Oneida Tribal Executive Committee was slowly learning the process of establishing a written governmental record other than meeting minutes. Resolutions became routine items on the General Tribal Council agendas, and, when approved, they were enough direction to the Executive Committee to be executed. One resolution approved in 1940 directed the Executive Committee to establish a revolving credit fund.[26] The next year, the General Tribal Council passed its first piece of legislation under the provisions of its IRA constitution: it established a land committee with a list of policies for making land assignments.[27]

By the end of World War II, the Wisconsin Oneidas had 2,168 acres. Their tribal assets totaled $93,557.01. Oneida Executive Committee members were paid forty cents per meeting. Nearly everything the Wisconsin tribal government decided to do had to be approved by the BIA, including this payment of forty cents per meeting![28] The tribal government was forced to rely on the BIA for office support, funding, and even advice, and the Oneida Executive Committee had little direct authority to implement solutions. In 1946, the Executive Committee moved to request that the BIA send out notices of arrears, collections, evictions, foreclosures, and so forth, because of the lack of clear policies on how to handle these matters. The committee had neither the equipment nor staff to deal with the situations at hand. They also requested that members of the Executive Committee be reimbursed three dollars for attending each tribal meeting.[29] After much lobbying, in 1949 the secretary of the interior approved an amendment to Article IV of the IRA constitution that enumerated the powers of the Oneida Executive Committee — a major reorganization of the tribe's decision-making structure.[30] It is ironic that this tribal assertion for more self-rule came exactly at the time that the federal government was beginning its push to terminate American Indians, including the Wisconsin Oneidas.

Although the author sees the IRA as another failed government policy, generations of Oneida leadership have done their best to make the most of the "recognized" government that resulted from it. The Oneida Executive Committee struggled to understand its new constitution. They diligently moved forward in spite of language barriers, internal and external political pressures, and the lack of funds, lawyers or reliable advisors, an office or staff, and even of a communication network such as a phone system. Through sheer determination, the Oneida Executive Committee maintained the Oneida tribal government, establishing a strong foundation that allowed the Oneida Nation in Wisconsin to grow into the twenty first century.

Notes

1. Tom Porter, *And Grandma Said — Iroquois Teachings: As Passed Down through the Oral Tradition* (Philadelphia: Xlibris Corp., 2008), 273. The book is a transcription of Porter's oral teachings, including the Great Law of Peace.

2. Records of the Oneida Cultural Heritage Department (OCHD), Oneida Nation of Indians of Wisconsin (ONIW).

3. Laurence M. Hauptman, *The Iroquois and the New Deal* (Syracuse, NY: Syracuse University Press, 1981), 70–87.

4. For a detailed account of the historic, cultural, and religious importance of the condolence ceremony, see William N. Fenton, *The Great Law and the Longhouse: A Political History of the Iroquois Confederacy* (Norman: University of Oklahoma Press, 1998), 3–18, 135–242.

5. Oneida Nation of Indians of Wisconsin Constitution and Bylaws, Records of the Oneida General Tribal Council (OGTC), ONIW.

6. Indian Reorganization Act, *Stat.* 48, (1934): 984–988.

7. Minutes of the OGTC, 1937, ONIW.

8. Ibid.

9. Minutes of the Oneida Executive Committee (OEC), 1937, ONIW.

10. Ibid.

11. Ibid.

12. Ibid.

13. Ibid.

14. Ibid.

15. Minutes of the OEC, 1938, ONIW.

16. Ibid.

17. Ibid.

18. Ibid.

19. Minutes of the OGTC, 1939, ONIW.

20. Minutes of the OEC, 1939, ONIW.

21. Ibid.

22. Ibid.

23. Minutes of the OGTC, 1939, ONIW.

24. Minutes of the OEC, 1940, ONIW.

25. Minutes of the OGTC, 1940, ONIW.

26. Ibid.

27. Minutes of the OGTC, 1941, ONIW.

28. Minutes of the OEC, 1945, ONIW.

29. Minutes of the OEC, 1946, ONIW.

30. Minutes of the OGTC, 1949, ONIW.

A Contrast with Oneida

Menominee Termination and Restoration, 1954–1973

by Ada Deer

Unlike the Oneidas, who escaped termination, the Menominee Nation perhaps suffered more from this federal policy initiative than did any other Indian community. Here, Ada Deer, the former assistant secretary of the interior for Indian affairs, recounts the tragedy that befell her Menominee people and her work in eventually overturning this policy.

After her remarkable work in lobbying for the restoration of the Menominees to federal status, Deer taught at the University of Wisconsin School of Social Work and in the American Indian Studies program. She narrowly lost a bid for Congress in 1992 and subsequently served as assistant secretary of the Interior Department from 1993 to 2001.
— The Editors

OVER THE YEARS, I'VE HAD MANY CONTACTS with Wisconsin Oneidas. Albert King and some other Oneidas helped my father, Joseph Deer, build our family log cabin on the Wolf River in Menominee country. At different times I have had Oneida classmates — Audrey Skenandore was my classmate at Walter Allen Elementary School in Milwaukee. Three of my Upward Bound students were Oneidas: Sandra Schuyler, Bill Danforth Jr., and Raymond Christjohn. Over the years I have taught many students, including Oneidas; for example, Melissa Metoxen was my student at the University of Wisconsin–Madison. Herb Powless Sr. helped my brother Joe get a job, and I met former commissioner Robert L. Bennett in my days as an employee of the BIA in the 1960s. Dr. Robert Powless, another enrolled Oneida and former college president at Mt. Scenario College and former director of American Indian Studies at University of Minnesota–Duluth, is the only other American Indian student I remember during my attendance at the University of Wisconsin–Madison. Dr. Powless later brought me from Minnesota back to the University of Wisconsin–Stevens Point. While I was working in Washington, Ernest Stevens Sr. helped my people with the Menominee Restoration Act. When I came back home to Menominee, I visited Purcell Powless at Chicago Corners. You Wisconsin Oneidas have come a long, long way from those days. Bravo!

My people, the Menominee, were a federally recognized tribe from 1854 to 1954. They were terminated by an act of Congress in 1954 and restored to federal recognition in 1973.[1]

In 1929, we began a lawsuit against the federal government in the United States Court of Claims for mismanagement of our timber resources.[2] In 1951, the lawsuit was settled, and the Menominees were awarded eight million dollars [ten million dollars as a consequence of compounded interest]. Congressman Melvin Laird introduced legislation authorizing the release of the money on a per capita basis to individual Menominees. The bill passed the House of Representatives; however, the Senate held up the bill. That's when the trouble began. Senator Arthur C. Watkins of Utah, chairman of the Senate Indian Affairs Committee, insisted that before we could get the money, we had to agree to termination. Our people did not understand the full implications of what this meant. In 1953, Watkins and others claimed that we were fully ready to be released from bureau tutelage, that we were more assimilated than most other tribes, and that we were at the top of the list for termination. When the first vote was taken on whether we would accept it, very few Menominees came to the meeting.[3]

I question the legality of the vote, because only 174 people participated out of a tribal enrollment of more than 3,000 — 169 in favor and 5 against. The Menominees were poor and did not then have the education that we take for granted today. Some "white poo-bah" sold it to us. At the time, American Indians were too submissive to authority. It is easy to explain this: many of my people went to boarding schools, where they were brainwashed and subjected to rigid training. They were taught to accept and conform. That said, even though I use the term "white poo-bah," I am not anti-white — my mother was white.

A short while after that first vote, a second was taken. In this second vote, the Menominees rejected termination. One of our people, Ernest Neconish, with his cane in hand, came to every meeting. He never gave up. In 1959, he insisted:

> You Menominee people have the strength. These white people have no jurisdiction over our business. I'm telling you the whole truth. Band

together and throw out all these documents. I'm not going to give up. I
have backing by high spiritual power to understand my business.[4]

The Menominee termination went into effect in 1961. The state of
Wisconsin appointed a special committee to deal with it. The Menominee reservation was to disappear, to be absorbed by three counties under
state law; however, the Menominees in a vote rejected the idea of three
counties and insisted that a single county — Menominee County — be
formed out of the reservation.

One Menominee from Zoar, Wisconsin, reflected on the situation:
"One day I'm an American Indian. The next day I'm not!" The act of 1954
called for the "orderly termination of federal supervision over the property and members of the Menominee Indian Tribe of Wisconsin." Section
10 stated:

> Thereafter individual members of the tribe shall not be entitled to any
> of the services performed by the United States for Indians because of
> their status as Indians, all statutes of the United States which affect
> Indians because of their status as Indians shall no longer be applicable to
> members of the tribe, and the laws of the several states shall apply to the
> tribe and its members in the same manner as they apply to other citizens
> or persons within their jurisdiction....[5]

Under the act, tribal rolls were closed, tribal lands became subject to taxation, individual Menominees were no longer eligible for federal Indian
programs, and the Menominee Nation was no longer a federally recognized tribe.

The act had a devastating effect on our people. Our hospital, operated
by the Catholic nuns, was forced to close, because it didn't now meet
Wisconsin state standards. My mother, Constance, worked there; she
protested the planned closing and was fired as a result. Our tribal government — general council as well as advisory council — was soon abol-
ished. In its stead, a corporate structure — Menominee Enterprises, Inc.
(MEI) — was imposed under Wisconsin state law. Our lumber mill
was under new management, and MEI hired a white superintendent to

manage the operations. Many of the 3,270 tribal members were fired or forced out of their jobs.

The Menominees were shocked. We were never provided with any training sessions to deal with the implications of termination. Tribal members were given a bond that was to be worth three thousand dollars in the year 2000 and a certificate of beneficial interest "in accordance with the laws of the State of Wisconsin."[6] Our 160-acre homesteads assigned to each family became 22 acres [despite the fact that these homesteads never came under the Dawes Act and the allotment that followed]. The lawyers involved established a very complicated corporate structure that took away Menominee tribal decision making, namely meeting, talking, and voting.

My mother always told me that I should become more involved with the tribe. She said, "You are an Indian put on the planet by the Creator to help your people." I always believed that I should. I saw my mother always writing on behalf of the tribe, and I took her message to heart.

I returned to Wisconsin when Dr. Robert Powless offered me the directorship of Upward Bound at UW–Stevens Point, which was only two hours from my reservation. I started attending various meetings on the reservation. At most of these pro forma meetings, which were convened by state-dominated entities, the Menominees sat or stood in the back of the room and did not participate. They did not understand the legalese. After the initial presentations were made, the conveners would ask if there were any questions, believing no one would challenge them. I didn't sit back as most people did. I was known as a "loud mouth" even at a young age. When they didn't respond to my satisfaction, I stated: "*Excuse me*, that is no answer to the question!"

Many Menominees were both puzzled and surprised by my questioning and my assertiveness. People were curious about who I was because I had been away from the reservation for sixteen years attending college, going to graduate school, and working. My cousin, along with many others, criticized me. I had left the reservation, so what was I trying to do? I was not showing proper politeness and respect. I responded that I had a right to speak, reminding him that I had received a scholarship from the tribe to pursue my education but that I had not resigned from the tribe. I believe you need an excellent education to question authority and that we must invest in education for all our people to deal with continuous threats and attacks, such as those now confronting Indian gaming.

My people suffered a great psychic wound from termination — a cultural, economic, and political disaster. I believe that each person has to accept the responsibility to contribute to the tribe. Consequently, a number of us — not just me — founded DRUMS [Determination of the Rights and Unity of Menominee Shareholders], which was not simply an organization but a people's movement. Members included Lloyd Powless from Milwaukee, James White and his family from Chicago, Shirley Daley, Sylvia Wilber, Dr. Verna Fowler, and many others.[7]

Soon after the sales of our land began, some Menominee members began protesting. Others soon joined the struggle. Oscar Archiquette would come to support us, smile, and cheer us on. DRUMS gained steam, and support came from people off the reservation in Chicago, Milwaukee, and Minneapolis. At the same time some of our own Menominee people were individually benefiting by facilitating these land sales. We later received great support from Menominees on the reservation. We organized protest marches on the reservation and a major march from the reservation to Madison, where we met with Governor Patrick Lucey. He strongly supported our efforts for restoration. We gained support and legal assistance from the Native American Rights Fund and Wisconsin Judicare, and manpower from VISTA. We published a book, *Freedom with Restoration*, to inform the public and legislators.[8]

We began pushing for Congress to restore the Menominees to federal status. I dropped out of law school to work for Menominee restoration. One person told me I was dangerous without a law degree, but I would have been lethal with one. I lobbied in Washington for the act to restore Menominee status, and we had hearings on the bill. Ernest Stevens Sr. (Oneida), "Uncle" Louis R. Bruce Jr. (Mohawk), the BIA commissioner, and others from the BIA aided us. Then some lawyers involved wanted us to amend the 1954 termination act. I insisted on *repealing*, not amending, the 1954 act. That's why section 3(b) of the 1973 act states:

The Act of June 17, 1954 (68 Stat. 250; 25 U.S.C. 891–902) as amended is hereby repealed and they are hereby reinstated all rights and privileges of the tribe or its members under Federal treaty, statute, or otherwise which may have been diminished or lost pursuant to such Act.

We realized it would take a congressional act to reverse termination. With excellent legal assistance, first from Wisconsin Judicare and then from Native American Rights Funds, and additional help from NCAI, VISTA, the Friends Committee on National Legislation, and many others, we succeeded in our struggle to save our land and people with the passage of the Menominee Restoration Act. The Menominee Restoration Act of December 22, 1973, which was subsequently signed by President Nixon, was a historic reversal of American Indian policy.

Notes

1. Menominee Termination Act, *Stat.* 68 (1954): 250–252; Menominee Restoration Act, *Stat.* 87 (1973): 700ff (December 22, 1973).

2. For a modern history of the Menominees, see David R. Beck, *The Struggle for Self-Determination: History of the Menominee Indians Since 1854* (Lincoln: University of Nebraska Press, 2005).

3. For the best treatment of Senator Watkins, see R. Warren Metcalf, *Termination's Legacy: The Discarded Indians of Utah* (Lincoln: University of Nebraska Press, 2002), 3–16, 40–43. For Watkins's own writings on termination, see his "Termination of Federal Supervision: The Removal of Restrictions over Indian Property and Person," in *Annals of the American Academy of Political and Social Science* 311 (May 1957): 47–55.

4. Ernest Neconish quoted in Nicholas C. Peroff, *Menominee DRUMS: Tribal Termination and Restoration, 1954–1974* (Norman: University of Oklahoma Press, 1982), 78.

5. Menominee Termination Act, 250–252.

6. Ibid. For this period in Menominee history, see Beck, *The Struggle for Self-Determination*, 129–149.

7. According to Peroff, DRUMS "harassed, overthrew, and replaced the established Menominee governing elite...." It "instilled a new sense of pride and purpose in the Menominee people." Peroff, *Menominee DRUMS*, 163–164. See also Beck, *The Struggle for Self-Determination*, 110. Beck's account is the best analysis of federal mismanagement of Menominee forest resources. See ibid., 63 passim.

8. Deborah Shames, ed., *Freedom with Reservation: The Menominee Struggle to Save Their Land and People* (Madison, WI: National Committee to Save the Menominee People and Forests/Wisconsin Indian Legal Services, 1972).

Claims Arising

The Oneida Nation of Indians of Wisconsin and the Indian Claims Commission, 1951–1982

by Karim M. Tiro

The author wishes to thank Maura Kisseberth and Eliza Stoker for their assistance in preparing this essay for publication. This essay was previously published in American Indian Law Review 32 (2008).

Introduction

THE ONEIDA NATION OF INDIANS OF WISCONSIN is one of three Oneida tribes today whose members trace their descent to the Oneida tribe that existed in present-day New York state when the first Europeans arrived, and constituted one of the Five (later Six) Nations of the Iroquois League.[1] The Wisconsin Oneidas were a party to multiple claims before the Indian Claims Commission (ICC), usually as coplaintiffs with other tribes, including other Oneidas.[2] These claims ranged widely across the spectrum of issues the commission considered; in addition to their claims involving land ceded by treaty, the Wisconsin Oneidas were among the small number of tribes who filed accounting and mismanagement claims.[3]

An overview of the Wisconsin Oneidas' ICC claims provides a broad tour of the commission's areas of activity as well as a glimpse of that tribe's turbulent experience in the century following the American Revolution. Furthermore, the commission's legacy is dramatically illustrated by the relationship between the Oneidas' ICC suits and their landmark land claims in the federal courts.[4]

"Finally": The Origin and Purpose(s) of the Indian Claims Commission

According to Harvey D. Rosenthal, formerly the official historian of the ICC, the commission was created by Congress in 1946 "to deal *finally* with the long-standing claims of Native Americans against the Federal Government."[5] Rosenthal's italics signal that this "finally" was understood differently by distinct constituencies that supported the ICC's creation. The ICC's first supporters partook of a backward-looking regret for past wrongs, now to be rectified belatedly. But they were joined by others who looked forward to an ultimate reckoning as a way to hasten the dissolution of Indian identities. The commission's mandate thus encompassed disparate and contradictory rationales; nevertheless, this linguistic pliability was a necessary condition of the commission's creation in a democratic political system.[6]

The initial momentum behind the idea of a commission came from a new generation of bureaucrats who had been brought to Washington by Franklin D. Roosevelt. Men such as Secretary of the Interior Harold Ickes and his commissioner of Indian affairs, John Collier, demonstrated a high degree of interest in and respect for Native American cultures compared to most of their predecessors (and many of their successors as well). Recognizing the inherent injustice of the legal predicament of Native Americans, the policies they crafted, collectively dubbed the "Indian New Deal," militated for the strengthening of tribal structures.[7]

Indian tribes had long-standing grievances involving their treaties but had no access to the federal courts until 1875.[8] Even after that, the doctrine of sovereign immunity precluded suits against the United States unless the plaintiff successfully undertook the burdensome task of obtaining special enabling legislation from Congress. Legal action against states was inhibited by the Eleventh Amendment, and local hostility compromised Indians' ability to obtain redress in state courts.[9] Indians were caught in a legal tangle. In 1916, the federal government intervened in one notable case — *United States v. Boylan* — to defend land rights of the New York Oneidas but declined to take further action.[10]

Adjudication of such claims in the federal courts became less viable over time, in part because Native Americans were disadvantaged by poverty and unfamiliarity with the legal system. Through the 1920s, they filed increasing numbers of requests for legislation permitting their claims to proceed. Although some of these requests were granted, dealing with the requests drew significant resources from the government.[11] As a result, various proposals were made for the airing and adjudication of Indian claims, including, most notably, the 1928 Meriam Report.[12]

The proposals languished. Although some of the delay was undoubtedly related to the Great Depression and World War II, lack of action could also be attributed to policymakers who feared the consequences of the United States being subject to potentially staggering liability. Thus, legislators and bureaucrats closely scrutinized and criticized any proposed entity for the adjudication of claims. The process eventually moved forward, but it wasn't because of the adoption by growing numbers of an "enlightened" attitude toward Indian rights, or the creation of a viable plan for the commission. Instead, congressional approval was the product of increasing support for a new, assimilationist Indian policy known as termination. Termination promised to definitively end relations between the government and Native Americans. For proponents of termination, including President Truman, the ICC was viewed as an opportunity to discharge any lingering, residual debts, thereby ensuring that when the government closed the books on its relations with Indians, they would stay closed.[13]

Taking a wider perspective, Ward Churchill has argued that the United States took up the matter of Indian claims to burnish its international image in the run-up to the Nuremberg trials.[14] Certainly the treatment of minorities became a more sensitive subject during the cold war, and the ICC could be useful to deflect criticism.[15] Embraced by very different constituencies with very different goals, the ICC represented simultaneously the last major initiative of the Indian New Deal and the first of the termination era.[16]

Docket 75: The Wisconsin Land Claim

The first disposal of a Wisconsin Oneida case came in 1962. The Wisconsin Oneidas and Stockbridge-Munsees were coplaintiffs (under the umbrella moniker "Emigrant New York Indians") in a land claim related to their settlement in Wisconsin (then Michigan Territory).[17] In 1822, two Oneidas of the First Christian Party and several Stockbridges, led by the Oneidas' St. Regis Mohawk missionary Eleazer Williams, entered into a treaty with Menominees for rights to settle on their land.[18] Backed by western New York land speculators, Williams's goal was to secure a western home for all the Indians of upstate New York.[19]

The representatives on both sides who negotiated the cession had highly dubious authority to do so; nevertheless, according to a treaty signed on September 23, 1822, the "New York Indians" acquired the right to cohabitate with the Menominees on a tract of land that was eventually fixed at 3,931,000 acres.[20] President Monroe gave his approval to this treaty in March of 1823.[21] However, amidst complaints from the Menominees, a brewing war with the Winnebagos, and an emerging policy to move all the natives beyond the Mississippi, the federal government quickly backtracked on its recognition of the New York Indians' claims to Wisconsin lands. By the Stambaugh treaty signed in 1831, the federal government reduced the New York Indian acreage to 569,120, with provisions to reduce it further if more Indians did not emigrate from New York.[22] In the supplementary treaty of October 27, 1832, the New York Indians agreed to this simply to secure some guaranteed landbase after years of uncertainty.[23] Ultimately, through the treaty signed at Washington on February 3, 1838, Oneidas residing at Duck Creek near Green Bay agreed to receive a reservation of just 100 acres per capita.[24] As a result, a reservation was created for them amounting to 65,000 acres.[25]

The legitimacy of the treaty of September 23, 1822, between the "Emigrant Indians" and the Menominees was problematic, but the commission deemed that its mandate was only to look into whether the federal government "acted properly in its course of dealings with plaintiffs."[26] In 1957, the three commissioners, Arthur Watkins, T. Harold Scott, and William Holt, determined that it had not. Despite its initial recognition of the 1822 proceedings, in subsequent treaties, the United States failed to acknowledge the New York Indians as coholders of aboriginal title to lands in Wisconsin and permitted the "New York Indians" to be railroaded into accepting a smaller tract.[27] Thus, the federal government was now responsible to the "New York Indians" for their half interest in the nearly four million acres (minus whatever lands had in fact been secured to them). In 1962, the commission issued an opinion that, based upon a valuation of land at eighty cents per acre in 1832, the Oneida of Wisconsin and the Stockbridge-Munsee were owed the sum of $1,488,629.60.[28]

In 1964, the commission ordered the correction of a computing error, which reduced the award to $1,452,824.[29] The award was reduced by another $139,351 due to the court's practice of allowing the defendant to deduct "gratuitous offsets."[30] These offsets represented monies spent by the federal government for tribal benefit even if they had not been disbursed in connection with the transactions in question. Against the award the government claimed — and the commission allowed — sums as small as $40 expended for funerals for indigent Indians in 1936.[31] While the offsets included agricultural equipment, the bulk ($128,249.57) were for purchases or grants of land. The total final award in 1964 was $1,313,472.65.[32] Of this, the Oneidas' share, which was not appropriated until 1967, was $1,171,248.[33]

ICC land-claim awards were based solely upon the difference between what the Indians had been paid and "fair market value" of the land *at the time of purchase.*[34] By not adjusting the award to compensate for more than 150 years of inflation, the ICC gave the government an additional benefit by allowing payment of the judgment in twentieth-century dollars. The commission also adhered to the "no-interest rule" that applies to federal liability, taking the position that absent specific congressional authorization, it was unable to award interest.[35] But in adhering to the "no-interest rule," the ICC (and Congress) were not simply bowing to precedent: application of the no-interest rule protected the Treasury from awards that were large but justifiable. Given the fact that the Indians had been prevented from filing suit for so long, time and the no-interest rule essentially nullified awards for the Indians.

Docket 159: The Timber Stripping Claim

From the creation of the Duck Creek reservation in 1838, timber had been cut and sold off by individual tribal members, effectively denuding the forest on the sixty-five-thousand-acre tract. Occasional Oneida requests for intervention led the federal agent to periodically request individual Oneidas to stop, but no firm action was taken prior to 1870. At that time, suits were initiated against purchasers, compensation of about one thousand dollars secured, and unauthorized lumbering ended.[36]

Although the commissioners found that "the timber on the reservation was tribal property" and as such "could not be disposed of without the approval of the Government," they did not grant the Oneidas relief.[37]

The ICC cited the Oneidas' lack of "clean hands"[38] because the cutting and sale of the timber had been effected by individual Oneidas and countenanced by some of their chiefs. Although the federal Indian agent to the Oneidas had knowledge of the removal of the timber, he had not played an active role in the mismanagement of the reservation's timber resources. The absence of active involvement on the part of the agent distinguished this case from the successful Wisconsin timber case won by the Menominees before the Court of Claims in 1950.[39] Once again, taking a narrow view of the federal trust responsibility, the commissioners denied that the guardian-ward relationship implied a duty to intervene to protect reservation resources, because no such obligation was specified in the treaty that created the reservation.[40] On appeal, the Court of Claims rejected the commission's opinion that the government had no responsibility to protect the Oneida timber.[41] However, the court let stand the commission's decision on the grounds that the government's responsibility had been fulfilled (albeit minimally) by whatever actions the agent had taken.[42]

Docket 344: The Pennsylvania Land Claim

The Wisconsin Oneidas were a party to a claim filed by the Six Nations collectively, challenging the acquisition from them of roughly the northwestern third of Pennsylvania in 1784, as well as the Erie Triangle in 1789. It was dismissed unanimously in 1963 by the same three commissioners who had decided the previous two cases. At the heart of the commission's reasoning for the dismissal was the relationship between the United States and Pennsylvania under the Articles of Confederation. The ICC was authorized to hear claims against the federal government, but the treaties under which the Six Nations lost these lands were signed with the state of Pennsylvania.

The power of Congress over Indian affairs under the Articles of Confederation was poorly defined. Article IX granted Congress the power to "regulat[e] the trade and manag[e] all affairs with the Indians, not members of any of the States, provided that the legislative right of any State within its own limits be not infringed or violated."[43] According to James Madison, Article IX was "obscure and contradictory," and the definition of "Indians not members of any of the States" remained "a question of frequent perplexity and contention in the federal councils."[44]

The commission narrowly interpreted the power of the federal government to regulate Indian affairs under Article IX; it held that an official of the federal government would have violated the article by offering the Indians advice in their land negotiations with a state.[45] The commission reasoned that because the United States was barred from playing any role in the treaty, it could not be liable for its outcome. The claim to the area encompassed by Pennsylvania's charter boundaries that was ceded in 1784 was therefore dismissed.

Another issue that arose during litigation involved definitions of the geographical boundaries of the states. Surveys in 1786 and 1787 revealed that Pennsylvania had only a few miles of frontage on Lake Erie.[46] New York and Massachusetts had already relinquished their competing claims in the area, so the land reverted to the federal government. Pennsylvania promptly undertook to purchase the Indian title to what became known as the Erie Triangle in 1789.

Although circumstances therefore differed from the 1784 purchase, the commission dismissed the Six Nations' claim to the Erie Triangle on the grounds that they had not established exclusive use or occupancy over the area. In the commission's Eurocentric view, occupancy was defined as more or less synonymous with village location.[47] Absent the tribe's ability to establish proof of fixed residence in the area, the claim did not proceed.[48]

The Six Nations then appealed to the Court of Claims, which focused more on the 1784 U.S. Treaty of Fort Stanwix than the Articles of Confederation.[49] The court affirmed the commission's decision and denied the appellants' contention that the treaty created a fiduciary relationship between the central government and the Six Nations as a whole.[50] The court held that "the most significant part of the treaty was merely a peace pact...."[51] However, the court left open the possibility that the treaty might operate differently upon the "friendly tribes" referred to in Article II of that treaty, which read, "The Oneida and Tuscarora nations shall be secured in the possession of the lands on which they are settled."[52] Furthermore, the court stated, "If this separate provision is thought to have had greater meaning for these friendly tribes, it is enough to note that the lands on which they were settled did not include the Pennsylvania territory with which this case is concerned."[53] Thus, the adverse decision in Docket 344 did not preclude a different outcome for the Oneidas' claims to lands in New York.

Docket 84: The Accounting Claim

Another claim originating in the eighteenth century was an accounting claim that the Oneidas mounted in conjunction with the rest of the Six Nations and Stockbridge-Munsee. The Six Nations were parties to an agreement with the United States in 1792 and to the Treaty of Canandaigua in 1794. The United States entered into these agreements as part of an effort to win political support during a faltering Indian war in the west. On March 23, 1792, with a delegation of the Six Nations visiting Philadelphia, the president arranged an annual payment to them of $1,500 for "clothing, domestic animals and implements of husbandry, and for encouraging useful artificers to reside in their villages." The Senate gave its advice and consent, and the president ratified, but the stipulation was never fulfilled until it was superseded by the 1794 Treaty of Canandaigua. The Canandaigua treaty promised a $4,500 annual disbursement for similar purposes.[54]

The ICC found that the monies spent on the conversion of the Indians to European-style agrarianism fell $32,218 shy of the total $711,000 to which the treaty entitled them up to 1952.[55] The $4,500 never paid under the 1792 article raised the total sum owed the Indians to $36,718.[56] As in the other claims, this small sum might have appropriately been magnified to reflect their loss through the application of compounding interest. However, the ICC did not address the timing of the underpayments and again invoked the no-interest rule.[57]

Gratuitous offsets were also applied. The commission reduced the award by $5,340.17 because the government had paid the expenses of various Six Nations delegations between the years 1842 and 1905; the commission also deducted $1,448 paid for flour and beef for Stockbridge-Munsee Indians in 1865. Not all offsets presented by the government were allowed. Disbursements benefitting individual tribal members, such as expenditures for orphans, were rejected. Expenses paid for tribal delegations disputing improperly negotiated treaties were also rejected. In seeking to limit the award, the federal government presented sums as small as an $86.65 expenditure in 1942 to investigate marl deposits on a reservation. That expense, at least, was rejected because its benefit to the tribe was unknown.[58]

In 1973, after deducting offsets, the commission awarded the Six Nations and Stockbridge-Munsees $29,930.[59] Although the sum was trivial, the proceeding at least recognized the ongoing obligations imposed by the Treaty of Canandaigua, which is a touchstone of Iroquois sovereignty vis-à-vis the United States.

Docket 301: The New York Land Claim

Pre-1790 Claims

In 1951, the Oneidas of Wisconsin, New York, and Canada filed a claim for approximately six million acres taken in treaties with New York state between 1785 and 1846. The first decision was not handed down until 1969, after the United States sought partial summary judgment. On the basis of its appellate victory in the Pennsylvania claim discussed earlier, the United States had requested the dismissal of those Oneida claims preceding passage of the Trade and Intercourse Act in 1790.[60] These happened to be the treaties of greatest consequence to the Oneidas, because more than 90 percent of their land at the end of the Revolution was ceded in treaties at Fort Herkimer in 1785 and Fort Schuyler in 1788. If the United States succeeded in removing these treaties from litigation, the Oneida claim would be reduced to roughly 250,000 acres.

The commission rejected the government's motion for summary judgment. Commissioners Margaret Pierce, John Vance, Richard Yarborough, and Theodore McKeldin distinguished this case from the Pennsylvania claim. They stressed the difference between the Oneidas' relationship with the United States and that of the Six Nations as a whole (the Pennsylvania plaintiff) at the end of the Revolutionary War.[61] In light of the Oneidas' fidelity to the United States and ample contemporaneous congressional recognition thereof, the ICC held that Congress intended to deal with them differently and that Article II of the Fort Stanwix treaty had indeed created a special relationship. The federal government thus could be held liable because it failed to uphold its treaty commitment to its former allies that they "be secured in the possession of the lands on which they are settled."[62]

The majority of the commission did not share their predecessors' opinion that addressing the Oneidas' dealings with a state would violate the Articles of Confederation. In arriving at its own conclusion, the commission invoked its power to provide relief for "claims based upon fair and honorable dealings that are not recognized by any existing rule of law or equity."[63] The commission had the authority to consider moral claims, but in keeping with the court format to which it adhered, it generally limited itself to legal ones involving land or money.[64] In the absence of a more specific legal rationale, the most consistently progovernment commissioner, Jerome Kuykendall, dissented.[65]

In its 1976 opinion, the commission found that the 1785 and 1788 treaties had been improperly negotiated by New York state. With respect to the first transaction, the commission observed that "the Oneidas did not voluntarily part with their land.... They sold their land only in the face of unwarranted accusations and threats by Governor Clinton.... Under these circumstances the Oneidas had no choice but to sell the land which New York desired."[66] The 1788 treaty was similarly problematic. According to the opinion, "the Oneidas did not voluntarily sell their lands at the Fort Schuyler treaty. In fact, it is clear from the evidence that the Oneidas did not even realize they were selling anything."[67] The commission concluded:

> Both the 1785 and 1788 treaties were the type of transaction against which the United States had promised to protect the Oneidas. The evidence shows clearly, however, that the United States took no action to protect the Oneidas with regard to either of the treaties.[68]

The commission further concluded that the United States was aware of the transactions and that its intervention was not prohibited by the Articles of Confederation.[69] To reach the latter conclusion, the commission was forced to explore the ambiguous language of Article IX.[70] In the commission's reading of that article, "the United States was granted the exclusive right to manage Indian affairs with those Indians which maintained a tribal existence independent of any state, so long as the United States did not purchase from any of these tribes land located within the boundaries of any state." The commission overruled any inconsistent opinions in an earlier Docket 301 decision and in Docket 344.[71] Commissioner Kuykendall again dissented, challenging the political criteria used to define "Indians, not members of any of the States." He stated the commission's conclusions "are too categorical, are not supported by the historical evidence of record, and have no judicial support."[72]

The Court of Claims affirmed the commission majority in 1978.[73] In its opinion, it upheld the commission's finding that Article II of the 1784 Treaty of Fort Stanwix "incorporat[ed] the frequent pledges of protection made by the Continental Congress to the Oneidas and Tuscaroras with regard to their land."[74] The Court of Claims also decided that under Article IX of the Articles of Confederation "the central government may not have been able to forbid the transactions, [but] the nature of the chicanery practiced upon the Oneidas suggest that feasible levels of assistance…might well have averted the harm." Federal influence to mitigate the situation at the time was not only legal under the Articles of Confederation but was required by the Treaty of Fort Stanwix.[75] The United States' liability was thereby affirmed.

Post-1790 Claims

From 1969 onward, the ICC had considered the pre- and post-1790 claims separately in light of the Trade and Intercourse Act passed by Congress. The act stated that "no purchase or grant of lands…from any Indians or nation or tribe of Indians…shall be of any validity in law or equity, unless the same be made by a treaty or convention entered into pursuant to the constitution…."[76] Although the act explicitly established federal authority over Indian land cessions, the United States argued that this did not necessarily make it liable for actions in which it was not directly involved, hoping the commission would be persuaded by the fact that federal representatives had been present at only two of the twenty-five transactions in question. In a 1971 opinion, the commission refused to define the federal government's duty so narrowly. If the federal government had knowledge of the treaties but did nothing, it could still be held liable.[77] The government also argued that the act did not apply to New York as one of the original thirteen states, a position that the commission rejected on the basis of its own decision in *Seneca*[78] as well as the Supreme Court's in *Federal Power Commission v. Tuscarora Indian Nation*.[79]

The United States appealed in the Court of Claims, but without success. The appellate court reaffirmed the fiduciary relationship between the federal government and the Indians under the Trade and Intercourse Act. It remanded the case to the commission to establish whether or not the federal government had knowledge of each of the treaties in question (and therefore liability for any deficiencies therein).[80] The commission found in 1978 that the federal government had actual knowledge of three of the treaties and constructive knowledge of the remainder; it was thus liable for any deficiencies in all of them.[81]

The Oneidas won victories before the commission in their claims related to New York lands. However, Docket 301's decision was limited because of the paltry compensation available in the absence of interest or any adjustment for inflation. While the ICC considered the Oneidas' claim, the federal courts were finally expressly opened to Indian claims by Congress in 1966.[82] In 1970, the Oneidas filed a claim against the counties that now sat on their reservation. (As already noted, a tribal suit against the state was barred by the Eleventh Amendment.) The potential awards in claims in federal court far exceeded compensation offered by the ICC. Moreover, the ICC offered only money, while the federal court could potentially return land.[83] The early results were striking, most notably a Supreme Court decision permitting tribes to initiate land claims in federal court for violations of the Trade and Intercourse Act.[84]

Ultimately, under the ICC the United States would not offer the Oneidas an award exceeding $3.3 million. The Oneidas of New York were willing to accept the settlement, but the Oneida tribe of Wisconsin tabled it in 1980. The latter did so primarily out of an ongoing concern that it would compromise their more recent, more significant suit in federal court. The Wisconsin Oneidas did not trust their attorney's assurances that acceptance of the award would not have this effect.[85] In 1982, amid continued concern over the potential ramifications of the ICC claim in federal court, the Oneidas withdrew their ICC complaint.[86]

Finally? The Wisconsin Oneidas and the Legacy of the ICC

So, how far did the wheels of justice turn? They certainly did not move full circle, ushering in "a new era for the American Indian," as the rhetoric at the commission's creation promised.[87] Legal historian John R. Wunder has judged the ICC a "miserable failure."[88] Although the commission had been authorized to decide claims on moral grounds, by taking on the form of a court, it usually (but not always) based its decisions on more narrow legal grounds. Although not negligible, the monetary awards granted the Wisconsin Oneidas were certainly small. This was a typical outcome. It was a great irony that a commission created to identify and redress "unconscionably low" payments to Indians itself paid awards in dollars that had depreciated over nearly two centuries.

With a geographically favorable location and careful management by the tribal government, the Docket 75 claim played a small part in helping the Wisconsin Oneidas develop their reservation. Unlike many tribes, the Wisconsin Oneidas prudently devoted only a small portion of the award for distribution as per capita payments.[89] Legal critic Vine Deloria's overall assessment of the ICC was not much more favorable than Wunder's. At most, Deloria observed, the ICC helped "clear out the underbrush and allow the claims created by the forced political and economic dependency during the last century to emerge."[90] Docket 301 certainly had this effect: it was abandoned due to the insufficiency of the proposed settlement, but not before demonstrating the strength of some of the Oneidas' potential claims. According to George Shattuck, the attorney who crafted the Oneidas' 1970 suit in federal court, "a generation became discouraged" over their failure to make headway in the courts since *Boylan*, despite continued efforts. The ICC revived them.[91] The Oneidas have yet to recover substantial compensation in the form of money or land via the federal courts, but the various cases they have filed there make it obvious that the ICC did not end their attempts. Clearly, those who wished to see the matter of Indian claims resolved *"finally"* — in either sense — saw their hopes dashed.

Notes

1. The three Oneida tribes are the Oneida Nation of Indians of Wisconsin, the Oneida Indian Nation of New York, and the Oneida Nation of the Thames (Ontario). I use the

term "Oneida" inclusively to designate all Oneida groups party to a particular claim, and I use "Wisconsin Oneida" (or "New York Oneida") to designate that particular group when they acted separately from the others. In the ICC cases that relate to Wisconsin exclusively, "Oneidas" refers to the Wisconsin Oneidas only. Canadian tribes could not bring claims before the ICC.

2. *Oneida Nation of N.Y. v. United States*, 41 Indian Cl. Comm'n 391 (1978); *Oneida Nation of N.Y. v. United States*, 26 Indian Cl. Comm'n 138 (1971); *Six Nations v. United States*, 23 Indian Cl. Comm'n 375 (1970); *Oneida Tribe of Indians of Wis. v. United States*, 12 Indian Cl. Comm'n 1 (1962); *Emigrant N.Y. Indians v. United States*, 5 Indian Cl. Comm'n 560 (1957). ICC decisions are available online at Indian Claims Commission Decisions, http://digital.library.okstate.edu/icc/index.html (last visited March 11, 2008).

3. Michael Lieder and Jake Page, *Wild Justice: The People of Geronimo vs. the United States* (New York: Random House, 1997), 233–234.

4. *City of Sherrill v. Oneida Indian Nation of New York*, 544 U.S. 197 (2005); *County of Oneida v. Oneida Nation of N.Y.*, 470 U.S. 226 (1985); *Oneida Nation of N.Y. v. County of Oneida*, 414 U.S. 661 (1974); *Oneida Nation of N.Y. v. New York*, 860 F.2d 1145 (1988).

5. Imre Sutton, *Irredeemable America: The Indians' Estate and Land Claims* (Albuquerque: University of New Mexico Press, 1985), 35.

6. Harvey D. Rosenthal, *Their Day in Court: A History of the Indian Claims Commission* (New York: Garland, 1990), 73.

7. Graham D. Taylor, *The New Deal and American Indian Tribalism: The Administration of the Indian Reorganization Act, 1934–45* (Lincoln: University of Nebraska Press, 1980), 17–18.

8. "The Supreme Court, 1984 Term — Indian Land Claims," *Harvard Law Review* 99, no. 254 (1985): 260–261.

9. Nell Jessup Newton, "Indian Claims in the Courts of the Conqueror," *American University Law Review* 41 (1992): 769–771; Ward Churchill, "Charades, Anyone? The Indian Claims Commission in Context," *American Indian Culture & Research Journal* 24 (2000): 47; "The Supreme Court, 1984 Term — Indian Land Claims," *Harvard Law Review* 99 (1985): 260; John Eduard Barry, "Oneida Indian Nation v. County of Oneida: Tribal Rights of Action and the Indian Trade and Intercourse Act," *Columbia Law Review* 84 (1984): 1852, 1858–1860.

10. *U.S. v. Boylan*, 256 F. 468 (N.D.N.Y. 1919), *aff'd* 265 F. 165 (2d Cir. 1920), *appeal dismissed*, 257 U.S. 641 (1921); Anthony Wonderley, *Oneida Iroquois Folklore, Myth, and History: New York Oral Narrative from the Notes of H. E. Allen and Others* (Syracuse, NY: Syracuse University Press, 2004), 192–210, esp. 204–09; John Tahsuda, "The Oneida Land Claim: Yesterday and Today," *Buffalo Law Review* 46 (1998): 1003–1005.

11. Rosenthal, *Their Day in Court*, 18–19; Lieder and Page, *Wild Justice*, 53–57.

12. Rosenthal, *Their Day in Court*, 52; Lewis Meriam, *The Problem of Indian Administration* (Baltimore, MD: Johns Hopkins University Press, 1928).

13. Churchill, "Charades, Anyone?," 52–53; Lieder and Page, *Wild Justice*, 60–61; William T. Hagan, " 'To Correct Certain Evils': The Indian Land Claims Cases," in *Iroquois Land*

Claims, ed. Christopher Vecsey and William A. Starna, 20 (Syracuse, NY: Syracuse University Press, 1988). On the Oneidas of Wisconsin, see Laurence M. Hauptman, "Learning the Lessons of History: The Oneidas of Wisconsin Reject Termination, 1943–1956," *Journal of Ethnic Studies* 14 (1986): 31–52.

14. Churchill, "Charades, Anyone?," 51–52.

15. Laurence M. Hauptman, *The Iroquois Struggle for Survival: World War II to Red Power* (Syracuse, NY: Syracuse University Press, 1986), 190.

16. John R. Wunder, *"Retained by the People": A History of American Indians and the Bill of Rights* (New York: Oxford University Press, 1994), 89–91; Lieder and Page, *Wild Justice,* 60–61.

17. *Emigrant N.Y. Indians v. United States,* 5 Indian Cl. Comm'n 560 (1957).

18. Ibid., 569–575.

19. Ibid.

20. Ibid., 572–574.

21. Ibid., 574.

22. *Treaty with the Menominee, Stat.* 7 (1831): 342, 346.

23. *Treaty with the Menominee, Stat.* 7 (1832): 405; *Appendix to Treaty with the Menominee, Stat.* 7 (1832): 409; *Emigrant N.Y. Indians,* 5 Indian Cl. Comm'n 603–604.

24. *Treaty with the Oneidas, Stat.* 7 (1838): 566, art. 2.

25. The Oneidas filed a claim that they had not received the correct acreage. However, since the extent of land they did receive was considered an offset against their award in this case, the claim was dismissed. *Oneida Tribe of Indians of Wis. v. United States,* 18 Indian Cl. Comm'n 433 (1967).

26. *Emigrant N.Y. Indians v. United States,* 5 Indian Cl. Comm'n 607, 621.

27. Ibid., 625.

28. *Emigrant N.Y. Indians v. United States,* 11 Indian Cl. Comm'n 359, 385–386 (1962).

29. *Emigrant N.Y. Indians v. United States,* 13 Indian Cl. Comm'n 560, 573-a, 573-b (1964).

30. Rosenthal, *Their Day in Court,* 29–31, on the history of this practice prior to its adoption by the ICC.

31. *Emigrant N.Y. Indians,* 13 Indian Cl. Comm'n at 562.

32. Ibid., 573-c.

33. Loretta Metoxen, *The New York Emigrant Claim and What We Did with It,* pamphlet (Oneida, WI: Oneida Land Claims Commission), undated.

34. Newton, "Indian Claims," 820.

35. Ibid., 820–821.

36. *Oneida Tribe of Indians of Wis. v. United States,* 12 Indian Cl. Comm'n 1, 2–5 (1962); *United States v. Cook,* 86 U.S. (19 Wall.) 591 (1873); *E.E. Bolles Wooden Ware Co. v. United States,* 106 U.S. 432 (1882).

37. *Oneida Tribe*, 12 Indian Cl. Comm'n 2.

38. Ibid., 20.

39. *Menominee Tribe of Indians v. United States*, 95 Ct. Cl. 232 (1941); Lieder and Page, *Wild Justice*, 232–233.

40. Commissioner T. Harold Scott differed from his colleagues on this point, stating that there were instances in which such a relationship existed absent specific language, although he did not say this was one of those instances. *Oneida Tribe*, 12 Indian Cl. Comm'n 23.

41. *Oneida Tribe*, 165 Ct. Cl. 487, 493–494 (1964).

42. Ibid., 487,494–500.

43. Articles of Confederation, art. 9; *Six Nations v. United States*, 12 Indian Cl. Comm'n 98, 118 (1963).

44. James Madison, *The Federalist No. 42*, in *The Federalist Papers*, reprint, New York, New American library/mentor book, 1961, 280-288.

45. *Six Nations*, 12 Indian Cl. Comm'n 118.

46. Donald H. Kent, *History of Pennsylvania Purchases from the Indians* (New York: Garland, 1974), 202–204.

47. *Six Nations*, 12 Indian Cl. Comm'n 120–121.

48. Ibid., 119–121.

49. *Treaty with the Six Nations, Stat.* 7 (1784): 15.

50. *Six Nations v. United States*, 173 Ct. Cl. 899, 906–907 (1965).

51. Ibid., 899, 906.

52. *Treaty with the Six Nations* (1784): 15, art. 2.

53. *Six Nations*, 173 Ct. Cl. 899 n.6.

54. *American State Papers — Indian Affairs* (Washington, D.C.: Gales & Seaton, 1832), 1:225, 229; *Six Nations v. United States*, 23 Indian Cl. Comm'n 387, 390–392 (1970); *Treaty with the Six Nations, Stat.* 7 (1794): 44, art. 6.

55. *Six Nations*, 23 Indian Cl. Comm'n 392–395.

56. Ibid., 391, 396, 400.57.

57. Ibid.

58. *Six Nations v. United States*, 32 Indian Cl. Comm'n 440–452 (1973).

59. Ibid., 453–459.

60. *Oneida Nation v. United States*, 20 Indian Cl. Comm'n 337 (1969).

61. Ibid., 349–350. Theodore McKeldin served only temporarily and was replaced by Brantley Blue in May 1969.

62. Ibid., 341–342; *Treaty with the Six Nations* (1784), art. 2, 15.

63. *Oneida Nation of N.Y. v. United States*, 26 Indian Cl. Comm'n 583, 585–589, 624 (1971); *Indian Claims Commission Act, Stat.* 60 (1946): §2, 1049, 1050.

64. Lieder and Page, *Wild Justice*, 66–67, 201; Sutton, *Irredeemable America*, 45.

65. *Oneida Nation*, 20 Indian Cl. Comm'n 351; *Oneida Nation*, 26 Indian Cl. Comm'n 591; Lieder and Page, *Wild Justice*, 205.

66. *Oneida Nation of N.Y. v. United States*, 37 Indian Cl. Comm'n 522, 526 (1976).

67. Ibid., 529.

68. Ibid., 530.

69. Ibid., 535, 546.

70. Ibid., 536–546.

71. *Oneida Nation*, 26 Indian Cl. Comm'n 583, 588; *Six Nations*, 12 Indian Cl. Comm'n 86, 118.

72. *Oneida Nation*, 37 Indian Cl. Comm'n 556 (Kuykendall, chairman, dissenting).

73. *United States v. Oneida Nation of N.Y.*, 217 Ct. Cl. 45 (1978).

74. Ibid., 57–59.

75. Ibid., 61–62.

76. *An Act to Regulate Trade and Intercourse with the Indian Tribes, Stat.* 1 (1793): ch.19, §8, 329, 330, www.yale.edu/lawweb/avalon/statutes/native/na025.htm. The 1793 version of the act was the version in effect in 1795, when the first of the purchases in question took place.

77. *Oneida Nation of N.Y. v. United States*, 26 Indian Cl. Comm'n 138, 145–147 (1971).

78. *Seneca Nation of Indians v. United States*, 20 Indian Cl. Comm'n 177, 182 (1968).

79. 362 U.S. 99 (1960).

80. *United States v. Oneida Nation of N.Y.*, 477 F.2d 939, 945 (Ct. Cl. 1973).

81. *Oneida Nation of N.Y. v. United States*, 43 Indian Cl. Comm'n 373, 468 (1978).

82. 28 U.S.C. 1362 (2006).

83. George C. Shattuck, *The Oneida Land Claims: A Legal History* (Syracuse, NY: Syracuse University Press, 1991), 10–11. The Oneidas did not, however, request the return of land in this suit. They asked for the rental value of the land lost by a single agreement in 1795 over a two-year period, 1968–1969.

84. *Oneida Indian Nation v. County of Oneida*, 414 U.S. 661 (1974); Tahsuda, "The Oneida Land Claim," 1007.

85. In 1978, the appellate court had rejected the Wisconsin Oneidas' request to postpone the proceedings because of potential implications for the other claim, as well as their attempt to dismiss their attorney. *Oneida Nation*, 217 Ct. Cl. 50–52, 52 n.5. Also in 1978,

the Indian Claims Commission denied a petition of the counties of Madison and Oneida in New York to intervene in the commission proceedings. *Oneida Nation of N.Y. v. United States*, 41 Indian Cl. Comm'n 391 (1978); Barry, "Oneida Indian Nation v. County of Oneida," 1861 n.68; Dr. John E. Powless, telephone interview with author, August 28, 2007; Shattuck, *The Oneida Land Claims*, 201; Kristina Lyn Ackley, "We Are Oneida Yet: Discourse in the Oneida Land Claim" (PhD dissertation, SUNY-Buffalo, 2005): 121–136.

86. Barry, "Oneida Indian Nation v. County of Oneida" 1861 n. 68; Tahsuda, "The Oneida Land Claim," 1006 n. 22.

87. Lieder and Page, *Wild Justice*, 64.

88. Wunder, *"Retained by the People,"* 114.

89. Fifteen percent of the award was used for the acquisition of land that was subsequently developed for economic and tribal use. Personal payments were limited to interest derived from the remainder of the award; the principal and interest remain under the control of a tribal committee. Metoxen, *The New York Emigrant Claim*. On the distribution of ICC awards generally, see Lieder and Page, *Wild Justice*, 257–263.

90. Vine Deloria Jr., *Behind the Trail of Broken Treaties: An Indian Declaration of Independence* (Austin: University of Texas Press, 1985 [1974]), 228.

91. George Shattuck, telephone interview with author, July 15, 2007; Ackley, "We Are Oneida Yet," 118; Hauptman, *Iroquois Struggle for Survival*, 179–203.

The Wisconsin Oneidas and Termination, 1943–1956

by Laurence M. Hauptman

IN THE IMMEDIATE POST–WORLD WAR II ERA, the Wisconsin Oneidas once again faced a perfect storm that threatened their tribal existence. Instead of allotment, they now confronted what policymakers dubbed "termination." As was true of most American Indian communities of the era, they were impoverished and had significant internal differences of opinion about what strategies to use to counteract this renewed threat; nevertheless, the Wisconsin Oneidas drew from their past to successfully fend off federal policy initiatives aimed at ending their status as a federally recognized Indian nation.

The New Deal policies had both positive and negative impacts on the Wisconsin Oneidas. On one hand, the WPA Oneida Language and Folklore Project instilled pride, and efforts to reclaim some submarginal lands did occur. On the other hand, a new level of bureaucracy in Indian affairs stymied efforts for more extensive reform. In addition, Commissioner of Indian Affairs John Collier's exaggerated claims that the Indian New Deal policies would lead to true self-rule by the Indians fueled efforts to end federal involvement during and after World War II.

The often-overwhelmed four-member Oneida government that operated under the IRA constitution and bylaws had to contend with staggering problems: the devastating poverty in their community and the racism toward them in the surrounding Brown-Outagamie County region, as well as the threatening clouds coming from Congress. At the height of the termination threat, the League of Women Voters found that fewer than 10 percent of Oneidas had graduated from high school.[1] Two years later, in 1958, a second study conducted by the University of Wisconsin found that only 40 percent of Oneidas had full-time employment.[2] Faced with these extreme challenges and told by BIA officials that termination was inevitable, the Wisconsin Oneidas found themselves divided on what course to choose: to make the best of a bad situation by seeking reparations in the

Indian Claims Commission, or to fervently reject any and all efforts at termination, which to some Oneidas seemed a hopeless effort at the time. In the end, they chose both paths.

The failure of the United States government to deal effectively with any and all of the Oneidas' massive problems worked to reinforce Oneida suspicion of Washington's Indian-policy makers. In their dealings with the non-Indian world, the Oneidas had experienced a long history of government ineptitude and corruption: the forced emigration westward from New York, the Dawes Act of 1887, corrupt Indian agents who failed to protect them from land swindlers and timber strippers, the nonrecognition of Oneida land claims, and many other examples. The government's historic failure to carry out the trust relationship with Indians provoked Oneida ire.

Under intense congressional fire, the 1943–1944 commissioner of Indian affairs John Collier admitted that the Indian New Deal had not accomplished many of his objectives.[3] Many congressmen during World War II and in the postwar era saw the BIA as overly bureaucratic, terribly ineffective, and damaging to Indian self-esteem and economic development, as well as to the Indians' path to assimilation into mainstream America. To Congress, as well as to many Indians of the time, the BIA was a self-perpetuating agency that did not serve Indian nations or individual needs effectively enough to warrant its continuance. In every hearing on Capitol Hill, liberals and conservatives alike rebuked the bureau for fostering guardianship, paternalism, and segregation, especially since the Indians had played an important role in the nation's defense during World War II. Congressmen of many political persuasions believed the Indians had to be "emancipated" from bureau control and for their own good.

On June 11, 1943, the Senate Committee on Indian Affairs issued Report No. 310, which ostensibly summarized the findings of the committee's lengthy hearings — Survey of Conditions of the Indians of the United States — begun in 1928. In effect, however, Report No. 310 (and a subsequent supplemental report issued by the committee) was largely an indictment of the Indian New Deal. The report called for the dismemberment and ultimate liquidation of the Indian Bureau, concluding with thirty-three recommendations, each calling for the elimination of certain bureau service functions.[4] In 1943, the House of Representatives adopted a resolution sponsored by Karl Mundt of South Dakota, calling for a separate investigation of Indian affairs. The report that followed this investigation insisted that the goal of policy was to encourage the Indian "to take his place in the white man's community on the white man's level and with the white man's opportunity and security status." The report was also highly critical of the bureau for failing to provide adequate economic and educational opportunities and for not encouraging the removal of restrictive regulations on Indians. In direct challenge to Commissioner Collier, the report suggested that the Indians be allowed to withdraw from the Indian Reorganization Act through the electoral process.[5]

Collier soon realized that Congress would not allocate to the bureau all the monies needed for Indian services for economic development, education, and health. In bureaucratic self-defense, in February 1944 the commissioner recommended to Congress that the BIA be "relieved of federal supervision" over tribespeople who met certain parameters and concentrate its responsibilities on fewer tribes. In testimony in 1944, Collier classified Indians into three categories according to their "level of acculturation": (1) 93,000 Indians; (2) 124,000 semi-acculturated Indians; and (3) 150,000 acculturated Indians. Those so-called acculturated Indians in the third category were to be "released" from bureau supervision entirely. Among the tribes Collier listed as acculturated peoples "capable" of operating without the bureau were the Wisconsin Indians at the Tomah agency, which included the Oneidas. Culturally myopic and southwest-oriented in his judgments of "Indianness," Collier, in his political compromise with Congress, had given generous credibility to the postwar movement for withdrawal of federal services from the Iroquois. At the same hearing, he urged the creation of an Indian Claims Commission in an effort to solve the Indian "problem." The New Deal had gone stale. A new age of termination, which stressed assimilation into "mainstream America," was now under way.[6]

Instead of pushing for Oneida termination, between 1952 and 1956 the BIA focused on Menominee termination. Just as Collier had to abandon his New Deal positions under the threats of congressional budgetary cuts, postwar bureau officials had to signal retreat as well. In hearings before the

Senate Post Office and Civil Service Committee on February 8, 1947, under severe congressional pressure to cut the bureau's budget by "emancipating" some Indian groups, acting commissioner of Indian affairs William Zimmerman Jr. proceeded to divide the Indians into three categories, much as Collier had done three years earlier. Zimmerman believed that the first group of ten tribes, which included the Menominees and the Iroquois in New York, could be "released" immediately from federal supervision. The second group of twenty included the Indians of the Great Lakes Agency, including the Oneidas and other Wisconsin tribes, who, according to the acting commissioner, could be "released" in two to ten years. A third group was composed of thirty-five other tribes who could be "freed" from control sometime in the future. Zimmerman, as had Collier before him, defined criteria for Indian Bureau withdrawal: degree of acculturation, economic resources and condition of the tribe, willingness of the tribe to be relieved of federal supervision, and state willingness to take over federal responsibilities.[7]

In the same year, Senator Hugh Butler of Nebraska introduced three bills affecting the Iroquois. One of the bills called for the final computation of the annuity provided by the United States to the Iroquois, which included the Oneidas of Wisconsin. Although the other two bills dealt exclusively with state criminal and civil jurisdiction over Iroquois in New York, the Wisconsin Oneidas made their presence felt at the federal hearings held in March 1948. At the session, Senator Arthur Watkins, a pro-terminationist legislator, asked Andrew Beechtree, representing the Wisconsin Oneidas, why his tribesmen were willing to continue to collect the fifty-two cent annuity per year from the federal government instead of agreeing to a larger lump-sum final settlement. Beechtree insisted that it was because of Indian pride. Beechtree had previously indicated: "Yet, you would lose the identity of this Indian because someone seems to think that the Federal outlay of approximately five thousand dollars a year in the execution of this treaty is endangering the economic structure of this great Nation."[8]

By the 1950s, the Wisconsin Oneidas were in desperate shape economically and politically. Although New Deal repurchasing had resulted in holdings of slightly more than two thousand acres of tribal lands, the

Oneida government literally operated "out of some councillor's garage." There was little money to pay outstanding bills, no salaries for officers except for the meager per diem payments for the once-a-month tribal meeting, and no reimbursement to individuals and/or to official tribal delegations sent to Washington, Madison, or regional gatherings.[9] Separated by religion, geography, and history, Oneidas struggled to survive on a landbase divided in checkerboard pattern among individual owners as a result of the Dawes Act. Since the 1887 act, at the death of an allottee, lands had been further divided into even smaller parcels. Over time, these so-called heirship lands came to be jointly owned by more than one Indian who had inherited equal portions of the original allotment under provisions of the Dawes Act. By the 1950s, in some instances, hundreds of Indians held an interest in the same allotment. BIA regulations, which Oneidas and other Indians criticized as excessive, required the consent of a majority of owners before heirship lands could be partitioned and sold. The land often sat idle or was leased, because in many cases heirs could not be found. Congressional bills of the 1950s tried to deal with this heirship mess, which still affects American Indians, by removing much of the regulation on these lands; however, these bills provided little or no protection against alienation of lands from Indian hands.[10]

The Oneida Nation of Indians of Wisconsin also had to contend with the new commissioner of Indian affairs, Dillon S. Myer, appointed to office by President Harry Truman in 1950. Myer, a career administrator who had served in numerous posts in the Department of Agriculture, had headed the War Relocation Authority from 1942 to 1944 and had been a commissioner of the Federal Housing Authority since 1946. Strangely, it was Myer's wartime experience with another minority group, the Japanese Americans, that led Secretary of the Interior Oscar Chapman to recommend him to President Truman for commissioner of Indian affairs. As head of the War Relocation Authority, Myer had supervised the tragic removal and detention of tens of thousands of Japanese Americans, who were held at special camps, some of which were located on Indian reservations. In suggesting that Truman appoint Myer, Chapman discussed his qualifications for the job: "He did an outstanding job in the maintenance and relocation of the Japanese evacuated from the Pacific Coast region, which program was fraught with many troublesome aspects, including the maintenance of good public relations during the emotionalism of war." Chapman added: "I feel that this total experience well fits him for the position of commissioner of Indian affairs."[11]

Almost immediately upon assuming office, Myer focused his agency's attention on the step-by-step transfer of bureau functions. Building on early Interior Department plans for federal withdrawal, Myer was also aided by the postwar climate of the country. The cold war with the Soviet Union and the early days of the Korean War had produced a sense of extreme American nationalism and lower tolerance of differences, both outside and inside American society. Increasingly, many Americans saw Indian reservations not as Native people's homelands but as strange anomalies irrelevant to modern times. Moreover, the increased awareness of civil rights and growing repudiation of segregation during the Truman administration helped reinforce the overly optimistic belief that reservation life segregated Indian peoples from the benefits of joining the mainstream of American life.[12]

Other factors also aided Myer's policies. Commissioners Collier and Zimmerman had previously indicated the readiness of certain tribes for federal withdrawal. In addition, Commissioner Myer had at his disposal massive surveys that reinforced his position. The Special Presidential Commission on the Organization of the Executive Branch of the Government, better known as the Hoover Commission, filed a task force report on Indian affairs in 1949 that, among other suggestions, advocated the transfer of federal programs to the states, urged policies that would encourage and assist Indians to leave the reservation and enter the mainstream of American life, and called for the "ending of tax exemption and of privileged status for Indian owned land and the payment of the taxes at the same rates as for other property in the area."[13] Myer's predecessor as commissioner, John Nichols, a former member of this task force, had announced in early 1949 that "the time should soon arrive when Indian peoples would be dealt with as other Americans and that all special designations and treaty restrictions would be set aside."[14] Myer had also contracted with Princeton University in 1950 to furnish an independent and detailed analysis of bureau functions in order to help determine a national

Indian program. The report of this academic group concluded that Indians should be given services that were ordinarily provided for other citizens by other state, local, or federal agencies. It recommended that the bureau assist the "Indians in the process of assimilation into society as co-equals of other citizens — a process which should result in the eventual termination of Bureau activities."[15]

The Myer program of termination was aided substantially by a new BIA rapprochement with Congress. The Indian Service cooperated with Congress at every turn, even at a loss of its supervisory role in its dealings with certain tribes and the transfer of all health-care administration from its control. Secretary Chapman had certain qualms initially about House Joint Resolution 490, introduced by Congresswoman Reva Bosone of Utah in 1950, which required the BIA to designate tribes for termination and produce a workable, two-stage federal withdrawal program by January 1952. Yet, in the end, Secretary Myer and the commissioner enthusiastically endorsed the program, with Myer and his successors giving the tribes the false impression that termination was inevitable for all Indians.[16] In 1952, Congressional Resolution 698 required that the bureau name "tribes, bands, or groups of Indians now qualified for full management of their own affairs" and recommend "legislation for removal of legal disability of Indians by reason of guardianship by the federal government."[17] The BIA's lengthy response, which appeared in House Report 2503, answered the congressional request by naming the Wisconsin Oneidas as being ready for termination.[18] Instead of pushing forward on Oneida termination between 1952 and 1956, the BIA focused on Menominee termination.

The cooperation between congressional leaders and Interior Department personnel continued even after Myer left office in 1953. Glenn Emmons, the new commissioner, an opponent of the New Deal and an ally of pro-terminationist New Mexico senator Clinton Anderson, agreed with much of Myer's thinking. During his early tenure at the BIA, Emmons joined with congressmen who sought to dismantle the bureaucracy of Indian affairs, discourage Indian dependence, and promote Indian "progress" by assimilating Indians into mainstream white society. He believed, as did Myer before him, that Congress should speed up removing the excessive restrictions on Indian trust lands, which even many Indians

182 A Nation within a Nation

viewed as overly paternalistic.[19] On August 15, 1953, Congress passed Public Law 280. With a few exceptions, the act transferred criminal and civil jurisdiction over Indian affairs to Wisconsin and four other states. The Oneida Nation of Indians of Wisconsin was one of the Indian nations directly affected by this legislation.[20]

Besides jurisdictional transfer, by September 1952 the BIA had developed an Oneida "withdrawal programming report." The Great Lakes Area Field Office, which prepared the report, concluded that the Oneida "tribe is ready for complete withdrawal of Bureau responsibility for services and termination of trusteeship responsibilities." The report insisted that the BIA was furnishing "very little service to these Indians" and that numerous Oneidas "have demonstrated ability to get along in the competitive world." The report, however, warned that there were two drawbacks to complete termination: (1) the need for legislation to "assist in clearing the land status," or more specifically the heirship problem; and (2) "treaty obligations involving annuity payment."[21]

One month later, in October 1952, BIA officials began to sell their withdrawal program to the Oneidas. In response, the Oneida Tribal Executive Council, headed by Dennison Hill, Irene Moore, Charles A. Hill, and Mamie Smith, expressed dissatisfaction with the ability of the political structure created under the Indian Reorganization Act to solve the Oneidas' many problems. The Tribal Executive Council maintained that the Indians' major needs were housing as well as economic and educational programs, not new termination legislation. They also expressed their dissatisfaction with the shifting nature of BIA policies from year to year and asserted that tribal consent was necessary before federal withdrawal could take effect.[22]

Throughout 1953, the bureau intensified its campaign to convince both Indian and Wisconsin politicians of the value of Oneida termination. Once again, Don C. Foster, the BIA area director; E. J. Riley, the administrative officer of the BIA's Great Lakes Consolidated Agency; Commissioner Myer; and Acting Commissioner W. Barton Greenwood worked out a "deal to offer the Oneidas a $60,000 lump-sum payment to commute the Canandaigua Treaty."[23] Myer, writing to Wisconsin senator Joseph McCarthy, tried to counteract the unfavorable publicity about the

BIA and its policies toward the Oneidas. He told McCarthy that he and the Oneida Tribal Executive Council were jointly negotiating for the "complete independence of the Oneida Tribe of any need for the special services and the supervision of the Bureau."[24] On May 15, bureau officials replied to a questionnaire prepared by the House Committee on Interior and Insular Affairs. The BIA's summary statement reiterated that the Oneidas were "ready for complete withdrawal of Bureau responsibility for services and for termination of trusteeship responsibilities," and once again raised the problems of unclear land status and treaty obligations involving annuity payment. Yet, the BIA's answers to the questionnaire gave the impression that complete Oneida termination was inevitable.[25]

In December 1953, Riley held a major meeting with Oneida tribal leaders at Parish Hall of the Episcopal Church of the Holy Apostles in Oneida, Wisconsin. At the meeting, he presented a proposed congressional bill "to settle once and for all, the problem of perpetual annuities," which, according to Riley, was "costing his office $2,200 a year to pay the Oneidas their $1,800 yearly annuity." Riley insisted that the proposal was "not one dreamed up by the Bureau of Indian Affairs"; he placed the blame on Congress, which was seeking a solution to what it called the "Indian problem." After maintaining that the bill did not abrogate the Canandaigua Treaty, the BIA official further pointed out to the Indians that "many Indian tribes had shown a desire to withdraw from the protective custody of the Federal government" and cited the cases of the recent move in that direction by tribes of California and Oregon. Despite his insistence that the legislation under consideration did not pertain to federal withdrawal, Riley, under intense questioning by tribal leaders, tried to convince the assembled Indians "that the Bureau of Indian Affairs is going to continue." Significantly, during this questioning, Riley discussed the proposed Menominee termination bill as further proof of congressional intentions to enforce termination. The Oneidas answered Congress by voting 53–0 at the meeting to reject a final cash settlement of annuities under the Treaty of Canandaigua.[26]

Despite this rejection, talk of fully terminating the Oneida Nation of Indians of Wisconsin continued until as late as 1957. This movement fueled efforts at terminating the Oneidas' Wisconsin Indian neighbors, the

Menominees. On January 4, 1954, Assistant Secretary of the Interior Orme
Lewis wrote to Vice President Richard Nixon, listing all the tribes that the
Interior Department considered capable of termination. Two weeks later,
bills calling for the termination of the Klamaths, Menominees, and other
tribes were introduced into Congress. Following Lewis's memorandum
nearly to the letter, these bills, which became law, called for the end of the
federal-Indian relationship and federal services for these tribes.[27]

The Oneidas, despite their earlier unanimous opposition to termination at the December 1953 meeting at the Parish Hall, were soon weakened
by severe political divisions that erupted in the early 1950s. Although the
vast majority of Oneidas continued to oppose commutation of the
Canandaigua Treaty, the issue of termination became intertwined with
the volatile political world of Oneida. Throughout the early part of the
decade, the tribal council at Oneida, headed by Julius Danforth and later
Dennison Hill, Irene Moore, and Mamie Smith, faced major political
battles with a group of powerful Oneidas living in Milwaukee. These
urban Oneidas, who had chosen the city for employment opportunities,
were led by Oscar Archiquette and Morris Wheelock, the founders of the
original tribal elected system at Oneida under the Indian Reorganization
Act of the 1930s.[28]

The Milwaukee group saw the political advantage of leading the fight
against termination and using the issue to come to power again at Oneida.
This same group, which had opted for economic development and tribal
political reorganization in the 1930s at the expense of pursuing tribal land
claims, by the 1950s had done a complete about-face. Now they were
among the leaders of the Oneida land-claims movement and were pas-
sionately urging the preservation of the Canandaigua Treaty. This long-
established Milwaukee community had never lost contact with kin in the
Green Bay area. Moreover, they had established an Oneida "fact-finding
committee" to investigate the actions of their political opponents at
Oneida in the 1950s. Although denigrated by the tribal council as the
"fraud-finding committee," the Milwaukee Oneidas played an important
role in the Oneida fight against termination during the Eisenhower
administration.[29]

A frequent correspondent to the commissioner of Indian affairs, Archiquette would repeatedly file Oneida objections to policies and policy-makers. Although largely self-taught, he would not hesitate to do battle with Commissioner Emmons in arenas far distant from Green Bay. By the mid-1950s, Archiquette, along with Wheelock and Chauncey and Ruth Baird, had developed a strategy to counter efforts at termination: they would find out the itineraries of key BIA personnel and then follow them to meetings, where the Oneidas would ask embarrassing questions, disrupt the gatherings altogether, or just keep tabs on the progress of termination legislation. It was precisely this strategy that contributed importantly to the BIA's reduced efforts to push termination for the Oneidas.[30]

The culmination of federal efforts to terminate the Oneidas occurred in the fall of 1956 at Des Moines, Iowa. Three members of the tribal council, Moore, Danforth, and Cecil Skenandore, attended an Indian affairs conference sponsored under the auspices of the BIA's Minneapolis area office. The meeting, which had been planned since the early spring, became a forum for Commissioner Emmons and his staff's efforts to terminate the Winnebagos (Ho-Chunks), Chippewas, Potawatomis, Stockbridge Munsees, and Oneidas. From October 18 through 20, the commissioner; BIA Area Director R. D. Holz; his assistant R. M. Kelley; program officers M. P. Mangan and Peter Walz; and Superintendent Riley pointed to the Menominees and presented termination as congressionally mandated and inevitable. Using the Menominee example as a model, Mangan, realizing the Indians' concerns about improving the disastrous conditions of Wisconsin tribesmen, described the intended program in glowing economic terms:

> The rules are Congress would provide in [the legislation] a period of years to accomplish this termination. For those tribes who go through the process in order to instruct those who want to get training and to help adjust to living without special status as Indians, as is now going on at Menominee, they (the government) would provide this special, very intensive training and educational program. A million dollars a year is authorized now. Under that we have a contract with the State of Wisconsin for over ¼ million dollars a year for the Menominee program. We have people down at the University of Wisconsin; other people are on

job training and on vocational training programs over at Green Bay, at
Milwaukee. They may get several years [for this] program. They are furnished transportation with their family to the training center and subsistence cost. That program will last as long as this termination program,
for 4½ years. That is intended to catch everybody that either graduated
from high school or already have their families if they want more training and it is intended that they get intensive training so that they will be
on a sound economic basis after this transition period is ended. They will
have a good background to provide for their own families. It is a program
with more facilities than they have had for several years. Would that fill
the needs to catch up for your people and those in trainable years? The
Congress provides that when this transition period ends, that the status
of these people as Indians will end and they have the same status as any
other citizen of the U.S. It does cut them off for help or benefits of general appropriations for Indians.[31]

Moore, Danforth, and Skenandore had arrived at the meeting with
their own carefully worked out agenda. At a tribal council meeting held
three days prior to the Des Moines conference, they had agreed to push for
federal monies for postsecondary education, for the improvement of the
drainage on land acquired during the New Deal, and for the building of a
convalescent home for tribal members. Curious as well as fearful about the
policy of termination, the Indians agreed to raise the issue of what could
be done with their "CCC building in the future if Oneidas are disbanded."
If federal withdrawal should occur, the Oneidas, financially strapped at the
time, agreed among themselves that the seventeen-acre CCC site would be
best turned over to Wisconsin and held in trust by the state as the "Oneida
Memorial Park."[32]

Immediately upon gaining an audience with Commissioner Emmons at
Des Moines, Moore, Danforth, and Skenandore pushed on these matters.
Although the commissioner indicated a willingness to lobby with Congress
to increase Indian higher-education appropriations, he refused the Oneida
request to waive repayment of their already-outstanding educational loans.
Emmons insisted that the building of a convalescent home for the Oneida
aged was "something that could be worked out with the state." The com-

missioner then agreed to push legislatively for the transfer of the seventeen-acre Oneida CCC property to Wisconsin after federal withdrawal, provided state officials and Oneidas agreed to the move. The BIA officials then rejected supporting the drainage project; the BIA considered it a county and state project because of the checkerboard nature of white and Indian land patterns at Oneida.[33]

Concern for the poor economic conditions at Oneida were utmost in the minds of the three Indian delegates.[34] Danforth explained and emphasized to the commissioner that there just was not "enough land to go around to those who live on these assignments" and that too many Indians wanted a share "of what is called tribal land." He and the other Oneidas complained that they did not even have money to purchase needed farm equipment.[35]

The Oneidas, unable to secure individual bank loans because of limited collateral resulting from poverty and because title to their small land-base remained in tribal hands, were so economically hard-pressed that their delegates at Des Moines even raised the possibility of obtaining individual fee patents on tribal land. Moore, herself a dairy farmer working forty acres of tribal lands, contracting seventy acres of allotted lands, and leasing twenty acres, indicated that as many as 75 percent of the Oneidas would want fee patents to their land.[36] Yet Moore was also a shrewd and realistic Indian politician, and she was not advocating this terminationist course of action but indicating the size of the economic crisis at Oneida. She understood, as had Oneida politicians before her, that her Indian political opponents such as Wheelock and Archiquette would use any hint of cooperation or collaboration with the BIA against her and her council. Although in a desperate crisis, neither Moore nor other Oneidas were willing to sacrifice their historic land claim against New York state, which they were afraid would be jeopardized if they agreed to federal withdrawal.[37]

It is important to note that Commissioner Emmons and his staff had inadvertently undermined their "sell" of termination. The Oneida delegation had heard similar promises before. Toward the end of the conference with the Oneidas, Emmons suggested that what the Oneidas really wanted was to be just like the white home owners in Des Moines, earning their way and paying real estate taxes on their lots. Because taxation of Indian lands had been a vehicle of white dispossession of Oneidas in both New York in the first half of the nineteenth century and subsequently under allotment policies in Wisconsin, the Oneida delegates reacted negatively to Emmons's statement. Skenandore questioned him, asking: "Could it be set up so that if they [the Oneidas] had a patent that they couldn't sell it?" Emmons's reply alarmed the Indians and undoubtedly reminded them of past troubles: "From a law standpoint if an Indian says, 'I am competent and I want a fee patent,' you can't turn around and tie him up with restrictions. The government does not have any right to tell you what you have to do for the next 10 years."[38]

BIA officials then further exacerbated the situation. Seemingly oblivious of Indian perceptions of the BIA, Commissioner Emmons suggested that the Oneidas speed up termination by working with the bureau and Congress to pass a tribal resolution in support of federal withdrawal legislation. Superintendent Riley then brought up what he referred to as the "one stumbling block," namely the Oneidas' refusal to accept the one lump payment of $60,600 in lieu of the Oneida annuity under the Canandaigua Treaty. Although the Wisconsin tribesmen had by 1956 agreed to let the annuity accumulate rather than take the fifty-two cents per person per annum, the Oneidas were unanimous now in opposing a payoff of what they considered a sacrosanct treaty; they also feared jeopardizing any land claims or other suits pending before the Indian Claims Commission. Despite assurances by Emmons and Mangan that nobody "is going to deny the continual obligation, either by annual payments or by exposing the United States to a court case on your part," the three Oneida delegates went home even more convinced that termination was a threat to tribal existence.[39] The delegates had gone to Des Moines with a belief that termination was inevitable and that the issuance of fee patents was one possible solution to their tribal economic crisis, but they returned completely opposed to these federal initiatives.

Meanwhile, Archiquette, who had traveled to Des Moines and kept tabs on the three delegates, soon saw the political advantage of presenting his Milwaukee-based Oneidas as the "anti-terminationist" group. He'd been denied an audience with Commissioner Emmons at the Des Moines meeting, and Archiquette used this rebuff to solidify his image as a defender of the Oneidas against the BIA federal withdrawal plan. Though not invited, Archiquette had learned at Des Moines that bureau officials had once again suggested that the Oneidas work with and support congressional efforts in this direction.[40] Thus, now the two major factions in the Oneida polity had come to the same conclusion about United States Indian policies of the Truman-Eisenhower administrations: federal withdrawal was a mistake. Suspicious of bureau intentions and aware that real estate tax delinquency had contributed to the loss of more than sixty-five thousand acres in Wisconsin, both Oneida groups — reservation and Milwaukee leadership — rejected termination.

Although the tribal council and the Milwaukee-based group were both significant, it is important to note the United States Congress did not fail to terminate the Oneidas simply because the Oneidas took a stand. Unlike their Wisconsin neighbors the Menominees, who owned more than 200,000 acres in 1954, the Oneidas held only 2,209 acres of tribal lands. The Oneidas owned no timber land, and they had a major heirship land problem. In the mid-1950s, the Oneidas had not even a long-shot chance for economic self-sufficiency. Their poor economic condition, which had led more than half of the 3,500 Oneidas to migrate from the environs of Green Bay, stood in sharp contrast to the Menominees' and undoubtedly made the Wisconsin congressional delegation think twice about carrying out termination, for fear that the state would assume an increased financial burden.

Thus, fearing repeating the mistakes of the past, the Oneidas rejected termination in the fall of 1956. Although federal efforts continued in this direction for another two years, the Oneidas had weathered the storm and survived as Iroquois people in their Wisconsin homeland. Despite being politically divided, the Oneidas had remembered their past. Emmons's arguments in favor of termination appeared to them to be a carbon copy of the promises made to the Wisconsin Oneidas about their lands at the time of the Dawes Act. It is significant that the Menominees had never been allotted and had never faced the same tragic experiences under the Dawes Act and under the workings of the federal competency commission during World War I. In addition, the Menominees' major claim had been settled by an official award from the United States Court of Claims in

1951, unlike the major Oneida land claim, which still has not been resolved. Fearing undermining their claims, which they had been pursuing for more than a century and a half, the Oneidas rejected a one-time lump-sum final payment of their annuity. Thus, the Oneidas avoided the same fate as their Wisconsin Indian neighbor to the northwest.

Notes

1. (Wisconsin) League of Women Voters, *Report* (Appleton, WI: 1956).

2. "A Report on the Labor Force and the Employment Conditions of the Oneida Indians," special study with approval from Oneida leaders of Wisconsin by research assistant Douglas Thorson, University of Wisconsin–Madison, October 1958.

3. House Committee on Indian Affairs, *Bill to Authorize Investigation of Indian Affairs: Hearings on H.R. 166*, Part I, 78th Cong., 1st sess., 1943, 16–17; Part II, 78th Cong., 2d sess., 1944, 52–91.

4. Senate Committee on Indian Affairs, *Survey of Conditions of Indian Affairs, Partial Report*, No. 310, 78-1, serial 10756, 1943; Senate Committee on Indian Affairs, *Survey of Conditions of Indian Affairs, Supplemental Report*, 1944.

5. U.S. Congress, *House Report No. 20910*, 78-2, serial 10848 (Washington, D.C., 1945).

6. House Committee on Indian Affairs, *Bill to Authorize Investigation of Indian Affairs*. See the excellent works by Kenneth R. Philp, "Termination: A Legacy of the Indian New Deal," *Western Historical Quarterly* 14 (April 1983): 165–180; and Philp's *Termination Revisited: American Indians on the Trail to Self-Determination, 1933–1953* (Lincoln: University of Nebraska Press, 1999).

7. Senate Committee on Civil Service, *Officers and Employees of Federal Government: Hearings on S.R. 41*, 80th Cong., 1st sess., 1947, 544–547. See also Philp, *Termination Revisited*, 71–75.

8. Senate Subcommittee of the Committee of the Interior and Insular Affairs, *New York Indians: Hearings on S. 1683, S. 1686, S. 1687*, 80th Cong., 2d sess., 1948, 45.

9. Cecil Skenandore, interview by Laurence M. Hauptman, July 23, 1985, Oneida, WI. Skenandore was a member of the Oneida tribal council in the 1950s.

10. Norbert Hill Sr., interview by Laurence M. Hauptman, July 28, 1982, Oneida, WI. In October 1978, I attended a meeting of the Oneida Tribal Business Committee with the late Mr. Hill, Oneida tribal chairman in the 1960s, in which the BIA and tribal representatives were still dealing with the question of heirship lands.

11. Oscar Chapman to Harry Truman, March 18, 1950, Truman MSS., OF6-C, TL. For more on Myer, see Richard Drinnon, *Keeper of the Concentration Camps: Dillon S. Myer and American Racism* (Berkeley: University of California Press, 1987).

12. Larry W. Burt, *Tribalism in Crisis* (Albuquerque: University of New Mexico Press, 1982), 1–13; Donald Fixico, *Termination and Relocation: Federal Indian Policy, 1945–1960* (Albuquerque: University of New Mexico Press, 1986), 49–69.

13. *Report of the Committee on Indian Affairs of the Hoover Commission*, Philleo Nash MSS., Box 44, TL.

14. Quoted in "Indian Commissioner Sees Tribes Treated Like Other American Citizens in Future," *New York Times*, May 5, 1949.

15. Quoted in Lawrence J. Hasse, "Termination and Assimilation: Federal Indian Policy, 1943 to 1961" (Ph.D. dissertation, Washington State University, 1974): 127.

16. Dillon S. Myer to Senator Herbert H. Lehman, Lehman MSS., "Indians" (American), J-WO-100-14, CU.

17. U.S. Congress, *House Report No. 2503*, 1952, 2–3.

18. U.S. Congress, *House Report No. 2680: Report with Respect to the House Resolution Authorizing the Committee on Interior and Insular Affairs to Conduct an Investigation of the Bureau of Indian Affairs*, 83rd Cong., 2d sess., 1954, 3–4.

19. Burt, *Tribalism in Crisis*, 15–30.

20. U.S. Congress, *House Concurrent Resolution No. 108. Stat. 67* (1953): 588–590. The origins of this act dated to at least 1949. U.S. Congress, *House Report No. 1362: Subjecting Indians and Indian Reservations in the State of Wisconsin to the Laws of the State, with Certain Exceptions*, 1949, with attached bill H.R. 2736, Alexander Wiley MSS., Box 50, "Indians," Wisconsin Historical Society, Madison, WI. Norbert Hill Sr., interview by Laurence M. Hauptman, July 28, 1982, Oneida, WI; Ruth Baird, interview by Hauptman, June 23, 1983, Green Bay, WI; Loretta Ellis Metoxen, interview by Hauptman, June 22, 1983, Oneida, WI.

21. Great Lakes Area Field Office, Ashland, WI, to Committee on Interior and Insular Affairs on Oneida Reservation, *Withdrawal Programming Report for Oneida Tribe of Wisconsin*, made September 25, 1952, submitted June 19, 1953, BIA CCF, 1949–1956, File # 17112-1952-077, RGLCA, RG 75, NA.

22. Oneida Executive Council to Dillon Myer, November 18, 1952, BIA Central Files, 1949–1956 #17112-1952-077, RGLCA, RG 75, NA.

23. Dillon S. Myer to Oneida Tribal Executive Council, February 10, 1953; Don C. Foster to E. J. Riley, February 19, 1953; Foster to W. Barton Greenwood, May 21, 1953; Foster to G. Warren Spaulding, June 25 1953; Greenwood to Congressman John W. Byrnes, October 19, 1953, BIA CCF, 1949–1956, File #17112-1952-077, RGLCA, RG 75, NA.

24. Dillon S. Myer to Senator Joseph McCarthy, March 19, 1953, BIA CCF, 1949–1956, File #17112-1952-077, RGLCA, RG 75, NA.

25. Reply (of May 15, 1953) to House Committee on Interior and Insular Affairs, *Questionnaire on Tribal Organization, etc., Supplement to Withdrawal Programming Report of Aug. 5, 1952*, BIA Central Files, 1949–1956, #17112-1952-077, RGLCA, RG 75, NA.

26. "Oneidas Again Face Problem of Annuity; Reject Offer," *Green Bay Press-Gazette*, December 18, 1953.

27. Orme Lewis to Richard M. Nixon, January 4, 1954, Box 43, Philleo Nash MSS., TL; U.S. Congress, *Congressional Record*, 83rd Cong., 2d sess., 1954, 100, 322–323, 407, 410.

28. Norbert Hill Sr., interview by Laurence M. Hauptman, July 28, 1982, Milwaukee, WI; Ruth Baird, interview by Hauptman, June 23, 1983, Milwaukee, WI; Nancy Lurie, interview by Hauptman, June 20, 1983, Milwaukee, WI. For an early academic portrait of the Milwaukee Indian community, see Robert E. Ritzenthaler and Mary Sellers, "Indians in an Urban Situation," *Wisconsin Archeologist* 36 (1955): 147–161.

29. Ibid.

30. Oscar Archiquette to commissioner of Indian affairs, February 1, 1954, with attached resolution of the Oneida Fact Finding Board, 1952; Glenn Emmons to Archiquette, February 23, 1954; Archiquette to Emmons, [November 20?] 1956; Chief, Branch of Credit Memorandum to Peter Walz, December 10, 1956; Thomas Reia to Oscar Archiquette, January 7, 1957, BIA CCF, 1949–1956, #17112-1952-0771, RGLCA, RG 75, NA. Baird interview, June 23, 1983; Hill interview, July 28, 1982. Oscar Archiquette, interview by Robert Venables, July 14, 1971, Shell Lake, WI.

31. Transcript of Indian Tribal Conference, Des Moines, IA, October 18, 1956, Oneida Indian Historical Society, Oneida, WI.

32. "Things to be brought up in Iowa," Oneida Tribal Memorandum, October 15, 1956, Oneida Indian Historical Society, Oneida, WI.

33. Transcript of Des Moines conference.

34. Skenandore interview, July 23, 1985.

35. Transcript of Des Moines conference.

36. Ibid.

37. Ibid.

38. Ibid.

39. Ibid.

40. Hill interview, July 28, 1982.

Federal Indian Policies and the Wisconsin Oneidas

From the Indian Reorganization Act (1934) to the Indian Self-Determination and Education Assistance Act (1975)

by Loretta R. Webster

BY 1930, THE ONEIDA TRIBAL GOVERNMENT was composed of chiefs whom many members viewed as having little or no power and acting at times as mere tokens of the federal government. The Dawes Act and the federal policy of assimilation had torn tribes apart and worn them down. Oneida people were models of "assimilation," yet no amount of education or hard work could dull the discrimination in and around the reservation. More than sixty thousand acres of the lands originally allotted to tribal members were now in the hands of successful white farmers.[1] The Oneidas who continued to live on the reservation found little or no employment except for seasonal jobs. A few who lived on the reservation could find full-time work in Green Bay, on the railroad, or in construction, but most had to leave the reservation to find jobs to support their families. Well more than the majority of Oneida reservation families lived on a near-subsistence economy: canning and drying summer vegetables, meat, fish, and fruit for the winter months; hunting for fresh meat in the winter; gathering wood for their cooking and heating; and relying on the church and its benefactors for clothes, household items, and other amenities. Little or no cash was part of this subsistence economy. The joke on the Oneida reservation was that the "Great Depression" in the United States actually raised their economy, because it brought stable WPA jobs to many Oneida families for a few years.[2]

The Meriam Report of 1928 chronicled the poor health, housing, education, and general living conditions on reservations throughout the United States. Average life expectancy for American Indians was around thirty-five years of age, and the dropout rate in high school was astronomical. Long-standing federal policy, which eliminated the Oneida family support systems and the language and cultural base through relocation, boarding schools, and the like, had generated many abusive behaviors in the family and community. The report recommended reforming the deplorable life on the reservations by increasing funding for health and education, ending the allotment policy, and encouraging tribal self-government.[3] These recommendations were eventually codified by the U.S. government in the Indian Reorganization Act (IRA) of 1934.[4] About this same time, the Johnson O'Malley Act provided special "educational funds" for Indian public school children and established the blood quantum level of one-quarter for services.[5] This one-quarter blood quantum level became the basis for Oneida enrollment in their constitution formulated under the Indian Reorganization Act of 1934.[6]

The Oneida Nation of Indians of Wisconsin was formed and accepted its constitution under the IRA in 1936. They became a "federally recognized tribal government" on December 21, 1936, when the U.S. secretary of the interior approved their constitution.[7] There was a close debate over the decision to accept an IRA constitution. The Oneida people agreed, in part, because the IRA authorized the federal government to accept lands in trust for tribal governments and their people, and even provided funds to repurchase lands lost through the allotment period. After the Oneida constitution was approved, the Bureau of Indian Affairs (BIA) purchased approximately 1,500 acres of land and put it in trust for the Oneida tribe. The title to these first purchases was held by the United States of America in trust for the Oneida Tribe of Indians of Wisconsin. A survey of the status of the title of lands within the Oneida reservation, taken shortly after the first officers were elected under the IRA, showed that 92 percent of the original 65,400-acre reservation was owned by non-Oneidas. This survey included the 1,500 acres that had recently been purchased for the tribal government.

The IRA provided the Oneidas with their present form of elected government. It also formulated the Indian preference rule in hiring, established a revolving loan fund for tribal development, and generally included other provisions directed toward improving the lot of American Indians and strengthening tribal self-government. The first chairman under the new Oneida constitution was Morris Wheelock, who was elected for a one-year term. As with any new project in Oneida, the newly elected government was slow to fully implement or even understand the meaning of the powers outlined in the boilerplate constitution.[8] IRA constitutions adopted by tribes across the country all read basically the same, with heavy control and oversight by the Department of the Interior through the BIA. Access to financial resources was also controlled by the BIA. The BIA revolving loan fund may have looked like a pot of gold for the elected volunteer IRA governments, but it was hopelessly inadequate when tribal governments attempted to use it to pull their reservation economy out of the mire of subsistence. It is hard to imagine the financial constraints under which the Oneida Executive Committee worked for decades after the IRA constitution was approved. For example, L. Gordon McLester III was elected as a councilman on the expanded Business Committee in 1969. He indicated that the nine elected members received five dollars a month to attend meetings, and occasionally his five dollar check was returned to him because of insufficient funds.[9]

The history of Oneida economic development shows that raising the level of income for Oneida people is closely entwined with the tribal ownership of land. A BIA report on tribal economic development stated that in 1937, the Oneida tribal government had no source of funds. The same year, the average annual individual Oneida income was $369.17 per year, much of this coming from farming, work in Green Bay and De Pere, and seasonal employment. Most of the Oneida homes were considered substandard, lacking electricity, running water, indoor bathroom facilities, or adequate space. Of the 65,400 acres designated as the Oneida reservation in 1838, the tribe and its members held only 3,644.76 acres by 1937.[10] During the Great Depression, the federal government provided a WPA project on the Oneida reservation, which provided stable jobs for many Oneidas from 1935 to 1941. This WPA project generated many volumes of stories, which the Oneida Cultural Heritage Department and the Oneida Language Program have cataloged for access by community members.[11] Oneidas who lived on the reservation indicated that their standard of living actually got better during the Depression because of the stable WPA jobs.

The economic situation of Oneida changed little until the 1960s, when the Johnson administration advanced the Economic Opportunity Act.

Under this act, for the first time in America's history, economically depressed communities such as reservations were provided grants to do their own planning and provide services to their constituencies. In 1965 the Head Start program began in the Parish Hall. In addition to adding many human service programs for the community, the Oneida leaders took advantage of this federal funding by developing one of the first Indian-owned industrial parks in the state. Through loans and grants from the Bureau of Indian Affairs and Department of Commerce (Economic Development Administration or EDA), the Oneida tribal leaders improved twenty-seven acres of heirship land located right in the middle of the Green Bay Industrial Park. This area became the Oneida Industrial Park, but because there was little or no money to do the full-time promotion necessary to fill it, the development stood virtually empty for many years.[12]

In 1970 the Oneidas constructed a building in their industrial park and started the Standing Stone Corporation. Money to start the corporation, a musical instrument repair business, was raised partially through selling shares to tribal members all over the country. A low-interest business loan was also negotiated from the BIA. Although it was generally felt that the BIA loan would not provide needed working capital to take the business to a profitable level, this was the tribe's only chance to develop a viable business.[13] As was the case with so many underfunded tribal businesses all over the country, the Standing Stone Corporation went bankrupt, in 1975. At this time, the Oneida tribal budget was around a million dollars, but it was all federal contracts that left no discretionary money for investment in businesses or lands that would generate their own funds for the Oneidas. If money could have been invested into Standing Stone, there would have been a good possibility for success. An elected Business Committee, which was still composed of volunteers, provided oversight for the many federal programs and tribal economic development efforts.[14] Other enterprises started by the Oneida tribe were similarly unsuccessful. These included waste management, several construction firms, a credit union, and an environmental laboratory. Luckily, these obstacles did not deter the tribal leadership from its fundamental goal of developing an economic infrastructure that was not tied so completely to federal and state contracts, or "soft" money.

Looking at the years from 1934 to 1975, it is amazing to realize that the newly elected Oneida government — which had no money, no lawyers, and little experience — managed to survive the never-ending pressures of federal Indian policy. Many of the new IRA-elected governments were in a similar situation, and in 1944, tribes came together to form the National Congress of American Indians (NCAI). This organization became the first major national lobbying group for tribal government causes and was composed solely of representatives of recognized Indian tribes. Although other national Indian organizations have since been formed, including the National Tribal Chairman's Organization, National Indian Health Board, National Indian Gaming Association, and others, NCAI remains a strong lobbying force for tribal governments. It formed a coalition of tribal governments, which shared expertise and strategy for dealing with such federal actions as the formation of the Indian Claims Commission, termination and relocation policies, and Public Law 280, discussed later, to name a few.[15] For many years, most tribal leaders depended entirely on NCAI for information and legal advice, which was directed solely at forming strong, independent Indian governments.

The Indian Claims Commission (ICC) was formed in 1946 to provide a forum for adjudicating the continuous complaints from tribal governments against the United States. It accepted claims brought by more than 170 Indian tribes, until it was disbanded in 1978. The Oneida Nation of Indians of Wisconsin filed two claims in the ICC forum. Their New York emigrant claim was filed in September 1967 for all grievances against the United States arising in the state of Wisconsin. Money to settle all Oneida grievances in Wisconsin was won and accepted by the Oneida Nation in 1977, shortly before the work of the ICC ended. By this time, Indian tribes realized that the return of land was not going to be part of the United States' redress of wrongs done to them, and they had the choice of accepting money or losing their claim. Attorney fees and "offsets" for money and services provided to the tribe by the United States reduced the Oneidas' award. Fifteen percent of the remaining settlement money for the Oneidas' New York emigrant claim was placed into a reservation development fund, and 85 percent was placed into a trust account that made per capita payments to all tribal members from the interest generated annually. This trust account still exists and continues to generate interest that is used to support Oneida tribal initiatives.[16]

The second claim filed with the ICC was the New York land claim. Although the Oneidas won their claim to 250,000 acres in the state of New York, they refused the settlement money, withdrew the complaint from the Indian Claims Commission, and filed it in the federal court system. They again were successful with their complaint when the Supreme Court confirmed in 1985 that the Oneida Nation still owned 250,000 acres in the state of New York, most of which was now illegally titled to non-Indians. The euphoria of this success was soon dampened as the Oneida leadership began negotiations for a settlement. These negotiations have now gone on for more than twenty years: at times a settlement seemed close and at other times a settlement seemed darn near impossible. The United States and the state of New York are again offering only money to settle, and through this they want to clear the title for all those non-Oneidas who are now living on the land. Only time will tell how this issue will be settled by the leadership of the Oneida Nation.[17]

In 1953, Congress passed House Concurrent Resolution 108, which established the federal termination policies that disastrously affected our Menominee neighbors. The Oneida Nation of Indians of Wisconsin was too poor to be terminated, but this did not relieve them from the fear of being terminated with every progressive step they made. The slow financial deterioration of the Menominees, under the imposed jurisdiction of the state, was played out in the national Indian forum. All tribes supported Menominee restoration to tribal status; however, that came only in 1973, after many years of struggle.[18]

Public Law 280 was also passed in 1953, and this time all the tribes in Wisconsin, except the Menominee tribe, became part of an experiment that transferred judicial authority for civil and some criminal complaints arising on Indian reservations to the state of Wisconsin. Because tribal governments were slow to regulate their territory and people through laws, the state of Wisconsin soon came to believe and act as if P.L. 280 had given it the authority to regulate the tribes with state laws. Several Supreme Court decisions, such as *California v. Cabazon Band of Mission Indians* in 1987, confirmed that tribal governments still had the right to regulate themselves, their people, and territory, even in a P.L. 280 state.[19] It comes down to the difference between a state's "criminal/prohibitory" laws and its "civil/regulatory" laws; "if the intent of a state law is generally to prohibit certain conduct, it falls within P.L. 280's grant of criminal jurisdiction, but if the state law generally permits the conduct at issue, subject to regulation, it must be classified as civil/regulatory and P.L. 280 does not authorize its enforcement on an Indian reservation."[20] For thirty years after P.L. 280 passed, this issue of civil jurisdiction was battled out in the courts by tribal governments. Here in Wisconsin, the Oneida Nation is still on guard to protect its right to regulate its members and its territory from state encroachment.

The legacy of P.L. 280 remains in Oneida, as it does throughout the state. It continues to muddy the jurisdictional authority between the state and tribes. It established what is now known as "concurrent" jurisdiction within reservations, where Oneida people may have the choice of going to either a state or tribal judicial forum to settle certain issues. The Appeals Commission regularly meets with judges from Brown and Outagamie counties to deal with local civil issues with conflicting jurisdiction, and there is now a national conference being planned to deal with this issue. The Oneida Business Committee has negotiated agreements between the tribe and the various state subdivisions within the reservation. It is confusing to many people, even tribal members, that the Oneida reservation completely encompasses the towns of Hobart and Oneida, and parts of the village of Ashwaubenon, city of Green Bay, and town of Pittsfield. On land owned by the Oneida Nation, these state subdivisions have little or no civil regulatory jurisdiction. On land owned by non-Oneidas, the Oneida Nation has little or no civil regulatory jurisdiction, even though the land is within the limits of its territorial jurisdiction. Throughout the reservation there are countless levels of concurrent jurisdiction.

Legal scholars have defined the times in which we now live as the self-determination era (1961–present). This era begins with the Economic Opportunity Act, passed under the Johnson administration. That was called the War on Poverty, and "disadvantaged" groups such as American Indians, blacks, and residents of Appalachia were given the opportunity to plan and apply for federal grants to help bring themselves out of poverty. The Oneida Housing Authority was formed in 1963 for the purpose of building decent homes under the Housing and Urban Development (HUD) program.[21] In 1965, the Head Start program began with eight tribal staff.[22] Oneida's Head Start program continues today, and the tribal leadership developed the expertise to create full-time jobs and a reservation economy with more and more contracts and grants from federal agencies such as Indian Health Service, Environmental Protection Agency, USDA, Education, Health and Social Services, Department of Labor, and Department of the Interior. Today, the tribe's Governmental Service Division is one of the largest income areas, second only to the Gaming Division.

In 1968, the Indian Civil Rights Act extended most of the protections of the federal constitutional Bill of Rights to tribal members in their dealings with the tribal government. This law included important provisions allowing states that had assumed jurisdiction under Public Law 280 to "retrocede," or transfer jurisdiction back to the tribes and the federal government.[23] The Oneida Nation, through its judicial system under the Oneida Appeals Commission and through its drafting of a new Oneida constitution, has discussed the gradual retrocession by the state courts on certain civil issues where there is presently concurrent jurisdiction. The Indian Civil Rights Act led to a major revision of the tribe's original constitution in 1969 with the addition of Article VI — Bill of Rights, which states: "All members of the tribe shall be accorded equal opportunities to participate in the economic resources and activities of the tribe. All members of the tribe may enjoy, without hindrance, freedom of worship, conscience, speech, press, assembly, association and due process of law, as guaranteed by the Constitution of the United States."[24] The concept of due process was further codified with the passage of the Oneida Administrative Procedures Act in 1991: "The Oneida Tribe shall ensure due process of law for the designated citizens through adoption of this act, pursuant to Article VI of the Oneida Tribal Constitution as amended."[25] The judicial forum for providing "due process of law" for the Oneida tribe is called the Oneida Appeals Commission. This commission was established at the same General Tribal Council meeting that approved the Oneida Administrative Procedures Act.

Another major advance in Oneida sovereignty is the Indian Self-Determination and Education Assistance Act, enacted by Congress in 1975. As a result of this act, the Oneida tribe has assumed administrative responsibility for such programs as education, health, and realty from federal agencies. Since 1996, the Oneida Division of Land Management has contracted with the Bureau of Indian Affairs to process transactions on Oneida trust lands.[26]

Amendments to the Indian Self-Determination and Education Assistance Act have authorized the designation of some tribes as being "self-governance tribes." The Oneidas were named a self-governance tribe as soon as they had the opportunity to apply for this designation, which allows a tribal government to contract for the administration of much of the services provided by the Bureau of Indian Affairs (BIA) for more than a century. Funds come to the Oneida tribal government directly from the BIA's budget and now provide millions of dollars for tribal administration of services.

This is a positive transition for tribes that have been able to meet the criteria for self-governance designation. This designation has created a parallel erosion of the BIA in its authority over tribes, its working budget, and the number of positions in BIA offices. There is much discussion and speculation about whether the BIA will continue to exist as an agency. Through strong self-determination policies, the federal government has already determined the BIA cannot continue to exist because of its past paternalistic management and outright mismanagement of tribal funds. Tribal governments across America are thriving in this self-determination era, and the BIA is not. These changes have created a different relationship between the two, and Oneida tribal leaders are continuing to debate how to address this new and changing relationship.

Notes

1. For this land loss, see Laurence M. Hauptman and L. Gordon McLester III, eds., *The Oneida Indians in the Age of Allotment, 1860–1920* (Norman: University of Oklahoma Press, 2006), 179–245.

2. For the conditions at Oneida, Wisconsin, around 1930, see Laurence M. Hauptman, *The Iroquois and the New Deal* (Syracuse, NY: Syracuse University Press, 1981): 70–77.

3. Institute for Government Research (Brookings Institution), *The Problem of Indian Administration*, comp. Lewis Meriam (Washington, D.C.: 1928).

4. *Indian Reorganization Act, Stat.* 48 (1934): 984–988.

5. Johnson O'Malley Act, 596.

6. See note 4.

7. Oneida Nation of Indians of Wisconsin Constitution and Bylaws, Records of the Oneida General Tribal Council (OGTC), ONIW, 1936.

8. Ibid., 1937–1940, ONIW.

9. L. Gordon McLester III, interview by author, August 14, 2004, Oneida, WI.

10. Records of the OGTC, 1937, ONIW.

11. See Herbert Lewis, ed., with the assistance of L. Gordon McLester III, *Oneida Lives: Long-Lost Voices of the Wisconsin Oneidas* (Lincoln: University of Nebraska Press, 2005).

12. Records of the OGTC, 1965, ONIW.

13. Ibid. (1970).

14. Ibid. (1975).

15. *Indian Claims Commission Act, Stat.* 60 (1946): 1049–1056; *House Concurrent Resolution 108* — termination bill, *Stat.* 67 (1953): B132; Public Law 280, *Stat.* 67 (1953): 588–590; relocation of American Indians to urban areas: ARCIA (1954): 242–243.

16. See the article by Karim Tiro in Part 3 of this book.

17. *Oneida Indian Nation of New York v. County of Oneida, New York,* 414 U.S. 661 (1974); *County of Oneida v. Oneida Indian Nation of New York,* 470 U.S. 226 (1985); *City of Sherrill v. Oneida Indian Nation,* 125 S.Ct. 1478 (2005).

18. See Ada Deer's article in this volume. For the Menominee termination legislation, see Menominee Termination Act, *Stat.* 68 (1954): 250–252. For the restoration of the Menominees to federal status, see Menominee Restoration Act, *Stat.* 87 (1973): 700.

19. *California v. Cabazon Band of Mission Indians,* 480 U.S. 202 (1987).

20. Ibid.

21. Records of the OGTC, 1963, ONIW.

22. Ibid. (1965).

23. Title II–VII of the Civil Rights Act of 1968 focuses directly on American Indians: *Stat.* 82 (1968): 77–81.

24. Records of the OGTC, 1969, ONIW.

25. Ibid. (1991).

26. *Indian Self-Determination and Education Assistance Act, Stat.* 88 (1975): 2203–2214.

Part 4

Portraits of Wisconsin Oneida Leadership

Introduction

ART 4 OF THIS BOOK EXPLORES community and national leadership. In the first portion, the biographical and autobiographical articles focus on the Wisconsin Oneidas' leadership in the years after World War II. Signs of a turnaround in Wisconsin Oneida fortunes began during the long tenure of Julius Danforth as tribal chairman. Danforth, who held office from 1947 to 1962, had an energetic tribal council, the key figure of which was Irene Moore. During this fifteen-year period, the Wisconsin Oneidas formally rejected federal termination policies, dismissing an offer of a lump-sum payout of federal treaty obligations. Second, they initiated several Indian Claims Commission cases dealing with compensation for loss of resources of their Wisconsin reservation and seeking compensation for lands lost through dispossession in their central New York homeland. Third, as Thelma McLester pointed out in Part 1, the Oneidas allowed two major studies — one by the League of Women Voters and the other by the University of Wisconsin — in order to examine and plan solutions for the economic problems the community faced. Fourth, the Oneida Nation Business Committee sent an official representative, Eva Danforth (whose essay begins Part 4), to the White House on August 15, 1962, to attend the formal presentation of the Declaration of Indian Purpose and meet President John F. Kennedy.[1] The Declaration of Indian Purpose had been drafted by 420 Indians who had attended a history-making convocation — the American Indian Chicago Conference at the University of Chicago. The declaration read as follows:

> In order to give due recognition to certain basic philosophies by which the Indian people and all other people endeavor to live, We, the Indian people, must be governed by high principles and laws in a democratic manner, with a right to choose our own way of life. Since our Indian culture is slowly being absorbed by the American society, we believe we have the responsibility of preserving our precious heritage; recognizing that certain changes are inevitable. We believe that the Indians should provide the adjustment and thus freely advance with dignity to a better life educationally, economically, and spiritually....[2]

Althea Schuyler, the tribal treasurer during this period, then describes the difficult conditions under which the four-member council operated. Ill-housed, overworked, and minimally paid, the council, prompted by Irene Moore's example, focused much of their attention on the tribe's immediate needs, tribal enrollment matters, and HUD grant writing to establish what became Site I Oneida housing. Moore was the first Oneida woman to be elected tribal chair and the second Native American woman — Lakota Josephine Kelley preceded her — to hold that post in the United States. Moore's oral history, included here, describes her life and how she became Wisconsin Oneida tribal chair.

The two essays that follow Moore's memoir focus on tribal leaders who worked with Moore and made their own mark on Oneida betterment right up to 1990. Dr. Norbert Hill Jr., the vice president of the Menominee College campus in Green Bay, and Megan Minoka Hill of Harvard University write about Norbert Seabrook Hill Sr., who held the office of tribal chairman three times and served for twenty years on the Tribal Council. L. Gordon McLester III then offers a sketch of Purcell R. Powless, who was tribal chairman from 1967 to 1990, the longest tenure of a tribal chairman in the modern history of the Wisconsin Oneidas. Both men returned to Oneida from careers off the reservation in urban centers during the latter part of Julius Danforth's tenure as tribal chairman. They first worked with Irene Moore to initiate federal programs in health care, housing, and education and develop an overall economic plan for the community that led to the purchase of an industrial park. Later, these two men, along with many others in the community, worked to develop bingo operations and, subsequently, a successful hotel-casino complex. Both men had the ability to work effectively on and off the Oneida reservation, as evidenced by the improved conditions at Oneida since the 1960s.

Part 4 concludes with the voices of two prominent Oneidas, Robert L. Bennett and Ernest Stevens Sr. Bennett served as United States Commissioner of Indian Affairs from 1966 to 1969, the second Native American to become commissioner of Indian affairs. Unlike many outspoken Oneida political figures, Bennett was skilled at operating behind the scenes as a strong opponent of termination. In this 1968 interview conducted by Joe B. Frantz, he offers an overview of his career and experiences in Washington.

The volume closes with an essay by Ernest Stevens Sr., who has been renowned for his leadership and political work for more than fifty years, in particular his work as a Washington policymaker in the 1960s and 1970s. In 1975, he was appointed by Congress to the American Indian Policy Review Commission. Stevens explores the complex notion of Indian identity, the paramount importance of maintaining Indian sovereignty, and the necessary steps for subsequent generations to succeed at this goal.

Notes

1. Kennedy hastily met with the Indian delegation and, according to Thomas Clarkin, gave short shrift in preparing for this meeting. Clarkin, *Federal Indian Policy in the Kennedy and Johnson Administrations, 1961–1969* (Albuquerque: University of New Mexico Press, 2001): 79–80. Yet, as Eva Danforth makes clear in her oral history, the meeting was viewed in a different way by the Indians, as both meaningful and productive.

2. For the American Indian Chicago Conference of 1961, see Nancy O. Lurie, "The Voice of the American Indian: Report on the American Indian Chicago Conference," *Current Anthropology* 2 (December 1961): 478–500; Laurence M. Hauptman and Jack Campisi, "The Voice of Eastern Indians: The American Indian Chicago Conference and the Movement for Federal Recognition," Proceedings of the American Philosophical Society 132 (December 1988): 316–329. For the "Declaration of Indian Purpose," see Francis Paul Prucha, ed., *Documents of United States Indian Policy*, 3rd ed. (Lincoln: University of Nebraska Press, 2000): 245–247.

Table 3. Wisconsin Oneida Governments Under the Indian Reorganization Act, 1937–1969

Year	Chair	Vice-Chair	Secretary	Treasurer
1937	Morris Wheelock	Anderson Skenandore	Lydia Powless	Harrison Smith
1938	Morris Wheelock	Chauncy Adams	Lydia Powless	Harrison Smith
1939	Mark Powless	Andrew Beechtree	Lydia Powless	Ray Parkhurst
1940	Ray Parkhurst	Oscar Archiquette	Lydia Powless	Anderson Cornelius
1941	Ray Parkhurst	Oscar Archiquette	Lydia Powless	Anderson Cornelius
1942	Ray Parkhurst	Oscar Archiquette	Lydia Powless	Anderson Cornelius
1943	Hyson Cornelius	Sherman Skenandore	Lydia Powless	Anderson Cornelius
1944	Hyson Cornelius	Julius Danforth	Luella Cornelius	Sherman Skenandore
1945	Hyson Cornelius	Julius Danforth	Ephrim Schuyler	Sherman Skenandore
1946	Hyson Cornelius	Julius Danforth	Andrew Beechtree	Sherman Skenandore
1947	Julius Danforth	Anderson John	Andrew Beechtree	Sherman Skenandore
1948	Julius Danforth	Anderson John	Andrew Beechtree	Sherman Skenandore
1949	Julius Danforth	Oscar Archiquette	Mamie Smith	Sherman Skenandore
1950	Julius Danforth	Oscar Archiquette	Mamie Smith	Sherman Skenandore
1951	Andrew Beechtree	Simeon Adams	Mamie Smith	Charles A. Hill
1952	Dennison Hill	Irene Moore	Mamie Smith	Charles A. Hill
1953	Dennison Hill	Irene Moore	Mamie Smith	Charles A. Hill
1954	Julius Danforth	Irene Moore	Mamie Smith	Norin John
1955	Julius Danforth	Irene Moore	Cecil Skenandore	Norin John
1956	Julius Danforth	Norbert Skenandore	Cecil Skenandore	Althea Schuyler
1957	Julius Danforth	Irene Moore	Cecil Skenandore	Althea Schuyler
1958	Julius Danforth	Irene Moore	Eva Danforth	Althea Schuyler
1959	Julius Danforth	Irene Moore	Eva Danforth	Althea Schuyler
1960	Julius Danforth	Irene Moore	Eva Danforth	Althea Schuyler
1961	Julius Danforth	Irene Moore	Eva Danforth	Althea Schuyler
1962	Julius Danforth	Irene Moore	Eva Danforth	Althea Schuyler
1963	Irene Moore	Lee McLester	Eva Danforth	Althea Schuyler

Year	Chair	Vice-Chair	Secretary	Treasurer
1964	Norbert S. Hill	Lee McLester	Woodrow Webster	Althea Schuyler
1965	Norbert S. Hill	Lee McLester	Jackie Wacek	Althea Schuyler
1966	Norbert S. Hill	Oscar Archiquette	Irad Cornelius	Jocelyn Ninham
1967	Purcell Powless	Oscar Archiquette	Loretta Ellis	Jocelyn Ninham
1968	Purcell Powless	Oscar Archiquette	Amelia C./Loretta E.	Jocelyn Ninham
1969	Purcell Powless	Irene Moore	Amelia Cornelius	Al Manders

Reminiscences of Working for the Wisconsin Oneida Tribal Government in the 1950s and 1960s, Part 1

by Althea Schuyler

I WAS BORN JUNE 20, 1925, ON THE ONEIDA RESERVATION. I grew up on a farm here at Oneida on County Trunk H. My father worked our farm for forty-three years. The house is still standing, but a fire burned down much of the farm. I didn't think I was poor growing up, since we always had food to eat. Yet we had a hard time in school, since we did not have nice clothes to wear. I attended high school for two years and then left Oneida for Detroit, where I worked in a defense plant. Later, I moved to Milwaukee, where I also worked in a defense plant. I later married into the large Schuyler family. I've been a widow for the past twenty-seven years.

In 1950, I moved back to Oneida with my husband, Lester. In 1958, my aunt, Irene Moore, encouraged me to run for the position of tribal treasurer. At the age of thirty-one, I was elected to this position on the Oneida Nation of Indians Business Committee. At that time, the vote was held at the Civilian Conservation Corps camp, but later, elections would be held at Chicago Corners.

I was tribal treasurer for ten years. I remember when the tribal government used to meet in the old CCC building where the Site II housing complex is today. The building had no running water, and we had to use the outhouse. The men would have to arrive early to stoke the fire before Tribal Council meetings. We froze our buns off! As tribal treasurer, I received ten dollars a month as salary. I worked with Julius Danforth, Purcell Powless, and Irene Moore [tribal chair]. She and I would work well into the night and even on Sunday to update tribal enrollments. These were critical years. We did not have any money. We worked hard on behalf of the tribe.

There were no subcommittees at that time, and the council's biggest job was to get Oneida people enrolled. There was a charge of one dollar to become enrolled, and the money was used to help with the paperwork and postage. I do not remember the budget other than the enrollment monies and funds from the BIA for a revolving loan fund for Oneida people to borrow to build homes, until the program ran out of funding. E. J. Riley, the BIA agent, would come down and check the books or records. I cannot recall major concerns except for the blood quantum issue. The people had to decide what the blood quantum would be to allow people to be enrolled.

At my church [Oneida Methodist] I was treasurer, member of the choir, and Sunday school teacher. I was also a foster mother for twenty years, and one of my three foster children was a Menominee. I served our elderly for thirty years before my retirement in 2005, cooking for the elderly through the Oneida Nutrition Program. Cooking and serving for the elderly has been the joy of my life. I appreciate our elders and what they have done for us. They are the backbone of our community, and I respect and love them. I am old now, but I still bring things to our elders.

Our tribe has come a long, long way. The Oneidas have become more and more prosperous. We must be more loving and kind to each other and respect our elders. God bless the Oneidas, and may they continue to enjoy what has been achieved.

Reminiscences of Working for the Wisconsin Oneida Tribal Government in the 1950s and 1960s, Part 2

by Eva Danforth

I WAS BORN NOVEMBER 20, 1925, ON THE ONEIDA RESERVATION. My family lived in Menasha, Wisconsin, but we moved back to Oneida when I was twelve or thirteen years of age. I graduated from East Green Bay High School in 1945 and would find summer work in Detroit, where I worked in restaurants and then in a defense plant.

I remember what the New Deal was like here at Oneida. We lived on twenty acres of "New Deal land" [reacquired by Oneidas under the Indian Reorganization Act] in a "New Deal house." My husband's parents lived adjacent to us. We had no money, so I couldn't pursue my education beyond high school. My husband and I had three children [including Jerry Danforth, Wisconsin Oneida tribal chairman].

I was always interested in politics and public speaking. In 1957, at the age of thirty-three, I decided to run for the office of tribal secretary. Although I was not successful that year, I did win in 1958. I remember that the voting was held at Chicago Corners, in the tribal building, and about seventy-five tribal members voted. The nation had no official address, so, as secretary, I received all tribal mail at my home. I would act as the postmaster, responsible for sorting and delivering mail to the proper member or office. Irene Moore and I used to sit at my kitchen table, reading and answering the mail.

As a council member, I was overworked and underpaid. I received fifteen dollars per month for regular meetings and five dollars for extra meetings. Yet the work was rewarding, everything that I expected. E. J. Riley, the BIA agent from Ashland, Wisconsin, would attend every council meeting and was there to assist the tribe when needed. During my tenure as tribal secretary, from 1958 to 1963, council meetings were held once a month and then steadily increased to three or four each month, when more decisions had to be made for land assignments and approval of enrollments to keep tribal rolls current.

[In the 1950s,] the closest thing to termination that I remember [was] Washington officials' efforts to give us sixty thousand dollars to end treaty obligations. Later, we received fifty-two cents per year under the [Treaty of Canandaigua of 1794]. We held a meeting in Parish Hall, and Ruth Baird and Oscar Archiquette tried to explain it and spoke against the federal government's plan. Archiquette spoke in the Oneida language at that meeting. We sent notices out of the meeting, and the proposal was rejected.

The American Indian Chicago Conference met in 1961. Although I did not go to Chicago, I was to be part of the follow-up. The conference organizers collected all the information from tribes all over the country, and they put it in a leather-bound book. We made our list of what we needed at Oneida. I went to the White House with American Indian Chicago Conference delegates, and we gave the book to President Kennedy in a ceremony in the Rose Garden. President Kennedy shook our hands and wanted to know what tribes we belonged to. The president told us that these matters would be his first concerns for legislative action once he went back to his office. And so help me, [they were]! That's when the Oneida [HUD] housing program got started.

The federal HUD grant established the first housing program, essentially a self-help project to build twenty homes on the reservation. We had to deal with the BIA's Indian Relocation Program whereby tribal members could relocate to other areas of the country to gain employment. Our major concerns in those years were improving education, health, housing, and the delivery of social services. I have no clear recollection of budget matters, other than there were not many of them!

Even without the telephone, adding machines, computers, e-mail, etc., we did a lot in those years.

Irene Moore

A Memoir

interview conducted by Madelyn Genskow (1976)

Childhood at Oneida

I WAS BORN IN ONEIDA ON OCTOBER 17, 1903. My mother was Ida Skenandore and my father Dennison Metoxen. My grandparents had migrated from New York. I was the oldest child in my family. During my childhood, my father was a farmer who cleared the land, farmed, and sold some of the timber. I remember him cutting down trees and carting them off. My father had maybe eight to ten cows. My mother, who made baskets, had a nice garden, and we had a variety of vegetables as well as sweet and Indian corn. Our farm was on Ridge Road, which is now County E, about three miles south of the Methodist church. I remember having to haul firewood for the house.

Boarding School Days

My father had gone to Hampton and had an eighth- through tenth-grade level of education. My mother was not an educated woman, although she had attended Tomah Indian School. Around the second or third grade, she was sent home because she had extremely poor eyesight, making it impossible for her to read.

I started school at ten years of age and was sent off to the Oneida Boarding School [States Indian Industrial School at Oneida, Wisconsin, which was run by the BIA]. I couldn't speak a word of English when I went there, and I would get into trouble because of it. Sometimes I would be saying "yes" when I should have been saying "no," and saying "no" when I should have said "yes." I was punished for it with a spanking on my hand. Of course we were punished if we were caught speaking our language. We were supposed to learn to speak only English. I was just sent there to learn, I guess, and I just took it in stride. I thought lots of my education. I was being educated and I tried to follow. That's what I had to be and I did learn. I made the grade every year, even though I didn't speak English. I think about it sometimes — kind of cruel. My parents would come there and visit maybe once a month. At Thanksgiving and Christmas, I would get to go home. Then they would bring us back again. I remember the food at the school. I didn't like tomatoes, even though that was all they gave us. I learned to like them. I was at the Oneida Boarding School for five years.

I had heard about how wonderful Carlisle was. I was kind of anxious to go there and so, after graduating from the Oneida Boarding School, I signed up for three years at Carlisle. When I arrived at Carlisle, I thought it was very nice: the cut grass, the beautiful grounds. At Carlisle, there were twelve hundred students, quite a change from the small school at Oneida. I liked it really well. I got along with all the students. We had four in each room. I was lucky to room with Fanny Silas, a Wisconsin Oneida, who was older, and I depended on her.

In the evenings, we had a religious assembly. We were also allowed to go to church off the school grounds in the town of Carlisle. There were several churches, and I went to the Methodist church. We would walk with one of the officers of the school down and back from the church. I liked it very much.

We had duties at the school. We were assigned to the laundry and, less likely, to the kitchen. The boys worked in the cooking department. The girls did the dishes and set the tables. Then we had to clean our rooms, make our beds. On the weekends we would change our sheets. We were taught history, which I always liked.

I was disappointed that after I had attended Carlisle Indian School for only one year, the United States government closed it down [in 1918] to use as a hospital facility for wounded American soldiers in World War I. I was transferred to Flandreau, where I spent four years. My sister Eva also attended Flandreau. I graduated with an equivalent of a high school degree. I even took chemistry and physics there. Yet it was a great disappointment to me, coming from such a wonderful school as Carlisle. Flandreau, South Dakota, seemed to me like wilderness.

Family Life

When I came home after graduation from Flandreau, I wanted to take a course in stenography, but we were too poor. My father worked in a paper mill, and so I applied for a job there. Later, I got a job in a department store in Appleton. I was making two dollars an hour, pretty good wages back then. I met my husband, Sim, at a picnic at Oneida. We would go to dances in Seymour or De Pere. He worked as a lumberjack at the time. After three years of dating, we were married in the Methodist church in Oneida. I worked for the church quite a bit. I stayed with my parents for a while when Sim went back to work again as a lumberjack in the woods. When he returned, we rented a house in Oneida. Our three daughters were born at home; we didn't go to hospitals. Back then doctors came to your house. Later Sim got a job in a stone quarry. He crushed stones to put on the roads. He was quite busy in the summer, early in the spring, and into the late fall. In the winter, he didn't work much, except for some part-time work in the woods. We would have to save money during the summer to get through the wintertime. I stayed home with my children, who were close together in age.

I was kept very busy, and there was nothing modern in those days. You washed clothes with a washboard. We had to deal with childhood diseases such as measles. My oldest daughter had chronic asthma, and we always feared she would choke to death. I used Indian medicine I got from my mother.

My mother made baskets and sold them, and I'm very sorry I didn't learn that art, since my mother was an extra good basket maker. A lot of my family were berry pickers. I would stay home with the little ones and get something to eat when they got home.

I always remember going to church on Christmas Eve in a sleigh, horses and all. All the children would receive a box of candy. I'll never forget it: quite a large box of star-shaped candy filled with nuts. They also gave us an orange or maybe an apple. We put up a Christmas tree. My mother kind of helped us. She had never had a tree herself or had put one up. We trimmed the tree with tinsel. We had cranberries, popcorn, etc., every year. We would get something else different that we could afford.

Tribal Government

During the Great Depression [Indian New Deal], United States government programs began to help restore some two thousand acres of Oneida lands. We organized a tribal council, too, under the Indian Reorganization

Act. Right after we got tribal land, I wanted to know more about what was happening. The Oneidas organized a tribal government. With the help of the BIA, we set up a constitution. I went to all those meetings so I knew what was going on all the time. I was interested right from the beginning. As a result of my attendance, I was asked to be on the credit committee. That's how I got started.

I became more interested in church work. I thought you should reach out into your community as far as you could to help people, and I thought of politics then as trying to do something to help things. I could see that people out here didn't have wells at the time. Oneidas would go a long way to someone who had a well who would let them use it and share it.

In 1963, I was asked whether I wanted to be nominated as chief [tribal chair]. At first, I turned it down, thinking that the chief of the tribe should be a man. But the chief at that time [Julius Danforth] could no longer serve, since his wife had become sick. At the time, the council was composed of four members: tribal chair Julius Danforth, me as vice chair, Althea Schuyler as treasurer, and Eva Danforth as secretary. Julius asked me if I would run. I was working on improving tribal housing, and I agreed to run for tribal chair because we were already in the middle of our housing project proposal and we felt that it would take too long to introduce a new person to what we were doing. I was subsequently elected in 1963, the first woman elected tribal chair of the Oneida Nation of Indians of Wisconsin [and second Native American woman to be elected tribal chair in Indian country]. My election got a lot of publicity; however, the next year (1964), I lost re-election by fifteen votes out of two hundred or three hundred votes cast.

I continued to be active in politics. We were working on improving housing. The only other pilot program in the country was in South Dakota. I had read in the newspapers the amount of federal government money available for housing, earmarked for black and other minority groups. I asked myself, Why aren't the Indians included in these programs? and I wrote to my senators [William Proxmire and Gaylord Nelson] to ask them about a big grant or money to borrow with no interest or very little interest and a small down payment. They wrote back after writing to the BIA. After the South Dakota pilot program, we became one of the first tribes to push for federal housing money. It took a while, and our own people thought the idea was too good to be true, but we did secure funding for housing in this way. I went to Washington, D.C., and attended a conference on housing. I acquired a lot of information on housing grants, but it was pretty hard to convince the Oneida people to vote for it, since they feared losing their lands (as had occurred in the allotment period [1906–1933]). We had an Oneida General Tribal Council meeting [where every enrolled member could express him- or herself and vote]. We agreed to organize the Oneida Housing Authority and then go ahead and ask for funds. The BIA sent a man [Skolaski] with the expertise to help us plan, organize, and apply for funding. We had a hard time finding a housing authority chairman. Floyd Acheson, a construction worker married to an Oneida woman, volunteered to run for the post, but only if a capable Indian wasn't there to run. An Oneida, Artley Skenandore, came to the fore and was elected to direct the Oneida Housing Authority. He administered it for three years.

The history taught at Carlisle and everywhere I went was that the Indians were savages and everything they did was not good. I thought about this a lot as I got older. I found out that the Indians weren't like that. I worked hard in our Seymour school district as a member of the education committee. I appointed Evelyn Smith and Gordon McLester to see what they could do to work with the school and to make contact with historians [such as Dr. Jack Campisi] who knew a lot about the Iroquois. I suggested that they start first with the Oneidas because they were part of the district and their children attended schools there. They convinced the school board and school administration to start revising the district's curriculum. They did a good job.

Norbert Seabrook Hill Sr.

by Megan Minoka Hill
and Norbert Hill Jr.

Rosa Hill Coenen and Richard Hill contributed to this essay.

FIGHTING UNDER THE NAME "CHIEF," Norbert S. Hill Sr. became the Golden Gloves champion in 1934 with an impressive record of sixty wins and four losses. Though just shy of six feet, he was quick on his feet and mastered a counterpunch that was known to intimidate his opponents. An ill-timed earache caused Norbert to bypass the Tournament of Champions and a potential bout with Joe Louis, but his boxing career became a metaphor that would guide his life as a nation builder, best remembered for the way he fought for his people.[1]

Early Influences

Born January 18, 1912, in Oneida, Wisconsin, to Dr. Lily Rosa Minoka and Charles Hill, Norbert was a natural leader.[2] The third of six children, he learned the importance of service, resourcefulness, and community empowerment at an early age.[3]

Norbert's mother, Dr. Hill, was his greatest inspiration and influence. She instilled in him a deep respect for community and an unwavering determination to better the living conditions of Indian people. He once said, "I was always involved because my mother was involved. I would hitch up the buggy or crank up the Model T to take her to doctor folks, and I recall hearing her discuss the changes that were occurring in the community." While she never engaged in politics, she observed and discussed the need for economic and social improvements. For example, she recognized the critical need to develop venues for youth leadership and told Norbert that he needed to drain the swamp to build a recreation area. He did. Her other observations, in combination with his political savvy and hard work, would eventually germinate into many other improvements throughout Oneida, such as the nursing home, the industrial park, and the post office. Norbert's endless supply of ideas, his dedication to his people, and his increasing efforts at implementation were instrumental motivating forces for development and progress for the Oneida Nation.

Education

While Norbert did not follow a traditional educational path, he was a life-long learner with an unquenchable thirst for knowledge. He read constantly to improve his understanding of the world and to cultivate new strategies to improve conditions in Indian country. He placed an equal value on life experience and formal education and often quoted his mother, who maintained that "going to school and getting an education were two different things and they didn't always happen at the same time."

His educational journey began at St. Joseph's Catholic School on the Oneida reservation.[4] At the age of fourteen, Norbert dropped out of Saint Joseph's, effectively skipping eighth grade, because his classes were not challenging. His love of adventure spurred him to enlist in the military. His age disqualified him for service, so, undaunted, he changed his birth year on the application and enlisted in the National Guard in 1926. (It was noted in the *Military News* that he killed a rattlesnake, barbecued it, and ate it, causing his staff sergeant to faint.) He was stationed at Wisconsin's Camp McCoy for two years before his superiors verified his age and suggested he return to school.

At that time he returned to Oneida and enrolled in St. Norbert's High School in DePere and then Green Bay West High School. In 1929, Norbert took a job at Morgan's Store in Oneida for ten cents per day. Even in those days, it was not a lot of money, but he was glad to have a job. He also spent time studying at the Haskell Institute, a Bureau of Indian Affairs high school located in Lawrence, Kansas. His sister Josephine was happiest when he attended Green Bay West with her, because she said going to school with Norbert was like going to school with a bodyguard. At Green Bay West, he played football and was the first Indian to score a touchdown against the crosstown rival, Green Bay East High, in 1931.[5] Because of his athletic ability, he was highlighted in local newspapers and scouted by Curly Lambeau for the Green Bay Packers.

Bored by the standard curriculum, Norbert decided to get his GED (general equivalency diploma) and travel the country to learn about other

Indians. To do this, he jumped trains, held onto the undercarriage, and visited new parts of the United States. He visited faraway Indian nations in Kansas, Montana, Oklahoma, and Iowa. As an ambassador would, he shared his experiences at Oneida and learned about the diverse Native cultures and conditions around the country. When possible, he joined farm teams and played baseball and basketball. Because of this experience, he grew to understand the values that distinguished Indian people and the commonalities that united them, which would ultimately inform his life's work.

Throughout his life, he returned to school when he needed to learn something to augment his personal knowledge and contribute to his professional work. In the 1940s, he completed vocational courses as a machinist under the GI Bill, and in the 1960s, he attended Macomb Community College in Warren, Michigan. The next decade, at the age of sixty-two, he attended the University of Wisconsin–Green Bay, where he took courses in urban planning and economics, so he would be still better able to help his people. Norbert was also a fellow at Chicago's Newberry Library, the nation's leading resource library for information on American Indians.

Urban Affairs

When the Great Depression hit in 1929, Norbert was able to secure only part-time seasonal work until 1936, when he joined a placement program through the BIA. He learned of an opening in Detroit for a machinist at the Ford Motor Company, and he took it. When he arrived, he took special courses at Cass Technical School to develop his technical skills.

While in Detroit, Norbert connected with Indians from a variety of tribes in the automobile industry and in the community, seeking a way "to help bring the Indian-ness back to the Indians in the city." He became an activist in labor unions and community organizations, and he initiated the first urban Indian organization in the United States, the North American Indian Club. He served as president four times, the only person to hold that distinction. He also helped to organize the veterans' post and served as commander. It was through the VFW that he learned how bingo could be harnessed as an economic-development tool for tribes, which would become a tremendous driver of the Oneida Nation's contemporary economy.

Still fond of his experience at Camp McCoy and armed with a desire to serve his country, Norbert joined the U.S. Navy Seabees Unit in 1942. He served for thirty-eight months in the Aleutian Islands and Hawaii, where he organized another Indian club. After the war, he returned to Detroit and married Eileen Johnson, a Cree from Alberta, Canada. Norbert and Eileen raised six children: Barbara, Norbert Jr., Rosa, Charles, Richard, and James.

He became a member of the Indian Council Fire, where he served for forty-six years, and a charter member of the Great Lakes Inter-Tribal Council, which in turn helped to develop the Office of Economic Opportunity and Head Start. In 1940, he joined the National Congress of the American Indian and would go on to serve as vice president of the American Indian Athletic Hall of Fame, chairman of the Resolutions Committee at the National Indian Educational Association, and member of the American Indian Relief Council. In addition, among other positions, he would be a member of the Oneida Business Committee for twenty years.

Norbert's determined, patient, and charismatic nature helped him to succeed as a community organizer. He instinctively understood human nature and the importance of formal and informal influences. His work with many associations taught him how to negotiate group dynamics, facilitate consensus, and — most important — get the job done. Unable to throw anything away, yet terribly organized, he was known to have at least seven different briefcases in his car at any given time — one for each organization he would meet with that week. Always running to meetings, he wore Nike shoes with suits. In 1981, when his family teased him about his footwear in Washington, D.C., he said, "You have to be good to your feet in this town!"

Oneida

Longing for his home, Norbert and his family moved back to Oneida in 1962, where Norbert devoted himself to the well-being of his reservation community. Norbert served more than twenty years in the Oneida tribal government, acting as chairman for three terms and as vice chairman from

1964 until his death in 1983. Over the course of his service, he revived the tribal judicial system and helped develop the Oneida Economic Development Plan and the Oneida Nursing Home Project. Some of his key achievements are:

Developing a thirty-year contract with the real estate division of the post office;

Helping secure 701 grants, which put the chair and other Business Committee members to work on a daily basis;

Participating in developing grants resulting in the construction of the industrial park, Standing Stone Building, Oneida Memorial Building, and Oscar Archiquette Building;

Obtaining Head Start funding for the tribe, separate from the funding received by the Great Lakes Inter-Tribal Council;

Helping to facilitate the purchase of the valuable land across from the Green Bay airport, where the Radisson Hotel and Oneida Casino are now located;

Obtaining a tax-exempt number from the IRS for his tribe; and

Obtaining the respect of Washington, D.C., politicians and department heads dealing with Indian programs. Because of Norbert's leadership, persistence, and patience, the tribe was viewed as accountable and able to sustain sound leadership.

Legacy

Norbert passed away on June 19, 1983, at the age of seventy-one, while attending the annual banquet of the Detroit Indian Club, the organization he had founded thirty years earlier. Over the course of his lifetime he assumed many roles: son, husband, father, friend, storyteller, academic, dancer, tribal leader, poet, community organizer, visionary, farmer, and boxing champion. Upon his death, the Oneida Nation of Wisconsin renamed the Sacred Heart Center in his memory on September 7, 1984. Today the Norbert S. Hill Center serves as the organizational center of the Oneida tribe.

N. Scott Momaday wrote: "A legacy is a gift from an ancestor, something handed down across time and space, and through the generations." In this way, Norbert's legacy continues to be realized today through the many gifts he left: hope, empowerment, dedication, and concern for the progress of Oneida people; a plethora of programs and policies in health, education, and welfare; and an example of dogged determination to improve the quality of life of all Indian people while retaining heritage, traditions, and integrity.

Notes

1. Louis won the Tournament of Champions later that year in the same weight category.

2. Lily Rosa Minoka Hill was the second American Indian woman doctor in the United States, graduating from the Woman's Medical College in Philadelphia in 1899. She operated a private practice in Philadelphia. When she married Charles Hill, they moved to the Oneida reservation, and she became known as the kitchen doctor.

3. Rosa and Charles had six children: Charles, Albert, Norbert, twins Jane and Josephine, and Melissa. Melissa passed away of chicken pox at the age of sixteen, while attending the Haskell Institute.

4. Norbert also attended a Bureau of Indian Affairs boarding school in Northern Wisconsin.

5. Noted in the *Green Bay Press Gazette*, 2006.

Purcell R. Powless

by L. Gordon McLester III

PURCELL R. POWLESS WAS BORN ON CHRISTMAS ÐAY on the Oneida reservation in Wisconsin in 1925. He is the son of Mark Powless and Margaret Stevens and is the second eldest of nine children. Purcell attended St. Joseph School in Oneida and Pipestone Indian School and graduated from Flandreau Indian School, South Dakota. Following graduation, he went to Davenport, Iowa, with his uncle, Eugene Powless, and got a job cleaning homes. Shortly after working with his uncle, Purcell joined the merchant marine and traveled around the world during World War II. He stayed in the merchant marine for three years and, following his tour of duty, came home to Oneida and married Angelina Skenandore on December 28, 1945. Purcell and his wife moved to Rock Island, Illinois, where he began his career as an ironworker. For thirty-five years Purcell worked in the high steel industry and is proud to have worked on such projects as the Mackinaw Bridge and hundreds of other steel construction jobs across the country. Purcell often worked on high steel with his brothers, John, Mark, and Eugene Powless.

In 1963, Purcell moved his family back to the Oneida reservation to a home with no plumbing or sewage, with an outhouse, and with a woodstove for heat. The house was on a dirt road. He commuted weekly from Chicago, where he worked on the construction of the Sears Tower.

In 1967, Norbert S. Hill Sr. approached Purcell to run for chairman of the Oneida Business Committee. Elected as tribal chairman in 1967, Purcell remained at the helm for twenty-three years. He remains the longest-seated chairman in the history of the Oneida Nation. Approximately two hundred voters came to the polling place to elect a four-member council. At that time the council was not a salaried body, but members received five dollars per meeting once a month. For the first council, Purcell served with Vice Chairman Oscar Archiquette, Treasurer Joy Ninham, and Secretary Loretta Metoxen. In 1969, the group changed from a four- to a nine-member council.

When Powless was elected, the Oneida Nation had very little money, and unemployment on the reservation was more than 60 percent. The Oneida Head Start project was in its second year, and the tribe relied on federal funds. Within the next fifteen years, Powless was successful in leading the Wisconsin Oneidas to the beginning of an era that would change the quality of life on the Oneida reservation and raise the standard of living in Oneida above the poverty level. By 1982, the Oneida Nation had expanded its budget to include private and federal funding for health care, education, and housing, and it provided jobs for approximately five hundred employees. The establishment of Oneida bingo had occurred during this period and was a major financial boost to the tribe's swelling budget.

In 1976 two initiatives forced the Oneida people to become more resourceful in securing funds to meet the needs of the growing reservation. One goal was to bring to fruition the dream of a nursing home for Oneida elders. The other was to find a way to help subsidize the operation and maintenance of a newly acquired community recreation facility. Through a community-development block grant from HUD, the Oneida had built a recreational building that needed a source of funding for the insurance and utility costs that would allow the building to stay open.

The solution was found in bingo, which would turn out to be the lead-in to the passage of the regulatory act that allowed gaming on Indian reservations — the goose that laid the golden egg. Powless credits the dedication and commitment of the Oneida women who worked tirelessly to bring bingo from a small-time penny-ante game to one of the most lucrative economic initiatives ever experienced by any tribe in Wisconsin.

Congressional passage of the American Indian Gaming Regulatory Act in 1988 opened the doors to casino gaming in the Nation. It required a signed compact with the state of Wisconsin on various issues. The compact was secured for Class III gaming in 1990.

The quality of life on the Oneida reservation has improved tremendously. When Purcell moved to Chicago with his wife and five children in 1959, he left a reservation that had four taverns, two grocery stories, two gas stations, dirt roads, no sewer or water, and virtually no industry. Children were bused to five different school districts, law enforcement was nearly nonexistent, and the closest health-care facility was ten miles away. Most community social functions were organized through the local churches. Housing was substandard, and tribal lands were barely thirteen hundred acres.

By the time Purcell R. Powless retired from office in 1991, however, the Oneida Nation had achieved tremendous growth toward self-sufficiency. By then the Nation had a nursing home, a clinic, a police department, an extensive social services department, a communications department, an elementary school, an industrial park, a convenience store, a tobacco enterprise, a hotel, modern housing units, a landbase of six thousand acres, services for the elderly, expanded educational programs, day care, a fitness center, an Oneida language preservation program, a land office, agricultural and farming projects, environmental programs, a library, recreational facilities and programs, and employment opportunities.

Now happily retired, Purcell lives on the original allotment of his grandfather, John D. Powless.

An Interview with
Robert L. Bennett

by Joe B. Frantz

Too often, Native Americans who work for the federal government have been viewed with suspicion by members of their communities back home. Even though their motivation for this type of employment is usually a combination of family economic survival and the hope that they can help other Native Americans, they are frequently and sometimes ruthlessly criticized as "Bureau Indians" or "apples." One such case is that of Robert L. Bennett, a Wisconsin Oneida and the second Native American to become commissioner of Indian affairs.¹ Born on the Wisconsin Oneida reservation on November 16, 1912, Bennett was a graduate of Haskell Institute in Lawrence, Kansas, and later Southwestern University School of Law.

In 1933, he was hired as a junior clerk by the BIA and sent to Utah. He later served at the Navajo Agency at Window Rock, Arizona, worked with Indian World War II veterans in Phoenix, and was sent to Aberdeen, South Dakota, as a job-placement officer and later assistant director. He rose to the position of BIA area director for Alaska. Throughout the 1950s and early 1960s, Bennett gained a reputation as an economic-development specialist.² In 1962, he was appointed deputy commissioner of Indian affairs under Dr. Philleo Nash, a fellow Wisconsinite. Supported for the commissionership by Secretary of the Interior Stewart Udall, Bennett's nomination was unanimously confirmed by the United States Senate on April 13, 1966. At a White House ceremony two weeks later, President Lyndon Johnson swore in Bennett as commissioner of Indian affairs.

Bennett, who died in July 2002, was a transitional figure in the history of federal Indian policy. He knew how to hold his tongue and operate as a team player in the dysfunctional setting of the BIA as well as with Interior Department officials. In the 1950s and 1960s, at a time when Indians were a very low priority in Washington and Congress mandated "federal withdrawal," outsiders such as Robert Burnette, the former tribal chairman of the Rosebud Sioux, saw Bennett as "too nice a guy to rock the boat."³ To others, such as policy reformer and historian Alvin Josephy Jr. (a non-Indian), Bennett was viewed as a two-faced bureaucrat.⁴ Yet recent historical writings have revealed another side to this man.

Historians R. Warren Metcalf and Thomas Clarkin clearly show that Bennett had a strong dislike for those pushing termination. Metcalf insists that Bennett had contempt for Senator Arthur Watkins, termination's "main man" in Congress, and was furious with Watkins's proposal to terminate the Paiutes, who had not consented to the policy. Though he was a strong opponent of termination, Bennett's work was largely behind the scenes. He had helped found the National Congress of American Indians in 1944, but he was excluded from a leadership position because of the NCAI's restrictions on having BIA personnel in its governing body. Clarkin goes further, presenting Bennett as a subversive working on behalf of Indian communities in the Interior Department. Although he never pushed for new legislation while he was commissioner, Clarkin insists that Bennett used his bureaucratic skills to sidetrack efforts to continue termination policies.[5]

As commissioner of Indian affairs from 1966 to 1969, Bennett did not lose track of what was happening at Oneida. His childhood friend, Norbert Hill Sr., was a major political figure on the reservation, serving as tribal chairman during the same years as Bennett's commissionership, and the two never lost touch. Bennett also made trips to Wisconsin in this period to visit his sister Prudence on the reservation. Hence, the Wisconsin Oneidas had a knowledgeable man with a detailed road map to guide them through the maze of the federal bureaucracy. They knew what grants were available and how and where to pursue funding. This was Bennett's secretive role, a "Deep Throat" providing inside information about Johnson's Great Society.[6]

The following interview of Robert L. Bennett (RB) was conducted by Joe B. Frantz (JF) on November 13, 1968, in Washington, D.C. — The Editors

JF: This is an interview with Mr. Robert L. Bennett, who is the commissioner of Indian affairs for the Department of the Interior, in his office in Washington, D.C., on November 13, 1968. Joe B. Frantz is the interviewer. Commissioner Bennett, would you identify yourself for us at the outset? I gather you have been Indian commissioner longer than anyone in the history of the service.

RB: I have been the commissioner of Indian affairs for over two and a half years, and this exceeds the record of some twenty-six months by the only other commissioner of Indian affairs who was of Indian blood. He was Colonel Ely Parker, who was on the staff of General Grant. It also happens that I am the first career public servant to hold the position of commissioner of Indian affairs, having started out in the Bureau of Indian Affairs in 1933.

JF: Where are you from originally?

RB: I'm originally from Oneida, Wisconsin, which is a small Indian community near Green Bay, Wisconsin. My association with Indian affairs goes back to the time I was a student in a government boarding school at Haskell Institute, Lawrence, Kansas, from which I graduated in 1931....

JF: ... Then after finishing Haskell Institute, did you go with the government?

RB: Yes. I've spent some thirty-six years now with the government, most of it with the Bureau of Indian Affairs in various locations. The only time I wasn't in the Bureau of Indian Affairs was when I was in the Marine Corps during World War II, and also when I spent some time with the Veterans Administration in Arizona outlining training programs for Indian veterans of that state.

JF: And you became a commissioner, then, when?

RB: April 27, 1966, I was sworn in as commissioner of Indian affairs....

JF: The Bureau of Indian Affairs, though, goes back nearly to the start of this country, doesn't it?

RB: Yes, it does. For a time it was in the military department and then, in about 1824, it was transferred to the civilian agency. It has been in existence since that time....

JF: Had you known the president [Lyndon Johnson] previous to being named the commissioner?

RB: No, I had not known the president previous to being named commissioner...and my association with him has been primarily through Mr. Stewart Udall, the secretary of the interior.

JF: I presume it was Mr. Udall who recommended you to the president?

RB: Yes, it was Mr. Udall who recommended me, and this grows out of the president's policy of trying to find career people to head up various programs of the federal government. As you know, Mr. Johnson has felt for some time that in some of these programs, it is better to have career people head up the programs rather than political appointees; and it just so happened that I was selected from the Bureau of Indian Affairs to become the commissioner....

JF: Yours has been a quite full administration. Let's get down to some of it. For instance, there has been a complete turnaround, as I gather, in this matter of Indian termination policy.

RB: Yes, there has. This was stated first of all by the president when he gave emphasis to the developmental aspects of his policy, both in terms of human and resource development, as far as the Indians were concerned. He became quite explicit about the termination policy in his special message of March 6 [1968]. Prior to that, he had also stated to Secretary [John] Gardner of Health, Education, and Welfare that he was opposed to unilateral termination, and this message was given to over three hundred tribal representatives in the national meeting in Kansas City in February 1967. So all throughout his public announcements, he has taken this position. This has since been followed, you know, by the passage of Senate Concurrent Resolution No. 11, introduced by Senator [George] McGovern of South Dakota, who is chairman of the Subcommittee on Indian Affairs. This resolution states the sense of Congress also that there must be programs developed by and with the Indian people for their development and less concern be given to any kind of policy which would unilaterally terminate the federal government's responsibilities to Indian people.

JF: Well, now, approximately two decades ago, there was enough popular thinking along this line that Congress did establish a policy of unilateral termination. Why do you think you had this switch?

RB: Well, I think because the whole political climate has changed since 1950. I think that if such a policy were being considered in Congress today in the light of the responsibility which the nation feels to various disadvantaged groups, such a resolution as HR 108 would not pass the Congress. The fact that Senate Concurrent Resolution No. 11 was passed, which is almost in opposition to Resolution 108 of the 1950s, indicates that there is a change in the whole national political climate.

JF: Now, what does this [suggest] to the person of the future — what is going to happen?

RB: Well, I think the president outlined a sort of very broad blueprint in his special message when he stated that the kind of relationship he wanted to see between the federal government and Indian people is one of partnership, in working at their various problems, which would include the participation and the thinking and decisions of the Indian people, along with the resources that the federal government and other governmental agencies have to offer. And I interpret this partnership to mean one in which the people in the federal government sit down and work with Indian people because they want to and not because they have to. And I think once we get this kind of spirit in terms of our relationship with the Indian people, that, with Indian leadership playing a vital role, progress will be accelerated.

JF: Previous to this, the idea had been for the federal government to withdraw as a partner. Is that correct?

RB: During the policies of the 1950s, it was a program which was also entitled, in addition to "terminating the trusteeship," the "withdrawal of services from Indian people." And history has proven that in many areas where services have been withdrawn, the local community has not been able to step in and provide the services formerly provided by the federal government. But I think — again referring back to the changed national political climate brought about largely by the policies of President Johnson — the federal government is helping local communities to provide services for their citizens all over the country, not only just for Indians but for everybody. So it is within this context, I believe, that it has been possible to bring about the change in the policy with respect to Indians.

JF: Do you work with the Indian claims problems?

RB: Yes, we [do]. We have certain specific responsibilities. One of these specific responsibilities is, of course, to furnish all of the available information that we have to the tribes and their attorneys. We also have a responsibility to make loans to tribes who do not have the financing to develop information in support of their claims. The Claims Commission also asks for our recommendations whenever there are any compromise settlements between the United States and the tribes. We have to furnish a social-economic report on all tribes who win claims to the Congress before Congress authorizes the expenditure of the money by the tribe. And we also have to make our recommendations to the Congress as to the best method, usually through planning with tribes, in which any monies awarded to the tribes should be distributed.

JF: Well, now, when the Indian Claims Commission delivers a case to the Court of Claims, what is the procedure?

RB: When the Indian Claims Commission makes a decision, or the Court of Claims makes a decision, they furnish a report to the Congress of the United States and to the Treasury. The Treasury then requests an appropriation by Congress to pay the claim. When Congress makes this appropriation, the money is deposited in the Treasury of the United States to the credit of the tribe at 4 percent simple interest. Thereafter it is not available for expenditure until authorized by Congress. This means that the tribe, in cooperation with the Bureau of Indian Affairs, has to come up with a program which is presented to the Congress, and Congress then authorizes the use of funds, usually for whatever program purposes that may be requested by the tribe.

JF: Have you had any instances of Congress reneging on a Claims Commission recommendation?

RB: No, there have been no instances of [that]. There have been some discussions as to what possibly might be the best use the tribe might make of their money, but there is no case that I know of where any payment of a claim has been withheld by the Congress.

JF: Have you established a formula for the tribe's use of the money that is awarded, or is this worked out by the individual tribe?

RB: This is generally worked out by the individual tribes; however, our preference and the preference of most of the tribes is that a certain proportion of the money be available for investment purposes, while others...

JF: Investment in what?

RB: Well, this could be investment in businesses; it could be investment in the purchase of land; it could be any income-producing investment of any kind. And then we all know that with the economic situation on most of the reservations, particularly those in isolated areas, there is need for immediate expenditures in the way of housing and improvements of this kind. Most of the tribes also have a great concern about higher education, and a great many of the tribes set up either actual scholarship funds or, in some cases, trust funds, to support a scholarship program for higher education.

JF: Has the introduction of new claims about reached its peak, or did you envisage a continuing group of claimants?

RB: The time for the filing of claims under the Claims Commission Act of 1946 has expired.

JF: The Claims Commission was extended at one time...

RB: The Claims Commission has been extended several times, the most recent being five years from April 1967; but while the time of the Claims Commission has been extended, the time for filing claims has not been extended. The life of the Claims Commission has been extended to take care of the business brought about by the filing of claims prior to the time limit set in the Claim Commission Act, so that if there are any future claims that any tribe has against the United States, these can only be pursued if they get special authorization or what they call a jurisdictional act from the Congress.

JF: Can you give me approximately the total that has been awarded to date?

RB: It runs a little over $315 million. I think one of the first claims awarded was one of the largest, and it was $32 million to the Confederated Bands of Ute of Utah and Colorado. Some of the most recent awards, which have been quite substantial, are $15 million to the Cheyenne and Arapaho of Western Oklahoma; $6 million to the Spokane tribe of Washington. And so the individual awards range from $4,000 or $5,000 on up to the $32 million for the Ute Indian tribes.

JF: It seems to me that there is a popular misconception that you think of Indians as all being in the trans-Mississippi west. You do have a considerable concern with Indians to the east of the Mississippi, do you not?

RB: Yes, we do. Of course, there are those in Wisconsin, in Michigan east of the Mississippi, and then we have the substantial groups with which we are heavily involved — these are the Choctaw Indians of Mississippi; the Eastern Cherokee of North Carolina; and the Seminole and Miccosukees of Florida. We do have a limited kind of relationship with some of the Five [actually Six] Nations of New York also.

JF: What effect has the Civil and Criminal Jurisdiction Act of 1953 [P.L. 280] had on your policy in the Indian Bureau?

RB: Well, the Indian tribes have never been in favor of the extension of the civil and criminal jurisdiction of states over Indian reservations, and they have fought constantly since the enactment of this legislation to have it amended to provide for a consent feature, which would mean that the state could not extend civil or criminal jurisdiction over an Indian tribe unless it was with the consent of the tribe. In the recent so-called Open Housing or Civil Rights Act of 1968, this was included; so the way the Civil and Criminal Jurisdiction Act now stands as amended, it does require consent of the tribe for the extension of state criminal and civil jurisdiction. It also provides that where states have assumed or were given this jurisdiction by the 1953 act, they can retrocede their jurisdiction or the tribes can request retrocession. So I think the tribes feel they have won a great political victory as a result of getting a consent provision made a part of the Civil and Criminal Jurisdiction Act....

JF: You stay reasonably alert to what is going on in Congress in these sorts of social services or economic services, whatever they may be?

RB: Yes, we do. We watch all general legislation of that kind to be sure that Indian tribes are included. And then we also, of course, have specific legislation in certain Indian matters, too.

JF: Do you work through your Interior Committee in the two houses, or do you work with the specific committee that is considering the legislation?

RB: On all Indian legislation we work through our substantive committees of the Interior and Insular Affairs, both in the House and in the Senate. We also work on certain policy matters in funding, of course, with
the Appropriation Committees of both houses. When other committees
are considering broad, general legislation, we go directly to these committees with our recommendations. Quite often, the committees themselves refer broad legislative matters to the Department of the Interior for
its comments, and this provides us an opportunity to make recommendations.

JF: You have had a conscious policy of upgrading health services to the
Indians, have you not — of building hospitals and staffing them and trying to give a better grade of health service generally than has been the case
in the past?

RB: Yes, as you know, in 1953 the jurisdiction for health programs of
Indians was transferred from the Bureau of Indian Affairs to the Division
of Indian Health, which has its national offices out in Silver Spring,
Maryland. The Division of Indian Health is under the Public Health
Service in the Department of Health, Education, and Welfare; and I
know Dr. Rabeau, who was the director of Indian health. There has certainly been a very real effort in many health areas, so that there has been
an appreciable decline in infant mortality under the new programs; further, there has been a special program authorized for sanitation, Public
Law 121, under which the tribe and the Public Health Service developed
water and sewer project[s] in Indian communities. There is a strong emphasis also on the education of community health people, people who
will be able to orient individuals in the local Indian communities toward
better sanitation, better nutrition, and better health care. There also, of
course, has been an upgrading of the facilities and personnel in the Division of Indian Health, so I think there have been some real strides made
in improved health services. Much of this program comes about through
recommendations made by the National Indian Health Advisory Board,
which is made up of public citizens, including Indians, with whom the
Division of Indian Health meets. We also meet with them on a regular
basis on many mutual problems of concern to both of us, and we find

that these meetings are very successful and very informative, and quite often, both Dr. Rabeau and I issue joint statements of policy and agreement following these coordinated meetings.

JF: Has the Indian life expectancy rate run even with or behind the general population of the United States?

RB: It has run considerably behind, but there has been a marked improvement in life expectancy.

JF: Within the past decade?

RB: Within the past decade, that is correct. Most of the health problems, I believe, are of an environmental nature. By working together with the Division of Indian Health in improving the environment for Indian people, I am sure that much of their health problems can be eliminated. I believe that Indian people still have many illnesses which the general population doesn't have any more because of improved environment. With the sanitation program, with the health service, and with their improved housing and improved economic standard, we believe that we can eliminate many of these causes of illness.

JF: Other than your own personal energy and imagination, is there some routine or some established method of coordination of these various Indian services between the several departments here in Washington?

RB: Yes, there is a means to accomplish this. [President] Johnson, again in his special message [March 6, 1968], pointed out that he felt that there was this lack of coordination between the various departments, and since he of course is against any waste in government or loss of efficiency, he established under the vice president the National Council on Indian Opportunity. This is made up of six cabinet people and the director of the Office of Economic Opportunity, plus six national Indian leaders. This council almost has cabinet status, and one of their main functions is to be a coordinating force of all of the efforts being made at the federal level on behalf of Indians. Also this council has been given certain specific responsibilities to make recommendations to the president for policy....

JF: This was established by executive order?

RB: This was established by executive order the day following the president's special message of March 6. And the vice president has given the six Indian members special areas of responsibility, and each of these Indian leaders will be chairing various aspects of the Indian problem. Mrs. LaDonna Harris is the chairman on the off-reservation or urban Indians, and she is starting a series of meetings next week, beginning with a meeting in Minneapolis, Minnesota. This meeting will be held on November 22 and November 23. She will then have meetings in other larger urban areas to become acquainted with the problems that these people have. The president did single out this group of Indian people as needing special attention in his special message of March 6....

JF: Other than a sort of psychological shove, does the administration give any incentive to industry to establish plants on tribal lands?

RB: The one incentive that they do have, of course, is the training programs offered by the federal government. Another incentive is that if the capital investment is made by the tribes, this of course is not taxable, because this is real property held in a trust status by the secretary of the interior. So there is a tax incentive also in connection with some of the plants located on the reservations....

JF: Have there been significant changes in land ownership and leasing for Indians?

RB: There have been some significant changes, because we are concerned now with the development of Indian resources, and we are going in for developmental kinds of leases and programs, more than being concerned with immediate cash return. In the past, because we were concerned with immediate cash return which we sometimes did not feel was sufficient for certain resources, the resources have lain there twenty and thirty years without development. We are now taking a deeper look at the returns to the tribe, not only in terms of cash return but other benefits such as jobs and the attraction of other businesses because of the developmental-type program. And with this in mind, we have changed our attitude and are going in for more development leases. In long-term leases, our recommendation to the tribes is that they get what we call a "piece of the action." We don't like to see them just turn over the raw resource to some developer for ninety-nine years, out of which they get a little money each month or each year; we'd rather see the tribes participate as partners. In some cases, as indicated by the pictures I have in the office here of a winter ski resort of the Mescalero Apache, and then this summer resort here on the Warm Springs reservation, these are totally owned tribal facilities....

JF: In September you made a speech in Omaha in which you spoke of the fact that in these past several years the Indian was reaching a sort of new plateau in his search for identity and also had improved his tribal organization. I wonder if you could elaborate on those two things.

RB: I think with the present political climate of the country and as the attitude of people toward one another changes in the country, the Indian people have seen the opportunity to do something they've wanted to do for a long time, and that is to assert themselves as a group and as a distinct group. You find that even though they are carried by circumstances into large areas — here again, they congregate together. And in the city of Los Angeles alone, I don't believe there's a weekend goes by all summer that there isn't a big Indian ceremonial or powwow thing in one of the public parks in the city of Los Angeles. The Indian people, as I analyze it, seek several things. One, they seek their own identity as Indian people. And you'll find in Indian country that there are more ceremonials and there are more powwows, if you want to call them that, going on than ever before. There is more participation, particularly by younger Indians, than ever before. And I think even the costuming is being upgraded. You don't see any bedraggled feathers or old pieces of costumes like you used to see. They're coming back real strong. And then, secondly, is their tribal identification. They want to be identified as an Indian individual and with a tribal group. Now, this is the one thing, I think, that eventually every person will have to understand in connection with the relationship between the Indian tribe and the Indian government. In addition to whatever commitments the Indian people feel the federal government has made to them, the Indian people also want just as much recognition by the federal government that they are the Seneca Nation, the Navajo tribe, or the White

Mountain Apaches. They want the federal government to say to them and recognize, "You are the White Mountain Apaches," or "You are..." Whatever may be the future relationship from a legal point of view between the tribe and the federal government, they will resist any effort on the part of the federal government to say, "You are no longer a tribe of Indians," even though the federal government may not have any further commitments to them as a people. Then, third, the Indian people throughout the country, more than ever before, want to know what's going on in Indian Affairs. We started a publication here called *The Indian Record*. We started that less than two years ago as a voice coming from the commissioner's office to the Indian people. And we started with — our first edition was six hundred copies and now we are [at] fifteen thousand copies a month. And the Indian people act like they're almost starving for news of what's going on in Indian Affairs. And then there is a concern, of course, with their property rights in any commonly owned resources as tribal members. This has been highlighted by the claims that are being prosecuted against the United States. If they are a tribal member, they want to participate in whatever distribution is made of any awards made to them by the federal government.

I think the future for the Indian people is very bright. I think their hopes and expectations are higher than they have ever been before. And I think that the interest shown by the president and by the administration in the last few years in Indians is really beginning to show results in Indian country, not only in terms of what you see physically but in terms of attitudes. When you go out to Indian country, I can sense — I just have a feeling that there is something going on, that there [is] movement there....

JF: Vitality.
RB: That there's a vitality and these communities are again coming into their own.

JF: In the younger generation now, you went through a period [in] which you in a sense rejected the Indian background and tried to assimilate into the non-Indian world; and now...you have come back to the rediscovery of the Indian values while taking what is worthwhile, I judge, out of the non-Indian world. Is that correct?

RB: Yes, this is correct.

JF: Kind of a rediscovery on the younger generation's part?

RB: Yes, this is true. When I went to a government school, you know, there were such restrictions as speaking your own language and things of this kind; and they tried to divorce you from your Indian background just as quickly as possible. This kind of philosophy, of course, has since been rejected, and now the young Indian people are beginning to see that they will have a meaningful place. And as I stated in my talk about them and to them, it is up to the government and up to the tribes themselves to see that we provide a place for them....

JF:...I'm just trying to get an answer. What do you think the Indian attitude toward President Johnson and his administration in general has been?

RB: I think the Indian people are very responsive to the president. I think they recognize the fact that he has not only a passing or political interest but a very deep personal interest in them. He has shown this, certainly, at every opportunity that Indian people have had to meet with him. And he extended an invitation, and several hundred Indian leaders did attend my swearing-in ceremony on April 27, 1966, and they appreciated this very much.

JF: Where was this held? Was this held indoors or out?

RB: This was held indoors in the White House.

JF: That was a pretty good gathering.

RB: Yes, [it] was. All in all, I think they think a great deal of him and hold him in very high regard. And I think as time goes on and they begin to reflect back on history, that his stature is going to grow immeasurably with them....

JF: The Bureau of Indian Affairs has had, I don't need to tell you, a checkered history with some pretty inept leadership at times. Do you think —

leaving you out of it — do you think that it has finally sort of gotten itself a course and knows where it is going?

RB: I think that it has gotten itself a course because it has become, you might say, an advocate — I don't like to use the word, but almost a tool of the Indian people, and I think this is what its main function should be. It should be used by the Indian people to help them accomplish their goals....

JF: Well, the old-time attitude was a paternalistic, authoritarian sort of attitude.

RB: Oh, it definitely was, and one of the things we have to guard against continually now is the more subtle kind of paternalism which can easily creep into a federal bureaucracy or in the attitude of private agencies. Because sometimes, in our enthusiasm, we might get a little impatient with the progress they are making, but I think we have to measure it by the fact ...not is the bureau progressing, but are the Indian people progressing?

JF: Other than just giving yourself lectures about this, how have you avoided this subtle paternalism?

RB: Well, we have many kinds of orientation sessions, and in this orientation session with our staff, we also invite Indian leaders. So the Indian people...

JF: They orient you?

RB: Yes, and the Indian people know what we are telling our staff at the same time the staff knows it. So that there is this kind of, you might say, control that is being exercised by the Indian people themselves because they are sitting in these meetings and they hear what we are telling our staff, what we are expecting of them.

JF: When did this procedure begin?

RB: I started this about a year ago, and we've had several seminars throughout the Indian country along this line.

JF: Has it gotten some fairly rousing sessions?

RB: Oh, yes, I think we've had some real excellent sessions. And the kind of session I like is when we get into a room with a number of people where there are Bureau of Indian Affairs staff who might be Indians, and everybody is talking. It's getting to the point now where you can't tell whether that's a tribal or a bureau representative that is talking, because we're developing and trying to come up with this kind of partnership that I think the president was talking about. It's the spirit behind it more than anything else.

JF: Has there been any conscious effort to recruit Indians for employment in the Bureau of Indian Affairs?

RB: Oh, yes, we are making a very strenuous effort to recruit qualified Indians, and we are also providing training programs within the bureau, so that the Indian people can advance in the bureau. And we also have an approved orientation program whereby we hope to bring young Indians into the Bureau of Indian Affairs for seasoning for a couple of years, and then get them out into the other agencies of government or private industry. We have, I think, about a dozen young Indian girls now as secretaries over in the State Department.

JF: Oh, really?

RB: So we are beginning to not only provide employment in Indian Affairs for Indians, but we are also seeing ourselves as a means by which Indian people can acquire experience, sophistication, and move out into other areas....

JF: Approximately how many employees do you have?

RB: We have approximately fifteen thousand employees.

JF: What percentage would you say have a significant amount of Indian blood?

RB: About 50 percent, a little over half of our fifteen thousand employees are Indians; about one-third of our staff here in Washington are Indians....

JF: There is talk from time to time of sort of changing the nature of the Department of Interior to more of a Department of Conservation. In a case like that, do you think the Bureau of Indian Affairs should remain where it is, or do you think it belongs more naturally with, say, something like [Health, Education, and Welfare]?

RB: Well, my recommendation already has been that there should be an assistant secretary of the interior for the Bureau of Indian Affairs, and also for the programs of the islands and territories, because both of these agencies operate people-oriented programs....

Notes

1. For Bennett, see Thomas Clarkin, *Federal Indian Policy in the Kennedy and Johnson Administrations, 1961–1969* (Albuquerque: University of New Mexico Press, 2001), 227–270; Warren R. Metcalf, *Termination's Legacy: The Discarded Indians of Utah* (Lincoln: University of Nebraska Press, 2002), 12, 14, 132–160, 177–179; and Richard N. Ellis, "Robert L. Bennett (1966–1969)," in *The Commissioners of Indian Affairs, 1824–1977*, ed. Robert M. Kvasnicka and Herman J. Viola, 325–333 (Lincoln: University of Nebraska Press, 1979). For Bennett's own thoughts and writings, see Kenneth R. Philp, ed., *Indian Self-Rule: First-Hand Accounts of Indian-White Relations from Roosevelt to Reagan* (Salt Lake City: Howe Brothers, 1986), 83–86, 162–164, 209–211, 224–225; Robert L. Bennett, "New Era for the American Indian," *Natural History* 75 (February 1967): 6–11; Bennett "Building Indian Economies with Land Settlement Funds," *Human Organization* 20 (1961–1962): 159–163.

2. Bennett "Building Indian Economies with Land Settlement Funds," *Human Organization* 20 (1961–1962): 159–163.

3. Robert Burnette and John Koster, *The Road to Wounded Knee* (New York: Bantam Books, 1974), 161.

4. Alvin M. Josephy Jr. et al., eds., *Red Power: The American Indians Fight for Freedom*, 2nd ed. (Lincoln: University of Nebraska Press, 1999), 75.

5. Clarkin, *Federal Indian Policy in the Kennedy and Johnson Administrations*, 227–269; Metcalf, *Termination's Legacy*, 143–144.

6. Norbert Seabrook Hill Sr., interview by Laurence M. Hauptman, October 17, 1978, Oneida, WI.

Protecting Indian Sovereignty

by Ernest Stevens Sr.

The concluding article is by Ernest L. Stevens Sr., well known in Indian country as Ernie Stevens. On the scene for more than fifty years, he came to national prominence in the early 1970s. In 1975, Congress appointed Stevens to the American Indian Policy Review Commission to head a staff of young Indian professionals in developing this massive project. The highest post that had been occupied by an Indian in previous administrations was the commissioner of Indian affairs, which had been held by a fellow Oneida and friend and mentor to Stevens, Robert L. Bennett. As was true with others who emerged at that time, Stevens was passionate, outspoken, and articulate, and his talents were quickly recognized by Indian leaders in government such as Louis R. Bruce Jr., a Mohawk who was commissioner of Indian affairs when Ernie was called to Washington, D.C., and by Congressional leaders such as Senator James Abourezk and Representative Morris "Mo" Udall, who would later bring him onto their Indian committees for his charisma and leadership skills.

Stevens was born on February 17, 1932, and for the first five years of his life spoke only the Oneida language. His mother, Maria Hinton, and her family, the Christjohns of Oneida, formed the basis of his lifelong interest in the history and heritage of the Oneida people. Ernie's other defining characteristic is his devotion to self-improvement and education. He attended UW–Stevens Point, earned a B.S. degree in economics and business administration from Mt. Senario College, and was a Harvard MIT development fellow.

His experience is not confined to Indian issues. Stevens was appointed as a Federal Trade Commission hearing officer and also worked in the Department of Justice from 1970 to 1973. During this period he was also active in national Indian organizations, including being elected as first vice president of the National Congress of American Indians in 1973.

Though he worked within the system, Stevens never forgot his roots and has continued to follow the Oneida longhouse ceremonies and teachings. His wit and insight — along with his vast knowledge of Indian history — have made him a captivating orator. He is that rare combination of tribal elder, storyteller, and source of information for anyone fortunate to have known him or heard him speak.

Today, Stevens lives in retirement on the Oneida reservation in Wisconsin, where he is still called upon for guidance by both old and young Indian people. — The Editors

INDIAN IDENTITY IS A COMPLEX NOTION wrapped in legal theory, government definitions, and a public bias formed by many years of persistent, inaccurate information in schools and media. For Indian people living on the reservations of their ancestors, Indian identity is an infinitely more intricate concept, complicated by more than 560 remaining recognized Indian tribes and more than 175 distinct Indian languages, not to mention the processes of assimilation and the federal government's attempt to make blood quantum the ultimate criterion for Indian identity. Indians have had many conscientious and outspoken friends in Congress, the press, academia, and other forums, but we have also had our share of cynical and forceful enemies of tribal sovereignty and the rights of Indian people, a fact that must never be forgotten.

In recent years Indians have focused their energies on building their political capacities, and the fact that we now are able to come to the table and be taken seriously is a measure of our success. Along the way, we have also developed some powerful alliances in and out of government: Indian organizations made voting a primary issue during the most recent national election, and candidates in both parties looked to them for support. What that showed in a very visible way was that Indians are participating in the body politic and every other facet of American life and expression.

Though U.S. citizenship was forced upon us in 1924, we have maintained an intact bicultural identity, evident in our oral histories and knowledge of our ancestors as well as in the Native languages used both ceremonially and in daily affairs. But biculturalism is never easy. For instance, though American Indians have participated in the armed services of the United States in every war (I personally served two tours of combat duty in Korea), they did so knowing that the government they fought for often acted dishonorably to them and their ancestors.

This problem of maintaining our cultural integrity is clearly one for which Native people must be responsible. Indian children must be prepared to participate successfully in the larger society without losing connection to or compromising the intrinsic values of their ancestors. Therefore, education of our children to their highest capacity is absolutely necessary, as they will carry on the responsibility of protecting the sovereignty and culture that is our heritage. Indeed, of all the issues facing

Indian country today, the protection of tribal sovereignty — tribal self-government in its purest form, existing only to serve the people — remains the top priority of Native American leaders. While specific needs such as health care, education, and housing are essential, none of these needs can be fulfilled if tribal sovereignty is lost.

. . .

By the mid-twentieth century, years of dispossession and oppression had left tribes with diminished autonomy and more dependence upon federal support for their basic needs. This led to marginal tribal economies, little to no infrastructure, correspondingly fewer sophisticated internal systems, and minimal interaction with external local governments. That is certainly no longer the case. Tribal economies have increased for the past sixty years, particularly in the past twenty. Much of this growth is often attributed to gaming (which has been a significant factor), but there are other roots. A number of indirect developments also set the stage for the tribal economic reality that we know today.

The sixties and seventies were a time of great change for Indian people as well as for the general population. In the early 1960s, the fishing rights and taxation cases raised issues that were compounded by tribal assertion of constitutional treaty rights.

In 1975, the Indian Self-Determination and Education Assistance Act was signed into law, and the tribal infrastructure changed in an important way: for the first time, tribes became employers, managing their own programs for health care, housing, and education. This policy change provided employment opportunities for tribal members who had acquired professional degrees and practical experience. It also provided a training opportunity for middle managers, a critical segment of the workforce in any organization.

The social upheavals going on in the United States at this time, enflamed by the war in Vietnam, included Indian activists demanding recognition of their rights to self-government, identity, and culture. In the 1970s, the American Indian Movement (AIM) became a strong voice for tribal sovereignty. In 1972 they confronted and occupied the Bureau of Indian Affairs to demand reform of oppressive policies and accountability for management of the trust assets of Indian people. Although I was an employee of the government, I was trusted enough by both sides to act as a negotiator, and we succeeded in bringing about a peaceful settlement to the event. (While many of the issues regarding the independence of tribal governments have markedly improved, the issue of mismanaged trust assets by the BIA remains unresolved and is the subject of a complicated lawsuit pending in federal courts.)

In 1973, another significant event occurred: AIM occupied Wounded Knee, South Dakota, site of the last Indian massacre by the U.S. cavalry in 1890. Two of my sons, Ernie Jr. and Kelly, teenage boys at the time, participated in this armed confrontation.

In 1975, the Senate Select Committee on Indian Affairs was established, and among its first actions was a study of the relationship of tribes to the federal government and the local governments around Indian reservations. The committee's first chairman, Senator Abourezk of South Dakota, selected me to head the project, and this study became the basis for much of the subsequent congressional legislation. The Senate Select Committee studied the results at length, and the American Indian Policy Review Commission published a comprehensive report in 1977, which included recommendations for every phase of tribal governance and their relationship with states and the federal government. The economic and self-governmental progress in Indian country over the past forty years can be directly traced to these origins.

. . .

The transition that began in the 1960s and 1970s, when the Indian Self-Determination and Education Assistance Act led tribes to take direct responsibility for programs previously administered by the federal government, soon led to a new development: tribes began to venture into entrepreneurial commerce, primarily cigarettes and fireworks. Now a new set of legal battles began, over jurisdictional issues of civil regulation between states and tribes. The state won some of the cases, such as the right to regulate and tax cigarettes, the sale of fireworks, and the regulation of the sale of alcohol. However, the tribes also won some very important cases: the upholding of treaty fishing rights, the prohibition of state taxes on tribal trust lands, the right to religious freedom, and the right to apply Indian preference in employment law. Finally, the right to operate bingo was upheld in various federal jurisdictions and ultimately by the U.S. Supreme Court. The Indian Gaming Regulatory Act of 1988 was a direct congressional response to the trends of Indian people successfully using federal courts to assert their legal rights.

Native Americans had learned valuable lessons and gained invaluable experience in managing tribal affairs in the most practical way. The need to create tribal regulatory bodies could not have been clearer, and tribal leaders promptly took advantage of that opportunity. Today, most tribal governments have adopted constitutional elective systems and have developed organizational structures to manage their resources and economies. As the tribal economies have grown, so has the need to engage with the surrounding nontribal communities. It has become more common than not to find tribal leaders and tribal administrators meeting with local government leaders and administrators to address trends and plans that impact one another's interests. These government-to-government interactions require informed leaders, often aided by technical experts, to prepare for both long- and short-range plans in zoning, economic diversification, development of natural resources, and the preparation of future generations to address those responsibilities. Government-to-government relations are also a necessity in developing and maintaining formal agreements to jointly address police and fire protection, emergency disaster planning, and sharing of utilities. Such agreements for common cause reflect local and state governments' growing respect for tribal government, a direct recognition of the sovereignty of tribal governments.

. . .

Tribal governance in today's world requires specialized knowledge and experience. Some of these skill sets come from formal training in the professions of health care, law, business, engineering, and accounting. Other necessary leadership skills are acquired through experience: political involvement, awareness of the community's particular history, and participation in cultural activities. In the past, leadership in Native communities evolved from tradition and custom, and those whom the general public called "Chief" were actually spokespeople selected by those who could best assess their intellectual abilities as well as their strength of character. The needs of the pre-European Native community may have been very different from today's in terms of daily activity, but one need that has remained constant is the need for knowledge and leadership. The evolution of traditional law has provided both the criteria and processes for both. Courage, intelligence, and dedication were then and are today the basis for representation. The leadership and membership of organizations such as the National Congress of American Indians (NCAI), the National Indian Education Association (NIEA), the Native American Rights Fund (NARF), and the National Indian Gaming Association (NIGA) reflect those respected characteristics. These groups also frequently provide administrations of both parties with recommendations for appointments — reflecting a respect that wasn't always there in the past.

. . .

Today, the federal government still plays a major role in tribal self-governance. For example, the Department of the Interior issues regulations regarding the status of lands that tribes may hold in trust; Native American communities rely largely on allocations for critical Indian health services from the Department of Health and Human Services; federal courts, including the U.S. Supreme Court, continue to hear cases challenging tribal jurisdiction; and Congress continues to introduce new legislation and consider proposed amendments to existing laws that affect tribal government. This federal influence is as clear and present now as it was when I came to Washington in the early 1970s.

However, through their own initiatives in recent years, tribes have achieved milestones in health care, education, employment, and the general welfare of their communities. This progress, however, cannot be sustained without the steadfast protection of the right of tribes to govern themselves and control the activities on their reservations. Because of the potential impact on tribal sovereignty, organizations such as the NCAI, NIEA, NARF, and NIGA commonly appear at congressional hearings on Indian issues. Alert to any activity that could negatively impact tribal rights, members of these organizations closely watch both houses of Congress and immediately notify tribal leaders of the need for their attention, comments, and presence on a given matter. Educated, prepared tribal government officials and their representatives are asserting positive influence on federal institutions, fulfilling the concerns issued by the American Indian Policy Review Commission. These are the modern-day tools and weapons that must be used to protect tribal sovereignty.

As Native Americans we rely on the literal and actionable truth of the U.S. Constitution, and on the United States' commitment to the rule of law. Tribal lawsuits to protect hunting and fishing rights, land claims, and jurisdictional regulation are based upon that reliance. The United States' commitment to protect our sovereignty is questionable: our treaties have been undermined and otherwise ignored. Still, we have prevailed in federal and state courts by asserting that the Constitution is "the law of the land" and not an irrational emotional expression. Today's fight is essentially the same as it was in the past, but Indians have brought new energy in the form of their own representation to Washington. We are not relying on non-Native spokespeople to protect our interests. Some Native people are understandably embittered, while others have taken the challenging path of believing that we can respect the values of our ancestors while being good American citizens, in a thoughtful, determined, proactive way. That is both our responsibility and our children's, and to achieve it we rely on the Indian commitment to family and community. This commitment has never been lost; nor is it dependent on the outside for its vitality. It is the ultimate link we have to our ancestors.

Conclusion

The Indian nations viewed treaties as covenants, as moral statements which could not be broken unless by mutual consent.... The purpose of these intergovernmental contracts was not to give rights to the Indians — rights which as sovereign nations they already possessed — but to remove from them certain rights which they already had. In treaty making, tribes were the grantors and the United States the recipient, and rights were granted to the U.S. by or from Indian nations.... [R]ights to land, water, hunting, government, etc., which were not expressly granted away by the tribes in a treaty, or taken away by later federal statute, were reserved by that tribe. — Stan Webster (Oneida), Wisconsin Indian Resource Council[1]

*I*n *A Nation within a Nation: Voices of the Oneidas in Wisconsin*, the editors have examined much of twentieth-century Native American history from the inside outward. Past scholars have largely presented Native Americans in this era within the framework of fighting Washington officialdom — Native Americans attempting to overcome injustices or pushing for "self-determination" or "self-rule." With their linear worldview focusing on advancing progress, these twentieth-century studies view the Indians as "fighting for freedom" and rights within the American Constitution system. Yet, as Stan Webster's quotation suggests, Wisconsin Oneidas start with a different premise and have a distinct view: namely, that they, as well as the indigenous nations of the Americas, have always possessed an inherent sovereignty, which has been chipped away or overwhelmed by outside forces. As has been shown, the Wisconsin Oneidas maintain their own concept of sovereignty in more ways than just by lobbying in Washington, D.C., or in Madison, Wisconsin, for programs, funding, jobs, or legislation to extend their constitutional rights.

By maintaining kinship and protecting their territory, however relocated or reduced from aboriginal times, the Wisconsin Oneidas separate themselves from the outside. Their continued and determined efforts to gain recognition for past injustices, such as their dispossession from their original central–New York homeland, obscure their real concerns about maintaining their territory in Wisconsin, where the largest population of Oneidas resides today. While they can never separate themselves culturally or spiritually from their New York roots and other Iroquoian peoples, much of their focus is on maintaining, protecting, and rebuilding their community in Wisconsin. The Amended Treaty of Buffalo Creek of February 3, 1838, at Washington recognizes their Wisconsin Oneida Territory in a government-to-government manner, reinforcing their already-existing view that they are and were sovereign peoples, long before the appearance of non-Indians on the North American continent. It is important to note, as Webster writes, that the Amended Treaty of Buffalo Creek did not invent Oneida sovereignty, because these Indians, as do others, believed that they always had a separate estate and nationhood.

Although most Wisconsin Oneidas are dual citizens under American law, they see their relationship to Washington in a somewhat different manner from the way federal officials perceive it. To the Wisconsin Oneidas, military service has had a special place in the community's life and in maintaining their sovereignty. By paying tribute to these soldiers and earlier ones who have served in the United States armed forces, from the American Revolution to the Iraqi and Afghan Wars, they are telling outsiders that they have made sacrifices, often at a heavy cost, at difficult times in American history. By polishing this chain of alliance, established in the American Revolution and later in the Treaty of Canandaigua on November 11, 1794, Wisconsin Oneidas expect reciprocity from the American nation — namely, a recognition of these Indians' inherent right to maintain their own sovereignty, to hold onto their territory, to pursue their land claims, and to continue their separate governmental structure.

By maintaining tribal government, the Wisconsin Oneidas in many ways operate separately from municipal, state, and national governments. Although the outward form of this government — the Oneida Business Committee — appears to be a western-style corporate structure designed in the 1930s, the Oneida General Tribal Council, consisting of the entire enrolled Wisconsin Oneida population over the age of twenty-one, can override decisions. It should be noted that the Oneida governing body has frequently altered over the years, adjusting to new and changing times.

The Wisconsin Oneida leadership has dealt with the present with one eye on the future. In 1909–1911 and again in the 1950s, though federal officials presented termination as inevitable, the Oneidas rejected a lump-sum cash payout of their treaty rights. Their insistence on remaining a sovereign Indian nation recognized by federal treaty won out over a monetary award. With the passage of the Indian Claims Commission Act of 1946, the Wisconsin Oneida tribal government filed a series of cases in its pursuit of various claims, including their 150-year-old New York land claim. When their attorney, Marvin Chapman, insisted in one of these actions that they accept a financial settlement, both the Oneida Nation Business Committee and the Oneida Nation General Council overwhelmingly rejected it. In their view, the Wisconsin Oneidas were not looking for an immediate payout but were attempting to ensure that their sovereignty would not be sacrificed by accepting a financial settlement. Thus, they were ensuring that their later claims actions against two counties of New York state would not be jeopardized. In traditional Iroquoian terms, they were considering the welfare of Oneidas for seven generations to come.

Through planning, the Wisconsin Oneida tribal leadership has been able to strengthen the community's infrastructure. Indeed, their purchase of an industrial park in Green Bay in the late 1960s, long before it could turn a profit, showed the thinking of leadership at the time and reflected their concern for the future survival of the Wisconsin Oneida community. Not only did they maintain and protect their territory, they also have reacquired treaty lands lost under the allotment policies. Today, their reservation includes more than seventeen thousand acres, substantially more than the ninety acres they held in 1934, but only 26 percent of the lands they held under the Amended Treaty of Buffalo Creek. They have become a major economic force in Wisconsin. The Oneidas fully own and operate the Radisson Hotel and Conference Center, along with their Oneida Casino, situated just across from Green Bay's Austin Straubel Airport; the Baybank, a full-service bank; the Oneida Industrial Park, a thirty-two-acre land development project with Wal-Mart as its major tenant and anchor store, and with the Oneida Mason Street Casino adjacent to the site; Oneida Printing, a state-of-the-art printing business; Oneida Nation Farms, an agricultural operation on the reservation focusing on cattle and apple raising, which provides discounted food to tribal members; Oneida Retail Enterprise, a chain of four "One Stops," several smoke shops, and one gift shop that sell Pendleton blankets, gas, and discounted cigarettes and serve as mini-marts and mini-casinos; and Seven Generations Corporation, which leases a fifty-thousand-square-foot health facility to Belin Health Systems. Moreover, the Oneida Nation of Indians is an investor, with three other Indian nations, in a Marriott Residence Inn Capitol in Washington, D.C., and is a major shareholder in the Native American Bank, N.A. Recently, they contributed money for the renovation of the Green Bay Packers' Lambeau Field, which led to the renaming of a part of the facility as the "Oneida Nation Entrance Gate." While these enterprises could be interpreted as Oneida acculturation into the world of non-Indians, the editors believe that they are merely examples of Oneida adaptation to changing circumstances, aimed at maintaining and ensuring their inherent sovereignty well into the future.

Notes

1. Quoted in David E. Wilkins, and K. Tsianina Lomawaima, *Uneven Ground: American Indian Sovereignty and Federal Law* (Norman: University of Oklahoma Press, 2001), 117. Emphasis in the original.

Bibliography

Archives and Manuscript Collections

American Philosophical Society, Philadelphia.
  Fenton, William N., Papers.
  Speck, Frank, Papers.
Brown County Local History Room Library, Green Bay, WI.
  Scrapbooks, vertical files.
Columbia University, New York.
  Lehman, Herbert, Papers.
  Poletti, Charles, Papers.
Cornell University, Ithaca, NY.
  Reed, Daniel, Papers.
Cumberland County Historical Society, Carlisle, PA.
  Records of the United States Industrial School.
  Student vertical files.
  Carlisle School publications, curriculum, photographs.
De Pere Historical Society, De Pere, WI.
  Vertical files, photographic archives.
Dwight D. Eisenhower Presidential Library, Collections. Abilene, KS.
  Bennett, Elmer, Papers.
  Benson, Ezra Taft, Papers.
  Bragdon, John Stewart, Papers.
  Chilson, O. Hatfield, Papers.
  Eisenhower, Dwight David, Records as President, 1953–1961.
  Harlow, Bryce, Papers.
  Lambie, James M., Papers.
  Oral Histories: Anderson, Clinton; Bennett, Robert L.; Benson, Ezra Taft;
    Brownell, Herbert; D'Ewart, Wesley; Folsom, Marion; Lawrence, David;
    Lewis, Orme; Watkins, Arthur.
  Rogers, William P., Papers.
  Seaton, Fred, Papers.
  United States Advisory Committee on Government Organization Records.
  United States Commission on Intergovernmental Relations Records.
  White House Central Files: Official File, General File, President's Personal
    File, Confidential File, Alphabetical File.
  Whitman, Ann, Files: Administration Series, Diary Series, DDE Diary Series,
    Name Series.

Florida Southern College, Lakeland, FL.
  Haley, James A., Papers.
Franklin D. Roosevelt Presidential Library, Hyde Park, NY.
  Berle, Adolph A., Papers.
  Presidential Records: Official File, President's Personal File, President's Sec-
    retary's File.
  Roosevelt, Eleanor, Papers.
  Roosevelt, Franklin D., Records as Governor.
Georgetown University, Washington, D.C.
  Wagner, Robert F., Sr., Papers.
Hampton Institute. Archives. Hampton, VA.
  Oneida student records, institute publications.
Harry S. Truman Library, Independence, MO.
  Brophy, William A., Papers.
  Clifford, Clark, Papers.
  Myer, Dillon S., Papers.
  Nash, Philleo, Papers.
  Truman, Harry S., Papers: President's Secretary's File, White House Central
    Files.
Hartwick College, Oneonta, NY.
  Hanley, James, Papers.
Haverford College, Haverford, PA.
  Philadelphia Yearly Meeting, Indian Committee, Records.
Humanities Research Center, University of Texas.
  La Farge, Oliver, Papers.
John F. Kennedy Presidential Library, Boston, MA.
  Collections: Kennedy, John F., Records as Senator, 1953–1961; Kennedy,
    John F., Records as President, 1961–1963; President's Office Files; White
    House Central Files.
  Kennedy, Robert F., Records as Attorney General, 1961–1964.
Library of Congress, Washington, D.C.
  Hughes, Charles Evans, Papers.
  Krug, J. A., Papers.
  La Follette Family Papers.
  Lenroot, Irvine, Papers.
  Roosevelt, Theodore, Papers.
Lyndon B. Johnson Presidential Library, Austin, TX.
  Collections: Johnson, Lyndon B., Papers; Senate Files, 1952–1961; White
    House Central Files, 1963–1968.
  Oral History: Bennett, Robert L.

Milwaukee Public Museum.
    Ritzenthaler, Robert, Field Notes.
National Archives, Washington, D.C.
    Bennett, Robert L., Office Files, RG75.
    Bureau of Indian Affairs, Central Classified Files, 1907–1939, RG75.
    Chapman, Oscar, Office Files, RG48.
    Collier, John, Office Files, RG75.
    Ickes, Harold L., Office Files, RG48.
    Indian Claims Commission Records, RG279.
    National Council on Indian Opportunity Records, RG220.
    Office of Indian Affairs, Records, 1824–1880; 1881–1907, RG75.
    Records of the U.S. Industrial School. Carlisle, PA. Student files. RG75.
Nebraska State Historical Society, Lincoln, NE.
    Butler, Hugh, Papers.
New York State Archives, Albany, NY.
    Investigation case files related to eviction of Oneida Indians, 1909–1910.
    Investigation file of Governor Charles Evans Hughes.
    New York State Governor (Charles Evans Hughes), Records.
New York State Library Manuscript Division, Albany, NY.
    Beauchamp, William, Papers.
    Parker, Arthur C., Papers.
    Society of American Indians, Papers.
    Stillman, Lulu, Papers.
Oneida Indian Historical Society, Oneida, WI, Records.
    Newspaper clipping files.
    Transcript of Indian Tribal Conference, October 18, 1956, Des Moines, IA.
    Transcript "Things to be brought up in Iowa," October 15, 1956.
Oneida Methodist Church, Oneida, WI, Church Records.
Oneida Nation of Indians of Wisconsin, Oneida, WI.
    Oneida Cultural Heritage Department, Genealogical records, WPA Oneida Folklore and Language Project.
    Oneida Nation Museum, Photograph collection.
    Tribal Business Committee, Minutes, 1937–1969.
Princeton University, Princeton, NJ.
    American Civil Liberties Union Collection.
    Association on American Affairs Collection.
[Smithsonian] Cooper-Hewitt Museum, New York.
    Sybil Carter Indian Lace Association Collection: Pamphlets, Oneida Lace.

Smithsonian Institution, National Anthropological Archives, Washington, D.C.
Collections: American Indian Chicago Conference Collection, National Con-
gress of American Indians Collection.
Oral History: Bennett, Robert L. (interview conducted by Thomas Cowger).
St. John Fisher College, Rochester, NY.
Decker, George P., Papers.
University of Oklahoma, Western History Collection, Norman, OK.
Duke, Doris, American Indian Oral History Project.
Thomas, Elmer, Papers.
University of Rochester, Rush Rhees Library, Rochester, NY.
Dewey, Thomas E., Papers.
Parker, Arthur C., Papers.
University of Texas, Humanities Research Center, Austin, TX.
La Farge, Oliver, Papers.
University of Wisconsin Area Research Center, Green Bay, WI.
Archiquette, John, Diary.
Holy Apostles Episcopal Church (Oneida), Records.
Wisconsin Historical Society, Madison, WI.
Illinois-Wisconsin Indian Friends Committee, Papers.
McLaughlin, James, Papers.
Montezuma, Carlos, Papers.
Nelson, Gaylord, Papers.
Wiley, Alexander, Papers.
Yale University, New Haven, CT.
Collier, John, Papers, Sterling Library.
Pratt, Richard, Papers, Beinecke Library.

Miscellaneous Manuscripts

Jennings, Francis, et al., eds., *Iroquois Indians: A Documentary History of the Six Nations
and Their League.* Woodbridge, CT: Research Publications, 1985. Fifty micro-
film reels.
Larner, John W., ed., *The Papers of the Society of American Indians.* Wilmington, DE:
Scholarly Resources, 1987. Ten microfilm reels.
New York State Legislature. Assembly. *Report of the Indian Commission to Investigate
the Status of the American Indian Residing in the State of New York, ... March 17, 1922.*
Unpublished manuscript. [Popularly known as the Everett Commission
Report.]
The Papers of the Indian Rights Association. Glen Rock, NJ: Microfilm Corporation of
America, 1975.

Interviews

Archiquette, Oscar. Interview by Robert W. Venables, July 9, 1970, Shell Lake, WI.

Hauptman, Laurence M. Interviews: Ruth Baird, June 23, 1983, Green Bay, WI; Louis R. Bruce Jr., June 30, 1982, Washington, D.C.; Richard Chrisjohn, September 4, 1984, Hunter Mountain, NY; Ray Elm, October 20, 1984, Rome, NY, April 21, 1985, Syracuse, NY; Norbert Hill Sr., July 28, 1982, Oneida, WI; Nancy Lurie, June 20, 1983, Milwaukee, WI; Loretta Metoxen, June 22, 1983, Oneida, WI; George Shattuck, August 25, 1983, Syracuse, NY; Maisie Shenandoah, October 22, 1984, Rome, NY; Cecil Skenandore, July 23, 1985, Oneida, WI; Sol Tax, December 5, 1982, Philadelphia, PA; Jacob Thompson, April 15, 1972, May 6, 1976, New Paltz, NY; Lincoln White, July 1, 1982, Washington, D.C.; Jake Whitecrow, May 5, 1980, New Paltz, NY.

Government Publications

American Indian Policy Review Commission. *Final Report.* 2 vols. Washington, D.C.: GPO, 1977.

Cohen, Felix S. *Handbook of Federal Indian Law.* Washington, D.C.: U.S. Department of the Interior, 1942; Reprint, Albuquerque: University of New Mexico Press, 1971.

Haas, Theodore H. *Ten Years of Tribal Government Under IRA.* Washington, D.C.: U.S. Department of the Interior, 1947.

Kappler, Charles J., Comp. *Indian Affairs: Laws and Treaties.* 5 vols. Washington, D.C.: GPO, 1903–1941.

New York State Legislature. Assembly Document No. 51. *Report of the Special Committee to Investigate the Indian Problem.* (Whipple Report). Albany, NY, 1889.

Nixon, Richard M. *Public Papers of the Presidents of the United States, Richard M. Nixon, 1970.* Washington, D.C.: GPO, 1971.

United States Bureau of the Census. Census nos. 13–16, 1900–1930. Washington, D.C.

United States Congress. *Congressional Record,* 1900–1975. Washington, D.C.

United States Congress. House. Committee on Indian Affairs. *Hearings on H.R. 1198 and H.R. 1341: Creation of the Indian Claims Commission.* 79th Cong., 1st sess., March 2–3, June 11, 14, 1945.

———. Committee on Indian Affairs. *Hearings on H.R. 3680, H.R. 3681 and H.R. 3710: Removal of Restrictions on Indian Property and for the Emancipation of Indians.* 79th Cong., 2nd sess., 1946.

———. Committee on Public Lands. *Report No. 2355: Conferring Jurisdiction on State of New York with Respect to Offenses Committed on Indian Reservations with Such State.* Washington, D.C.: GPO, 1948.

————. Committee on Public Lands. *Report No. 2720: Conferring Jurisdiction on Court of New York with Respect to Civil Actions Between Indians or to which Indians Are Parties.* Washington, D.C.: GPO, 1950.

————. *Document No. 251: Oneida Indians: Letter from the Secretary of the Interior Transmitting Report of Negotiations with Oneida Indians for Commutation of Their Perpetual Annuities as Provided for by Act of March 3, 1911.* 62nd Cong., 2nd sess., 1911.

————. *House Report No. 2680: With Respect to the House Resolution Authorizing the Committee on Interior and Insular Affairs to Conduct an Investigation of the Bureau of Indian Affairs.* 83rd Cong., 2nd sess., 1954.

————. Select Committee to Investigate Indian Affairs and Conditions in the United States. *Hearing on H.R. 166: A Bill to Authorize and Direct and Conduct an Investigation to Determine Whether the Changed Status of the Indian Requires a Revision of the Laws and Regulations Affecting the American Indian.* Part I: 78th Cong., 1st sess., March 23, 1943. Part II: 78th Cong., 2nd sess., February 2, 1944.

————. Subcommittee on Indian Affairs of the Committee on Indian Affairs. *Hearings: Seizure of Bureau of Indian Affairs Headquarters.* 92nd Cong., 2nd sess., 1973.

————. Subcommittee on Indian Affairs of the Committee on Public Lands. *Hearings on H.R. 2958, H.R. 2165 and H.R. 1113: Emancipation of Indians.* 80th Cong., 1st sess., 1947.

United States Congress. House and Senate. *Joint Hearings Before Subcommittee of the Committees on Interior and Insular Affairs...pursuant to H. Con. Res. 108: Termination of Federal Supervision Over Certain Tribes of Indians.* 83rd Cong., 2nd sess., 1954.

United States Congress. Senate. Committee on Civil Service. *Hearings on S. Res. 41: Officers and Employees of the Federal Government.* 80th Cong., 1st sess., 1947.

————. Committee on Interior and Insular Affairs. *Hearings: The Nomination of Robert La Follette Bennett...to Be Commissioner of Indian Affairs.* 89th Cong., 2nd sess, April 1, 1966.

————. Committee on Interior and Insular Affairs. *Report No. 1489: Conferring Jurisdiction on Courts of New York over Offenses Committed by Indians.* Washington, D.C.: GPO, 1948.

————. Committee on Interior and Insular Affairs. *Report No. 1836: Conferring Jurisdiction on Courts of New York with Respect to Civil Actions Between Indians or to which Indians Are Parties.* Washington, D.C.: GPO, 1950.

————. Committee on Public Lands. *Report No. 1362: Subjecting Indians and Indian Reservations in Wisconsin to Laws of the State.* Washington, D.C.: GPO, 1949.

————. Special Subcommittee on Labor and Public Welfare. *Report No. 501: Indian Education: A National Tragedy—A National Challenge.* Report of the Special Subcommittee on Indian Education, Committee on Labor and Public Welfare. 91st Cong., 1st sess., 1969.

———. Subcommittee on Indian Affairs of the Committee on Interior and Insular Affairs. *Hearings on S. 1017 and Related Bills: Indian Self-Determination and Education Program.* Washington, D.C.: GPO, 1973.

———. Subcommittee on Indian Affairs of the Committee on Interior and Insular Affairs. *Hearings: Occupation of Wounded Knee.* 93rd Cong., 1st sess., 1974.

———. Subcommittee on Indian Affairs of the Committee on Interior and Insular Affairs. *Hearings on S. 1017 and Related Bills: Indian Self-Determination and Education Program.* Washington, D.C.: GPO, 1973.

———. Subcommittee on Indian Affairs of the Committee on Interior and Insular Affairs. *Hearings on S. 1683, S. 1686, S. 1687: New York Indians.* Washington, D.C.: GPO, 1948.

———. Subcommittee to Investigate the Administration of the Internal Security Act and Other Internal Security Laws of the Committee on the Judiciary. *Hearings: Revolutionary Activities Within the United States: The American Indian Movement.* 94th Cong., 2nd sess., 1976.

———. Subcommittee of the Committee on Indian Affairs. *Hearings on S. Res. 79: Survey of Conditions of the Indians in the United States.* 43 Parts. 70th–76th Congress. Washington, D.C.: GPO, 1928–1943.

———. Subcommittee of the Committee on Interior and Insular Affairs. *Hearings on S. 1683, S. 1686, S. 1687: New York Indians.* Washington, D.C.: GPO, 1948.

———. Subcommittee of the Committee on Interior and Insular Affairs. *Hearings on H.R. 303: Transfer of Indian Hospitals and Health Facilities to Public Health Service.* 83rd Cong., 1st sess., 1954.

United States Department of Health, Education, and Welfare. Indian Health Service. *Indian Health Program, 1955–1980.* Washington, D.C.: GPO, 1980.

United States Department of the Interior. *Indian Health: A Problem and a Challenge.* Washington, D.C.: GPO, 1955.

United States Indian Claims Commission. *Decisions of the Indian Claims Commission.* New York: Clearwater Publishing Co., 1973–1978. Microfiche edition.

———. *Final Report.* August 13, 1946–September 30, 1978. Washington, D.C.: GPO, 1979.

United States *Statutes at Large.*

Court Cases

California v. Cabazon Band of Mission Indians. 480 U.S. 202 (1987).

City of Sherrill v. Oneida Indian Nation. 125 S. Ct. 1478 (2005).

County of Oneida v. Oneida Indian Nation of New York. 84 L.Ed. 2d 169 (1985).

New York Indians v. United States. U.S. Court of Claims. Doc. No. 17861 (1905).

Oneida Indian Nation v. County of Oneida. 414 U.S. 661 (1974).

United States v. Boylan et al. 265 F. 165 (2d Cir. 1920), appeal dismissed 257 U.S. 614 (1921).
United States v. Cook. 19 Wall 591 (1873).
ICC CASES:
> Docket 75: Wisconsin Land Claim. 5 ICC 609 (1957).
> Docket 84: The Accounting Claim. 23 ICC 390 (1973).
> Docket 159: Timber Stripping Claim. 12 ICC 1 (1962).
> Docket 344: Pennsylvania Land Claim [*Six Nations v. the United States*]. 12 ICC 86 (1963).
> Emigrant New York Indians. Docket 75: 5 ICC 553 (1957). 5 ICC 607 (1957).
> *Oneida Nation v. United States.* 26 ICC 583 (1971).
> *Oneida Nation v. United States.* Docket 301: 26 ICC 138 (August 10, 1971 and December 29, 1971).

Newspapers and Magazines

Akwesasne Notes (Mohawk Nation)
Brown County (WI) Democrat
Chicago Tribune
De Pere (WI) Journal Democrat
The First American (Washington, D.C.)
Green Bay Advocate
Green Bay Press Gazette
Indian Truth (Philadelphia, PA)
Indians at Work (Washington, D.C.)
Indians' Friend
Milwaukee Indian News
Milwaukee Journal
Milwaukee Sentinel
New York Herald
New York Herald Tribune
New York Times
Progressive
Quarterly Journal (Society of the American Indians)
Red Man (Carlisle Indian School)
Southern Workman (Hampton Institute)
Syracuse (NY) Herald American
Syracuse (NY) Herald Journal
Syracuse (NY) Post-Standard
Washington Post

Books, Booklets, and Pamphlets

Abernethy, Byron R., ed. *Private Elisha Stockwell, Jr., Sees the Civil War.* Norman: University of Oklahoma Press, 1958.

Abourezk, James G. *Advise and Dissent: Memoirs of South Dakota and the U.S. Senate.* Chicago: Lawrence Hill Books, 1989.

Adams, David Wallace. *Education for Extinction: American Indians and the Boarding School Experience, 1875–1928.* Lawrence: University Press of Kansas, 1995.

———. "From Bullets to Boarding Schools: The Educational Assault on American Indians." In *"They Made Us Many Promises": The American Indian Experience, 1524 to the Present.* 2nd ed., edited by Philip Weeks, 154–174. Wheeling, IL: Harlan Davidson, 2002.

Ambler, Marjane. *Breaking the Iron Bonds: Indian Control of Energy Development.* Lawrence: University Press of Kansas, 1990.

Ambrose, Steven, ed. *A Wisconsin Boy in Dixie: The Selected Letters of James K. Newton.* Madison: University of Wisconsin Press, 1961.

Anderson, Clinton P. *Outsider in the Senate: Senator Clinton P. Anderson's Memoirs.* New York: World Publishing Co., 1970.

Barsh, Russel L., and James Y. Henderson. *The Road: Indian Tribes and Political Liberty.* Berkeley: University of California Press, 1980.

Beck, David R. M. *The Struggle for Self-Determination: History of the Menominee Indians Since 1854.* Lincoln: University of Nebraska Press, 2005.

Benn, Carl. *The Iroquois in the War of 1812.* Toronto: University of Toronto Press, 1998.

Bernstein, Alison R. *American Indians and World War II.* Norman: University of Oklahoma Press, 1991.

Bieder, Robert E. *Native American Communities in Wisconsin, 1600–1960: A Study of Tradition and Change.* Madison: University of Wisconsin Press, 1995.

Bloomfield, Julia. *The Oneidas.* 2nd ed. New York: Alden Bros., 1907.

Boris, Eileen. *Art and Labor: Ruskin, Morris and the Craftsman Ideal in America.* Philadelphia: Temple University Press, 1986.

Britten, Thomas. *American Indians in World War I: At War and at Home.* Albuquerque: University of New Mexico Press, 1997.

Brophy, William A., and Sophie D. Aberle, eds. *The Indian, America's Unfinished Business: Report of the Commission on the Rights, Liberties and Responsibilities of the American Indian.* Norman: University of Oklahoma Press, 1966.

Burnette, Robert, and John Koster. *The Road to Wounded Knee.* New York: Bantam, 1974.

Burt, Larry W. *Tribalism in Crisis.* Albuquerque: University of New Mexico Press, 1982.

Cadwalader, Sandra L., and Vine Deloria Jr., eds. *The Aggressions of Civilization: Federal Indian Policy Since the 1880s.* Philadelphia: Temple University Press, 1984.

Campisi, Jack. "Oneida." In *Handbook of North American Indians*. Vol. 15, *The Northeast*, edited by Bruce G. Trigger, 481–490. Washington, D.C.: Smithsonian Institution, 1978.

———. "The Wisconsin Oneidas Between Disasters." In *The Oneida Indian Journey: From New York to Wisconsin, 1784–1860, Edited by* Laurence M. Hauptman and L. Gordon McLester III, 70–84. Madison: University of Wisconsin Press, 1999.

Campisi, Jack, and Laurence M. Hauptman, eds. *The Oneida Indian Experience: Two Perspectives*. Syracuse, NY: Syracuse University Press, 1988.

Carlson, Leonard A. *Indians, Bureaucrats, and Land: The Dawes Act and the Decline of Indian Farming*. Westport, CT: Greenwood Press, 1981.

Castile, George Pierre. *Taking Charge: Naive American Self-Determination and Federal Indian Policy, 1975–1993*. Tucson: University of Arizona Press, 2006.

———. *To Show Heart: Native American Self-Determination and Federal Indian Policy, 1960–1975*. Tucson: University of Arizona Press, 1998.

Castile, George, and Robert Bee, eds. *State and Reservation: New Perspectives on Federal Indian Policy*. Tucson: University of Arizona Press, 1992.

Chester, Greg. *The Battle of Big Sandy*. Adams, NY: Historical Association of South Jefferson County, 1981.

Child, Brenda J. *Boarding School Seasons: American Indian Families, 1900–1940*. Lincoln: University of Nebraska Press, 1998.

Christjohn, Amos, and Maria Hinton. *An Oneida Dictionary*. Edited by Clifford Abbott. Oneida: Oneida Nation of Indians of Wisconsin, 1998.

Clarkin, Thomas. *Federal Indian Policy in the Kennedy and Johnson Administrations, 1961–1969*. Albuquerque: University of New Mexico Press, 2001.

Clifford, Clark. *Counsel to the President: A Memoir*. New York: Random House, 1991.

Cohen, Felix S. *The Legal Conscience: Selected Papers of Felix S. Cohen*. Edited by Lucy Kramer Cohen. New Haven, CT: Yale University Press, 1960.

Colman, Henry. "Recollections of Oneida Indians, 1840–1845." In *Proceedings of the State Historical Society of Wisconsin at Its 59th Annual Meeting*. 152–159. Madison: State Historical Society of Wisconsin, 1912.

Cornelius, Melissa E., "Reminiscences of an American Indian." In *We Were Children Then*. Vol. 2, edited by Clarice Dunn and Gen Lewis. Madison, WI: Stanton, Lee Publishers, Inc., 1982.

Cowger, Thomas W. *The National Congress of American Indians: The Founding Years*. Lincoln: University of Nebraska Press, 1999.

Deloria, Vine, Jr. *Behind the Trail of Broken Treaties: An Indian Declaration of Independence*. New York: Dell Publishing, 1974.

———. *Custer Died for Your Sins: An Indian Manifesto*. New York: Macmillan, 1969.

———. *God Is Red*. New York: Grosset and Dunlap, 1973.

————. *The Indian Reorganization Act: Congresses and Bills*. Norman: University of Oklahoma Press, 2002.

————. *We Talk, You Listen: New Tribes, New Turf*. New York: Macmillan, 1970.

Deloria, Vine, Jr., and Clifford M. Lytle. *American Indians, American Justice*. Austin: University of Texas Press, 1983.

————. *The Nations Within: The Past and Future of American Indian Sovereignty*. New York: Pantheon Books, 1984.

Deloria, Vine, Jr., and David E. Wilkins. *Tribes, Treaties and Constitutional Tribulations*. Austin: University of Texas Press, 1999.

Dennis, Matthew. *Red, White and Blue Letter Days*. Ithaca, NY: Cornell University Press, 2002.

Drinnon, Richard. *Keeper of the Concentration Camps: Dillon S. Myer and American Racism*. Berkeley: University of California Press, 1987.

Eisenhower, Dwight D. *The Eisenhower Diaries*. Edited by Robert H. Ferrell. New York: Norton, 1981.

Ellis, Richard N. "Robert L. Bennett: 1966–1969." In *The Commissioners of Indian Affairs, 1824–1977*, edited by Robert M. Kvasnicka and Herman J. Viola, 325–332. Lincoln: University of Nebraska Press, 1979.

Episcopal Church Mission to the Oneidas. *Oneida: The People of the Stone: The Church's Mission to the Oneidas*. Oneida, WI: Episcopal Church of the Holy Apostles, 1899.

Fenton, William N. *The Great Law and the Longhouse*. Norman: University of Oklahoma Press, 1998.

Fixico, Donald. *Termination and Relocation: Federal Indian Policy, 1945–1960*. Albuquerque: University of New Mexico Press, 1986.

————. *The Urban Indian Experience in America*. Albuquerque: University of New Mexico Press, 2000.

Forbes, Jack D. *Native Americans and Nixon: Presidential Politics and Minority Self-Determination, 1969–1972*. Los Angeles: American Indian Studies Center, UCLA, 1981.

Foster, Michael, Jack Campisi, and Marianne Mithun, eds. *Extending the Rafters: Interdisciplinary Approaches to Iroquoian Studies*. Albany, NY: SUNY Press, 1984.

Garment, Leonard. *Crazy Rhythm*. New York: Times Books, 1997.

Glatthaar, Joseph T., and James Kirby Martin. *Forgotten Allies: The Oneida Indians and the American Revolution*. New York: Hill and Wang, 2006.

Greenstein, Fred I. *The Hidden-Hand Presidency: Eisenhower as Leader*. New York: Basic Books, 1982.

Greenwald, Emily. *Reconfiguring the Reservation: The Nez Perces, Jicarilla Apaches and the Dawes Act*. Albuquerque: University of New Mexico Press, 2002.

Grounds, Richard A., George Tinker, and David E. Wilkins, eds. *Native American Voices: American Indian Identity and Resistance.* Lawrence: University Press of Kansas, 2003.

Hagan, William T. *The Indian Rights Association.* Tucson: University of Arizona Press, 1985.

—————. "Reformers' Images of the American Indians." In *"They Made Us Many Promises": The American Indian Experience, 1524 to the Present.* 2nd ed., edited by Philip Weeks, 145–154. Wheeling, IL: Harlan Davidson, 2002.

—————. *Theodore Roosevelt and Six Friends of the Indian.* Norman: University of Oklahoma Press, 1997.

Haller, John S. *Outcasts from Evolution: Scientific Attitudes of Racial Inferiority, 1859–1900.* Urbana: University of Illinois Press, 1971.

Hauptman, Laurence M. "Designing Woman: Minnie Kellogg, Iroquois Leader." In *Indian Lives: Essays on Nineteenth and Twentieth Century Native American Leaders,* edited by L. G. Moses and Raymond Wilson, 159–188. Albuquerque: University of New Mexico Press, 1985.

—————. *The Iroquois and the New Deal.* Syracuse, NY: Syracuse University Press, 1981.

—————. *The Iroquois in the Civil War: From Battlefield to Reservation.* Syracuse, NY: Syracuse University Press, 1993.

—————. *The Iroquois Struggle for Survival: World War II to Red Power.* Syracuse, NY: Syracuse University Press, 1986.

Hauptman, Laurence M., and L. Gordon McLester III. *Chief Daniel Bread and the Oneida Nation of Indians of Wisconsin.* Norman: University of Oklahoma Press, 2002.

—————, eds. *The Oneida Indian Journey: From New York to Wisconsin, 1784–1860.* Madison: University of Wisconsin Press, 1999.

—————, eds. *The Oneida Indians in the Age of Allotment, 1860–1920.* Norman: University of Oklahoma Press, 2006.

Hertzberg, Hazel W. *The Search for an American Indian Identity: Modern Pan-Indian Movements.* Syracuse, NY: Syracuse University Press, 1971.

Hickey, Douglas R. *The War of 1812: A Forgotten Conflict.* Urbana: University of Illinois Press, 1989.

Hinton, Maria, transcriber and translator. *A Collection of Oneida Stories.* Oneida: Oneida Nation of Wisconsin, 1996.

Hitsman, J. McKay. *The Incredible War of 1812: A Military History.* Toronto: University of Toronto Press, 1998.

Holm, Tom. *Strong Heart, Wounded Souls: Native American Veterans and the Vietnam War.* Austin: University of Texas Press, 1996.

Horsman, Reginald. "The Wisconsin Oneidas in the Preallotment Years." In *The Oneida Indian Experience,* edited by Jack Campisi and Laurence M. Hauptman, 65–82. Syracuse, NY: Syracuse University Press, 1988.

Hosmer, Brian C. *American Indians in the Marketplace: Persistence and Innovation Among the Menominees and Metlakatlans, 1870–1920*. Lawrence: University Press of Kansas, 1999.

Hoxie, Frederick E. *Final Promise: The Campaign to Assimilate the Indians*. Lincoln: University of Nebraska Press, 1984.

————. *Talking Back to Civilization: Indian Voices from the Progressive Era*. New York: Bedford Books, St. Martin's Press, 2001.

Indian Rights Association, Annual Reports, 1883–1933. Philadelphia Indian Rights Association, 1883–1933.

Iverson, Peter. *Carlos Montezuma and the Changing World of the American Indian*. Albuquerque: University of New Mexico Press, 1982.

Jennings, Francis, et al., eds. *The History and Culture of Iroquois Diplomacy: An Interdisciplinary Guide to the Treaties of the Six Nations and Their League*. Syracuse, NY: Syracuse University Press, 1985.

Josephy, Alvin M., Jr. *Now That the Buffalo's Gone: A Study of Today's American Indians*. New York: Alfred A. Knopf, 1982.

————. *Red Power: The American Indians' Fight for Freedom*. New York: American Heritage Press, 1971.

Kellogg, Laura Cornelius. *Our Democracy and the American Indian: A Comprehensive Presentation of the Indian Situation as It Is Today*. Kansas City, MO: Burton, 1920.

Kelly, Lawrence C. *The Assault on Assimilation: John Collier and the Origins of Indian Policy Reform*. Albuquerque: University of New Mexico Press, 1983.

Kelly, William H., ed. *Indian Affairs and the Indian Reorganization Act: The Twenty Year Record*. Tucson: University of Arizona Press, 1954.

Kinney, J. P. *A Continent Lost, A Civilization Won: Indian Land Tenure in America*. Baltimore, MD: Johns Hopkins University Press, 1937.

Krouse, Susan Applegate. *North American Indians in the Great War*. Lincoln: University of Nebraska Press, 2007.

Kvasnicka, Robert, and Herman Viola, eds. *The Commissioners of Indian Affairs, 1824–1977*. Lincoln: University of Nebraska Press, 1979.

Lake Mohonk Conference of Friends of the Indian (and Other Dependent Peoples), *Annual Reports of Proceedings* (New Paltz, NY: 1883–1916, 1929).

[Wisconsin] League of Women Voters. *Study of the Oneida Indians of Wisconsin*. Appleton, WI: League of Women Voters, 1956.

Leupp, Francis E., *The Indian and His Problem*. New York: Scribner, 1910.

Lewis, Bonnie Sue. *Creating Christian Indians: Native Clergy in the Presbyterian Church*. Norman: University of Oklahoma Press, 2003.

Lewis, Herbert S., ed. *Oneida Lives: Long-Lost Voices of the Wisconsin Oneidas*. Lincoln: University of Nebraska Press, 2005.

Lieder, Michael, and Jake Page. *Wild Justice: The People of Geronimo vs. the United States*. New York: Random House, 1997.

Limerick, Patricia Nelson. *The Legacy of Conquest: The Unbroken Past of the American West*. New York: W. W. Norton, 1988.

Lindsey, Donal F. *Indians at Hampton, 1877–1923*. Urbana: University of Illinois Press, 1995.

Locklear, Arlinda. "The Allotment of the Oneida Reservation and Its Legal Ramifications." In *The Oneida Indian Experience*, edited by Jack Campisi and Laurence M. Hauptman, 83–100. Syracuse, NY: Syracuse University Press, 1988.

Lurie, Nancy O. *Wisconsin Indians*. Rev. 2nd ed. Madison: State Historical Society of Wisconsin, 2002.

Lurie, Nancy, and Stuart Levine, eds. *The American Indian Today*. Rev. ed. Baltimore, MD: Penguin, 1968.

Martin, Deborah B. *History of Brown County, Wisconsin: Past and Present*. 2 vols. Chicago: S. J. Clarke, 1913.

Mathes, Valerie Sherer. *Helen Hunt Jackson and Her Indian Reform Legacy*. Norman: University of Oklahoma Press, 1997.

McDonnell, Melissa L. *The Dispossession of the American Indian, 1887–1934*. Bloomington: Indiana University Press, 1991.

McLaughlin, James. *My Friend the Indian*. 1910. Reprint. Lincoln: University of Nebraska Press, 1989.

McLester, Thelma. "Josephine Hill Webster, 1883–1978: Supervisor of Oneida Lace Industry and First Woman Postmaster." In *The Oneida Indian Experience: Two Perspectives*, edited by Jack Campisi and Laurence M. Hauptman, 116–118. Syracuse, NY: Syracuse University Press, 1988.

———. "Oneida Women Leaders." In *The Oneida Indian Experience: Two Perspectives*, edited by Jack Campisi and Laurence M. Hauptman, 109–111. Syracuse, NY: Syracuse University Press, 1988.

McNickle, D'Arcy. *Indian Man: A Life of Oliver LaFarge*. Bloomington: Indian University Press, 1971.

———. *Native American Tribalism: Indian Survivals and Renewals*. Rev. ed. New York: Oxford University Press, 1973.

———. *They Came Here First*. Rev. ed. New York: Octagon, 1975.

Meriam, Lewis, et al. *The Problem of Indian Administration*. Baltimore, MD: Johns Hopkins University Press, 1928.

Metcalf, R. Warren. *Termination's Legacy: The Discarded Indians of Utah*. Lincoln: University of Nebraska Press, 2002.

Meyer, Melissa L. *The White Earth Tragedy: Ethnicity and Dispossession at a Minnesota Anishinaabe Reservation, 1889–1920*. Lincoln: University of Nebraska Press, 1994.

Myer, Dillon S. *Uprooted Americans*. Tucson: University of Arizona Press, 1971.

Nash, Philleo. "Anthropologist in the White House." In *Applied Anthropologist and Public Servant*, edited by Ruth Landman and Katherine Halpern, 3–6. Washington, D.C.: American Anthropology Association, 1989.

Nixon, Richard. *Memoirs of Richard Nixon*. New York: Grosset and Dunlap, 1978.

Oberly, James W. *A Nation of Statesmen: The Political Cluster of the Stockbridge-Munsee Mohicans, 1815–1972*. Norman: University of Oklahoma Press, 2005.

Orfield, Gary. *A Study of Termination Policy*. Chicago: University of Chicago Press, 1966.

Otis, D. S. *The Dawes Act and the Allotment of Indian Lands*. Edited by Francis Paul Prucha. Norman: University of Oklahoma Press, 1973.

Parman, Donald. *The Navajos and the New Deal*. New Haven, CT: Yale University Press, 1976.

Paul, Justin F. *Senator Hugh Butler and Nebraska Republicanism*. Lincoln: Nebraska State Historical Society, 1976.

Peck, Amelia, and Carol Irish. *Candace Wheeler: Art and Enterprise of American Design, 1875–1900*. New Haven, CT: Yale University Press and the Metropolitan Museum of Art, 2001.

Peroff, Nicholas. *Menominee Drums: Tribal Termination and Restoration, 1954–1974*. Norman: University of Oklahoma Press, 1982.

Pevar, Stephen L. *The Rights of Indians and Tribes*. 3rd ed. Carbondale: Southern Illinois University Press, 2002.

Philp, Kenneth R. *John Collier's Crusade for Indian Reform, 1920–1954*. Tucson: University of Arizona Press, 1977.

————, ed. *Indian Self-Rule: First-Hand Accounts of Indian-White Relations from Roosevelt to Reagan*. Salt Lake City, UT: Howe Brothers, 1986.

————. *Termination Revisited: Americans on the Trail to Self-Determination, 1933–1953*. Lincoln: University of Nebraska Press, 1999.

Pilkington, Walter, ed. *The Journals of Samuel Kirkland*. Clinton, NY: Hamilton College, 1980.

Porter, Robert Odawi, ed. *Sovereignty, Colonialism and the Indigenous Nations*. Durham, NC: Carolina Academic Press, 2005.

Pratt, Richard Henry. *Battlefield and Classroom: Four Decades with the American Indian, 1867–1904*. Edited by Robert M. Utley. New Haven, CT: Yale University Press, 1964.

Prevost, Toni Jollay. *Indians from New York in Wisconsin and Elsewhere*. Bowie, MD: Heritage Books, 1995.

Prucha, Francis Paul. *American Indian Policy in Crisis: Christian Reformers and the American Indian, 1865–1900*. Norman: University of Oklahoma Press, 1976.

————, ed. *"Americanizing" the American Indian: Writings by the "Friends of the American Indian," 1880–1900*. Cambridge, MA: Harvard University Press, 1973.

————. *The Churches and the Indian Schools, 1888–1912*. Lincoln: University of Nebraska Press, 1979.

————. *The Great Father: The United States Government and the American Indians*. 2 vols. Lincoln: University of Nebraska Press, 1984.

Richards, Cara E. *The Oneida People*. Phoenix, AZ: Indian Tribal Series, 1974.

Rosenthal, Harvey D. *Their Day in Court: A History of the Indian Claims Commission*. New York: Garland, 1990.

Shames, Deborah, ed. *Freedom with Reservations: The Menominee Struggle to Save Their Land and People*. Madison, WI: National Committee to Save the Menominee People and Forests/Wisconsin Indian Legal Services, 1972.

Shattuck, George C. *The Oneida Indians Land Claims: A Legal History*. Syracuse, NY: Syracuse University Press, 1991.

Smith, Robert, and Loretta Metoxen. "Oneida Traditions." In *The Oneida Indian Experience: Two Perspectives*, edited by Jack Campisi and Laurence M. Hauptman, 50–51. Syracuse, NY: Syracuse University Press, 1988.

Society of American Indians (SAI). *Report of the Executive Council on the Proceedings of the First Annual Conference, October 12–17, 1911*. Washington, D.C.: SAI, 1912.

Soltow, Lee. *Patterns of Wealthholding in Wisconsin Since 1850*. Madison: University of Wisconsin Press, 1971.

Stuart, Paul L. *The Indian Office: Growth and Development of an American Institution*. Ann Arbor, MI: UMI Research Press, 1978.

Sutton, Imre. *Irredeemable America: The Indians' Estate and Land Claims*. Albuquerque: University of New Mexico Press, 1985.

Szasz, Margaret Connell. *Education and the American Indian: The Road to Self-Determination Since 1928*. Rev. ed. Albuquerque: University of New Mexico Press, 1999.

Tanner, Helen Hornbeck, ed. *Atlas of Great Lakes Indian History*. Norman: University of Oklahoma Press, 1987.

Taylor, Graham D. *The New Deal and American Indian Tribalism: The Administration of the Indian Reorganization Act, 1934–1945*. Lincoln: University of Nebraska Press, 1980.

Thorson, Douglas. *Report on the Labor Force and Employment Conditions of the Oneida Indians*. Madison: University of Wisconsin, 1958.

Townsend, Kenneth W. *World War II and the American Indian*. Albuquerque: University of New Mexico Press, 2000.

Treat, James. *Native and Christian: Indigenous Voices on Religious Identity in the United States and Canada*. New York: Routledge, 1995.

Trigger, Bruce G., ed. *Handbook of North American Indians*. Vol. 15, *The Northeast*. Washington, D.C.: Smithsonian Institution, 1978.

Truman, Harry S. *The Autobiography of Harry S. Truman.* Edited by Robert H. Ferrell. Boulder: Colorado Assoc. University Press, 1980.

————. *Memoirs.* 2 vols. Garden City, NY: Doubleday, 1955.

————. *Off the Record: The Private Papers of Harry S. Truman.* Edited by Robert H. Ferrell. New York: Harper and Row, 1980.

Tsuk, Dalia. *Architect of Justice: Felix S. Cohen and the Founding of American Legal Pluralism.* Ithaca, NY: Cornell University Press, 2007.

Upton, Helen M. *The Everett Report in Historical Perspective: The Indians of New York State.* Albany: New York State American Revolution Bicentennial Commission, 1980.

Vecsey, Christopher, and William A. Starna, eds. *Iroquois Land Claims.* Syracuse, NY: Syracuse University Press, 1988.

Viola, Herman J. *Diplomats in Buckskin: A History of Indian Delegations in Washington City.* Washington, D.C.: Smithsonian Institution Press, 1981.

Washburn, Wilcomb E., ed. *The American Indian and the United States: A Documentary History.* 4 vols. Westport, CT: Greenwood, 1973.

Weeks, Philip, ed. *"They Made Us Many Promises": The American Indian Experience, 1524 to the Present.* 2nd ed. Wheeling, IL: Harlan Davidson, 2002.

Whipple, Henry B. *Lights and Shadows of a Long Episcopate: Being the Reminiscences and Recollections of the Right Reverend Henry Benjamin Whipple, D.D., L.L.D., Bishop of Minnesota.* New York: Macmillan Co., 1899.

Wilkins, David E., and K. Tsianina Lomawaima. *Uneven Ground: American Indian Sovereignty and Federal Law.* Norman: University of Oklahoma Press, 2001.

Wilkinson, Charles. *Blood Struggle: The Rise of Modern Indian Nations.* New York: W. W. Norton, 2005.

Wilkinson, Charles F. *American Indians, Time, and the Law: Native Societies in a Modern Constitutional Democracy.* New Haven, CT: Yale University Press, 1987.

Witmer, Linda. *The Indian Industrial School: Carlisle, Pennsylvania, 1879–1918.* Carlisle, PA: Cumberland County Historical Society, 1993.

Wonderley, Anthony. *Oneida Iroquois Folklore, Myth, and History: New York Oral Narrative from the Notes of H. E. Allen and Others.* Syracuse, NY: Syracuse University Press, 2004.

Wunder, John R. *"Retained by the People": A History of American Indians and the Bill of Rights.* New York: Oxford University Press, 1994.

Articles

Antone, Eileen M. "The Educational History of the Onyota'a:ka Nation of the Thames." *Ontario History* 85 (December 1993): 310–320.

Barsh, Russel L. "American Indians in the Great War." *Ethnohistory* 38 (1991): 276–303.

————. "BIA Reorganization Follies of 1978: A Lesson in Bureaucratic Self-Defense." *American Indian Law Review* 7 (1979): 1–50.

Bennett, Robert L. "Building Indian Economies with Land Settlement Funds." *Human Organization* 20 (1961–1962): 159–163.

————. "Indian-State Relations in Their Historical Perspective." *Journal of the Wisconsin Indians Research Institute* 3 (September 1967): i–v.

————. "New Era for the American Indian." *Natural History* 76 (February 1967): 6–11.

Boender, Debra R. "Termination and the Administration of Glenn L. Emmons as Commissioner of Indian Affairs, 1953–1961." *New Mexico Historical Review* 54 (October 1979): 287–304.

Campisi, Jack. "New York-Oneida Treaty of 1795: A Finding of Fact." *American Indian Law Review* 4 (Summer 1976): 71–82.

————. "Talking Back: The Oneida Language and Folklore Project, 1938–1941." *Proceedings of the American Philosophical Society* 125 (December 1981): 441–448.

Campisi, Jack, and Laurence M. Hauptman, "Talking Back: The Oneida Language and Folklore Project, 1938–1941," *Proceedings of the American Philosophical Society* 125 (December 1981): 441–448.

Cohen, Felix S. "Colonialism: U.S. Style." *Progressive* 15 (February 1951): 16–18.

————. "The Erosion of Indian Rights, 1950–1953: A Case Study in Bureaucracy." *Yale Law Journal* 62 (February 1953): 348–390.

Day, Gordon M. "Oral Tradition as Complement." *Ethnohistory* 19 (Spring 1972): 99–108.

Dowling, John H. "A 'Rural' Indian Community in an Urban Setting." *Human Organization* 27 (1968): 236–239.

Duncan, Kate L., "American Indian Lace Making." *American Indian Art* 5 (Summer 1980): 28–35, 80.

Hagan, William T. "Private Property: The Indians' Door to Civilization." *Ethnohistory* 3 (Spring 1956): 126–137.

————. "Tribalism Rejuvenated: The Native American Since the End of Termination." *Western Historical Quarterly* 12 (January 1981): 5–16.

Harmon, Alexandra. "American Indians and Land Monopolies in the Gilded Age." *Journal of American History* 90 (June 2003): 106–131.

Hauptman, Laurence M. "The American Indian Federation and the Indian New Deal: A Reinterpretation." *Pacific Historical Review* 52 (November 1983): 378–402.

————. "Governor Theodore Roosevelt and the Indians of New York." *Proceedings of the American Philosophical Society* 119 (February 1975): 1–7.

————. "Senecas and Subdividers: Resistance to Allotment of Indian Lands in New York, 1875–1906." *Prologue* 9 (Summer 1977): 105–116.

Hauptman, Laurence M., and Jack Campisi. "The Voice of Eastern Indians: The American Indian Chicago Conference and the Movement for Federal Recognition." *Proceedings of the American Philosophical Society* 132 (December 1988): 316–329.

Holm, Tom. "Fighting a White Man's War: The Extent and Legacy of American Indian Participation in World War II." *Journal of Ethnic Studies* 9 (Summer 1981): 69–81.

Horsman, Reginald. "Scientific Racism and the American Indian in the Mid-Nineteenth Century." *American Quarterly* 27 (May 1975): 152–168.

Kelly, Laurence C. "The Indian Reorganization Act: The Dream and the Reality," *Pacific Historical Review* 44 (1975): 291–312.

Koppes, Clayton R. "From New Deal to Termination: Liberalism and Indian Policy, 1933–1953." *Pacific Historical Review* 46 (November 1977): 543–566.

Lurie, Nancy O. "Menominee Termination: From Reservation to Colony." *Human Organization* 31 (Fall 1972): 257–270.

———. "The Voice of the American Indian: Report on the American Indian Chicago Conference." *Current Anthropology* 2 (1961): 478–500.

———. "Wisconsin: A Natural Laboratory for North American Indian Studies." *Wisconsin Magazine of History* 53 (Autumn 1969): 3–20.

Martin, Jill E. "A Year and a Spring of My Existence: Felix Cohen and the Handbook of Federal Indian Law." *Western Legal History* 8 (Winter–Spring 1995): 35–60.

———. "The Miner's Canary: Felix S. Cohen's Philosophy of Indian Rights," *American Indian Law Review* 23 (1998): 165–179.

McDonnell, Janet A. "Competency Commissions and Indian Land Policy, 1913–1920." *South Dakota History* 11 (Winter 1980): 21–34.

McDonnell, Melissa L. "Land Policy on the Omaha Reservation: Competency Commissions and Fee Patents." *Nebraska History* 63 (Fall 1982): 399–412.

Newton, Nell Jessup. "Indian Claims in the Courts of the Conqueror," *American University Law Review* 41 (1992): 769–771.

O'Grady, Terence J. "The Singing Societies of Oneida." *American Music* 9 (Spring 1991): 67–91.

Philp, Kenneth R. "Dillon S. Myer and the Advent of Termination, 1950–1953," *Western Historical Quarterly* 19 (1988): 37–59.

———. "Stride Toward Freedom: The Relocation of Indians to Cities, 1952–1960." *Western Historical Quarterly* 16 (April 1985): 175–190.

———. "Termination: A Legacy of the Indian New Deal," *Western Historical Quarterly* 14 (April 1983): 165–180.

Ricciardelli, Alex F. "The Adoption of White Agriculture by the Oneida Indians." *Ethnohistory* 10 (Fall 1963): 309–328.

Ritzenthaler, Robert E. "The Oneida Indians of Wisconsin." Public Museum of the City of Milwaukee *Bulletin* 19 (November 1950).

Ritzenthaler, Robert E., and Mary Sellers. "Indians in an Urban Situation." *Wisconsin Archeologist* 36 (1955): 147–161.

Stuart, Paul H. "Financing Self-Determination: Federal Indian Expenditures, 1975–1988." *American Indian Culture and Research Journal* 14 (1990): 1–18.

Udall, Stewart L. "The State of the Indian Nation—An Introduction." *Arizona Law Review* 10 (Winter 1968): 553–557.

Watkins, Arthur V. "Termination of Federal Supervision: The Removal of Restrictions Over Indian Property and Person." *Annals of the American Academy of Political and Social Science* 311 (May 1957): 47–55.

Zimmerman, William, Jr. "The Role of the Bureau of Indian Affairs Since 1933." *Annals of the American Academy of Political and Social Science* 311 (May 1957): 31–40.

Dissertations and Theses

Ackley, Kristina Lyn. "We Are Oneida Yet: Discourse in the Oneida Land Claim." PhD diss., SUNY Buffalo, 2005.

Basehart, Harry S. "Historical Changes in the Kinship System of the Oneida Indians." PhD diss., Harvard University, 1952.

Bell, Genevieve. "Telling Stories Out of School: Remembering the Carlisle Indian Industrial School, 1879–1918." PhD diss., Stanford University, 1998.

Bulkley, Peter B. "Daniel A. Reed: A Study in Conservatism." PhD diss., Clark University, 1972.

Campisi, Jack. "Ethnic Identity and Boundary Maintenance in Three Oneida Communities." PhD diss., SUNY Albany, 1974.

Dowling, John H. "The Impact of Poverty on a Wisconsin Oneida Indian Community." PhD diss., University of Michigan, 1973.

Geier, Philip Otto. "A Peculiar Status: A History of the Oneida Indian Treaties and Claims: Jurisdictional Conflict Within the American Government, 1775–1920." PhD diss., Syracuse University, 1980.

Hasse, Lawrence J. "Termination and Assimilation: Federal Indian Policy, 1943 to 1961." PhD diss., Washington State University, 1974.

Johannsen, Christina B. "Efflorescence and Identity in Iroquois Arts." PhD diss., Brown University, 1984.

Koppes, Clayton R. "Oscar L. Chapman: A Liberal at the Interior Department, 1933–1953." PhD diss., University of Kansas, 1974.

Matteson, Patricia. "'A Stain on the Blood': Indian-Loving and Nineteenth Century Women's Literary Strategies." PhD diss., University of Colorado, 1996.

Stovey, Patricia. "Parallel Souls: Studies on Early Twentieth-Century Native American Leaders in Relation to Black Activists W. E. B. Du Bois and Marcus Garvey, 1900–1934." Master's thesis, University of Wisconsin–Eau Claire, 2000.

Wanken, Helen M. "'Women's Sphere' and Indian Reform: The Women's National Indian Association, 1879–1901." PhD diss., Marquette University, 1981.

Contributors

Dr. Clifford Abbott is a professor of anthropology and linguistics at the University of Wisconsin–Green Bay, where he has taught for the past three decades. As the leading academic scholar of the Oneida language in the United States, he has worked with the Oneida Nation of Indians of Wisconsin since the 1970s in efforts to preserve and teach the language. He, Maria Hinton, and Amos Christjohn compiled *An Oneida Dictionary*, published in 1996.

Robert LaFollette Bennett, an Oneida, was the United States commissioner of Indian affairs from 1966 to 1969.

Dr. Jack Campisi, an anthropologist who served as the principal expert witness in the Oneida land-claims cases, has worked with more than three dozen American Indian nations from Maine to Alaska on issues related to federal recognition, Indian country, and land rights. He was the director of museum projects for the Mashantucket Pequot Tribal Nation, has served on the advisory board of the D'Arcy McNickle Center for the History of the American Indian at the Newberry Library, and has taught at Wellesley College. He is the author of *Mashpee: Tribe on Trial* (1991) and coeditor of *The Oneida Indian Experience: Two Perspectives* (1988).

Carol Cornelius is director of the Oneida Cultural Heritage Department of the Oneida Nation of Indians of Wisconsin. An Oneida, she is the author of two books on Iroquoian culture.

Franklin Cornelius is an Oneida veteran who served in Korea and Vietnam.

Judy Cornelius was the librarian at the Oneida library for eight years and has served on the Oneida Gaming Commission. An Oneida, she has been awarded a D'Arcy McNickle Fellowship from the Newberry Library in Chicago. Recently she served as treasurer of the Oneida Nation of Indians of Wisconsin.

Eva Danforth was Oneida Nation of Indians of Wisconsin tribal secretary from 1958 to 1963.

Jerry Danforth is an Oneida veteran and former tribal chairman of the Oneida Nation of Indians of Wisconsin.

Ada Deer was the assistant secretary of Indian affairs from 1993 to 1999. She led the fight for the restoration of the Menominees, her people, to federal status, which culminated in an act of Congress in 1973. She later became professor of Native American studies at the University of Wisconsin–Madison.

Madelyn (Cornelius) Genskow is a member of the Oneida Nation of Wisconsin. The daughter of the late Isaiah and Genevieve Cornelius, she was born and raised at her parents' farm on the Oneida reservation. Genskow was elected to be the first chairwoman of the founding board and was a volunteer supervisor for the Oneida office in Milwaukee (now called South East Oneida Tribal Services).

Laurence M. Hauptman is SUNY Distinguished Professor of History at the State University of New York at New Paltz. He is the coeditor of *The Oneida Indian Experience: Two Perspectives* (1988), *The Oneida Indian Journey* (1999), and *The Oneida Indians in the Age of Allotment* (2006). He and L. Gordon McLester III are the authors of *Chief Daniel Bread and the Oneida Nation of Indians of Wisconsin*, published by the University of Oklahoma Press (2002). In 1987 and in 1998, he was awarded the Peter Doctor Indian Fellowship Award by the Iroquois in New York for his research and writings on American Indian history.

Megan Minoka Hill, an Oneida, is an administrative fellow for the Harvard Project on American Indian Economic Development at the John F. Kennedy School of Government. She has served as a director of development for the Arizona State University Foundation, the director of development for the University of New Mexico's College of Arts and Sciences, and the director of individual giving and major gifts for the American Indian College Fund. Hill has also worked with indigenous communities to foster sustainable and culturally appropriate economic development in Siberia, New Zealand, Australia, and southern Africa.

Dr. Norbert S. Hill, an Oneida, is College of Menominee Nation vice president for the Green Bay campus. In New Mexico, Hill served as the executive director of the American Indian Graduate Center (AIGC), a nonprofit organization providing funding for American Indians and Alaska Natives to pursue graduate and professional degrees. Previous positions include executive director of the American Indian Science and Engineering Society (AISES), assistant dean of students at the University of Wisconsin–Green Bay, and director of the American Indian Educational Opportunity Program at the University of Colorado–Boulder. He founded *Winds of Change* and *The American Indian Graduate*, magazine publications of AISES and AIGC, respectively.

Maria Hinton is an Oneida elder and language teacher who has worked to preserve the Oneida language over the past thirty-five years. A graduate of the University of Wisconsin–Green Bay at the age of sixty-nine, she translated and transcribed *A Collection of Oneida Stories* (1996), which is used today by the Oneidas in their language program. She, her brother Amos Christjohn, and Clifford Abbott compiled the first major dictionary of the Oneida language, published in 1996.

Debra Jenny served as the teacher of traditional lacemaking at Oneida.

Dr. Patricia Matteson holds a PhD from the University of Colorado in women's and American Indian studies. She is currently working for the Mohonk Preserve in New Paltz, New York.

Betty McLester, an Oneida, is involved in reviving lacemaking, which was a major part of women's art traditions in the community from 1898 to 1953.

L. Gordon McLester III is the coordinator of the Oneida history conferences and founder of the Oneida Historical Society. A former tribal secretary of the Oneida Nation of Indians of Wisconsin, he is the president of Bear Claw and Associates. Besides writing a children's book on Oneida history, McLester is the coauthor of *Chief Daniel Bread and the Oneida Nation of Indians of Wisconsin* (2002) and coeditor of *The Oneida Indian Journey* (1999) and *The Oneida Indians in the Age of Allotment, 1860–1920* (2006).

Thelma McLester was the director of the Oneida Education Department for the Oneida Nation of Indians of Wisconsin. An Oneida, she has been awarded a D'Arcy McNickle Fellowship from the Newberry Library in Chicago and has written articles on the Oneidas' history for several scholarly presses and an encyclopedia. She has served as a trustee of Haskell Junior College and on the editorial board of *Voyageur* magazine.

Loretta Metoxen is an Oneida veteran, an Oneida tribal historian, and a former member of the Oneida Business Committee.

Edmund Powless, an Oneida veteran, fought in the Battle of the Bulge in World War II.

Althea Schuyler was Oneida Nation of Indians of Wisconsin tribal treasurer from 1956 to 1965.

Evelyn Smith-Elm, an Oneida elder, has served as a counselor for both the Oneida tribal school and for the Seymour school district. For many years, she has also been involved in service organizations of the Methodist Church.

Ernest Stevens Jr. is the executive director of the National Indian Gaming Association. He is a former member of the Oneida Business Committee.

Ernest Stevens Sr., an Oneida elder, worked as a Washington policymaker in the 1960s and 1970s. He served as staff director for committees of both houses of Congress, as assistant commissioner of Indian affairs, and as Federal Trade Commission hearing officer. In 1975, he was appointed by Congress to the American Indian Policy Review Commission. He is a former member of the Oneida Business Committee.

Kenneth W. Webster, an Oneida veteran, served in Vietnam.

Lewis Webster was a WPA storyteller. The WPA Oneida Language and Folklore Project, administered by Drs. Morris Swadesh, Floyd Lounsbury, and later Harry Basehart, collected hundreds of stories from Oneida elders between 1938 and 1942. Unlike other WPA projects of the time, these stories provide a unique portrait of an American Indian community because they were collected, transcribed, and translated by the Oneidas themselves.

Loretta Webster, an Oneida, is the former attorney for the Office of Land Management of the Oneida Nation of Indians of Wisconsin.

Index